Sheffield Silver Plate

# Sheffield Silver Plate

G. Bernard Hughes

PRAEGER PUBLISHERS

NEW YORK · WASHINGTON

BOOKS THAT MATTER

Published in the United States of America in 1970
by Praeger Publishers, Inc.
111 Fourth Avenue, New York, N.Y. 10003

© 1970, in London, England, by G. Bernard Hughes

Library of Congress Catalog Card Number: 72–114296

Printed in Great Britain

# Contents

# Preface

This book is intended for those who share my pleasure in Sheffield plate and those who are new to its beauty, its history and its importance among the discoveries and achievements of English craftsmen. I have endeavoured to explain what Sheffield plate is, and hence when the name Sheffield may be applied, and I have indicated how collectors may attribute periods to their pieces as closely as possible. I have studied Sheffield plate for many years, my first article, published in the *Daily Telegraph* more than 30 years ago, being followed by more detailed studies for such journals as *Country Life*.

Throughout the preparation of this book I have been helped and encouraged by a number of fellow enthusiasts. In particular I should like to mention Mrs V. S. Mitcheson who has lent me examples of Sheffield plate from her family collection, including pieces in which generations of daily use have revealed many constructional details. I am grateful, too, to Mrs Margaret Baggs, a descendant of Joseph Ashforth, the first plater to enter his mark at the Sheffield Assay Office after such marks became legal in 1784. Her copy of the rare *Robson's Birmingham and Sheffield Directory* has proved fascinating reading. Through the kindness of her sister Miss Grace Baggs, I have had the opportunity, too, to scrutinize the rare *Directory of Sheffield*, 1787. From Mr Mitchell-Withers, a descendant of Thomas Bolsover, I have received helpful information regarding his ancestor, and my thanks are due, too, to Miss Angela Salter, formerly Keeper of Applied Arts, City of Sheffield Museum, who arranged for my wife and myself to spend many hours inspecting piece by piece the Museum's authenticated and truly magnificent collection of Sheffield plate.

# 1. Introduction: silver plating on steel

From time immemorial men have sought ways of reproducing the appearance of precious metals with cheaper substitutes. Silver in particular, with countless domestic uses, has been widely imitated in its changing fashions of shape and decoration. Base metals have been plated by various means with veneers of silver leaf and foil so that the saving in material outweighed the cost of the labour involved and the effect produced was that of solid silver. Silver plating was practised in Imperial Rome. Some Roman coins minted in London, such as the copper *follis* or five-denarius piece, were silvered during the reign of Galerius, proclaimed Augustus in A.D. 304. It is important for the student of Sheffield plate to appreciate the scope of the alternatives that were available to sophisticated Georgians.

Until the eighteenth century silver plating was accomplished by processes of chemical amalgamation: the chapter rings on long-case and bracket clocks were silvered in this way. Several methods were described in detail in *The Laboratory or School of Arts*, London, 1740, including the following: 'Take calx of fine silver half an ounce, one ounce of sal-ammoniac, three ounces of salt. Mix and grind these together. When you use it, grind and temper it together with water, and rub your brass therewith. Anneal it brown and then quench it in water, wherein tartar has been dissolved; scratch it, and finish your work by polishing it.' Calx is defined as 'powder or friable substance produced by calcining a metal or mineral: formerly taken as the essential substance of the crude metal'.

A process for attaching leaves of pure silver to brass and copper was evolved in France early in the eighteenth century and continued in use until after the invention of electro-plating in the early 1840s. Known in England as French plating, this silvering, like the earlier methods, was impermanent and incapable of withstanding hard wear. The sharp edges on the object to be silvered were smoothed and the surface polished, and it was then heated at a charcoal brazier until almost red hot and plunged into nitric acid. After being cleaned up with pumice stone and water it was warmed until contact with water produced a slight hissing sound. The object was then placed on a hot iron mandril until the colour of the brass or copper changed to blue, when it was dipped into a very weak solution of nitric acid.

The actual silvering, known in the trade as charging, consisted of laying the silver leaves on the heated article and fixing them by steel burnishers of various shapes, great pressure being required to make the silver adhere firmly to the metal. The silverer always worked on two articles alternately. First he applied a double layer of silver leaf, then re-heated the piece to its original temperature and applied four more silver leaves, with heavy pressure from his burnisher. He continued charging in this way, four or six leaves at a time, until he had applied, in successive layers, 30 to 60 leaves according to the thickness of silver required. Finally he burnished until a smooth and uniform surface was obtained.

The Sheffield platers of England later used this process to repair accidental blemishes that occurred during manufacture, revealed only when the fused silver was burnished. Present-day restorers use French plating to conceal raw copper exposed on worn Sheffield plate.

The English process of close plating was patented in 1779 by Richard Ellis, goldsmith, George Street, Foster Lane, London, but a quarter of a century elapsed before it was taken up extensively in Sheffield and Birmingham. This was less costly than French plating but also consisted of applying silver leaf over base metals, including iron and steel. Small mastermen and their employees in this trade were known contemporaneously as 'platers on steel'. By this method a coating of silver beaten to paper thickness could be applied to a limited range of small domestic articles.

In the method generally adopted by close platers in the late eighteenth century the article to be plated was smoothed, polished and made absolutely clean. After being heated over a charcoal brazier until almost red hot, it was plunged first into a solution of sal ammoniac and then into molten tin. It was then wiped with tow so that no more than a thin film of tin covered the metal. Whilst still hot this was covered as closely and evenly as possible with foil of silver beaten to paper thickness and cut to the required size and pressed against the tin. On flat parts the silver was beaten with a small cloth-covered hammer to ensure complete contact with the tin, and in hollows it was forced into position by means of variously shaped wooden tools. A soldering iron was then passed lightly over its surface to melt the tin. This formed a solder which united the steel with the silver covering. Loose and overlapping fragments of silver leaf were brushed away and edges laid down by a further application of the soldering iron. Burnishing with a blood-stone or agate rendered joins invisible. Finally the piece was rubbed with a stick covered with soft leather dressed with rotten stone and oil, and finished with dry sifted rotten stone applied with calf skin. The surface then convincingly resembled silver plate. Taps and other complicated fittings for Sheffield plate tea urns and the like were often cast in brass and finished by close plating.

Ellis in his specification stated that the steel or iron to be plated was to be 'rubbed with borax; the gold or silver to be fitted close. The different solders used are as follows: one ounce standard gold [then 22 carats], four pennyweights fine silver, and three pennyweights fine copper; one ounce fine silver [without alloy], and two pennyweights spelter; one ounce sterling silver and twelve grains copper, copper-brass or spelter; the solder laid on as suits the different works. The particular art in soldering depends on the care in firing it.'

Close plating was applied to a limited range of small domestic articles of steel requiring either cutting edges or sharp points such as snuffers, skewers, cheese scoops, lobster picks, fish slices, pickle forks and the blades of dessert knives such as were mainly devised to meet the demands of the epicure. Sharp steel might be unrivalled for cutting meat, but close plating provided a range of edged and pointed table 'silver' for serving and eating lightly flavoured foods that would be ruined by acid-contaminated base metal. The finish was so immaculate that the inexpert found it difficult to distinguish it from Sheffield plate except by close examination. Exposure to extreme heat or prolonged dampness affected its permanency, however, causing blistering and flaking, and it could not stand up to long continuous wear. Close plating on iron and steel lacks the faintly bluish copper tinge of Sheffield plate. Close platers were usually stampers in a small way of business, working a foot-operated oliver fitted with shaping tools.

A more scientific method of close plating on steel was evolved in 1809 by Edward Thomason of Church Street, Birmingham. In his *Memoirs of Half a Century*, 1845, Thomason, by then a knight, recorded that in January 1810 he expanded 'the manufacturing rooms to add a new trade, the plating upon steel of knives, forks and spoons'. Rolled silver foil was used instead of silver leaf. According to his own account of this little-used process the intervening layer of tin was 'ingeniously expelled at a certain temperature when the rolled silver became attached firmly to the steel'. The iron or steel to be plated was smoothed, cleaned, coated with borax ground in water and then sprinkled with pure tin or silver solder. After being wrapped in silver foil bound with fine wire the piece was made red hot at a charcoal brazier: this attached the silver to the steel. The surface was then burnished and finished as if it were silver. This produced much finer results than ordinary close plating but was much more costly.

Thomason in his *Memoirs* regarded this craft as chiefly applicable to silver cutlery such as spoons, dessert forks and the blades of dessert knives, which he made in large quantities until the 1840s. Handles might be of sterling silver, ivory or mother of pearl, plain or carved. They were usually sold in cases of 12, 18 or 24 pieces. W. T. Rowlands, 92 Quadrant, Regent Street, London, advertised in *The Times*, 29 June 1838, dessert fruit knives and forks with 'silver plated on steel blades and with sterling silver blades', at the following prices per dozen pairs with silver ferrules: plain ivory handles, £2.17.6 and £8.18.6; carved ivory handles, £3.15.6 and £9.9.0; plain pearl, £3.18.0 and £11.11.0; carved pearl, £5.5.0 and £12.12.0; King's pattern, sterling silver handles, £6.15.0 and £13.13.0. Thomason declared that his process 'has never yet been used upon candlesticks, waiters, tea urns or articles of a similar description'.

The trade of plating on steel was established in Birmingham, to which it was virtually confined at the beginning of the nineteenth century when the Sheffield platers were faced with a war-time shortage of copper. The earliest close plater to be identified by Frederick Bradbury was W. Ellerby, London, who was operating in 1803. D. Hill & Co. appear to have been the first to have established the trade in Birmingham in 1806: a year later a further nine Birmingham close platers registered their marks at the Sheffield Assay Office.

The harness trade of Walsall employed close platers to ensure against rust on metal saddlery equipment, including many horse brasses. In 1839 fifteen were recorded as close platers of general work, nine of coach and harness equipment, five specializing on buckles, three on spurs. Nearby Bloxwich supported seven close platers. I have seen close platers at work in Walsall as recently as 1925.

In 1784 it was made legal to strike identification marks upon plated ware (see Chapter 7). Close plated steel, excluded from this Act, was in considerable demand during the Napoleonic wars because of the scarcity of copper for commercial purposes in England. The close platers on steel then applied to the Assay Office for permission to strike identifying marks on their ware. After the usual government delays this was granted in 1806. These marks differed from those on Sheffield plate in that they consisted of four separate marks cut into a single punch and arranged in the manner of the five punch marks struck on sterling silver. They usually consisted of the maker's name or initials split into three separate shields with the plater's device in the fourth shield. Registration at the Sheffield Assay Office was a legal obligation and in the case of a Sheffield plater also working as a close plater the two marks were required to differ. These marks were necessarily large and clumsy, rather a disfigurement to a small article. For this reason they were used by only a small percentage of close platers.

Close platers are listed and their marks illustrated in *The Old Sheffield Plate Register* published by the Sheffield Assay Office, 1909. This shows that 44 registered close platers operated in Birmingham and four in Sheffield between 1807 and 1849. The Sheffield men were Aaron Hatfield, Pepper Alley, 1808; B. Stot, Duke Street, 1811; J. Rodgers & Son, 1822; W. C. Hutton, 1831. Examples of their work are to be seen in Sheffield City Museum.

Birmingham close platers who registered their marks at Sheffield Assay

Office included W. Scot, 1807; J. Linwood, 1807; G. Gibbs, 1807; R. Silk, 1809; T. Butts, 1810; W. Woodward, 1814; H. Best, 1814.

It is possible by tracing registration marks of an individual firm to attribute periods of manufacture. For instance, William Hutton, Cannon Street, Birmingham, a plater on steel, first registered a mark on 19 November 1807 – *Hutton* in script to the left of an open-topped triangle with a pair of ears. This mark is often found on dessert knives and matching spoons and forks, nut-crackers, skewers, lobster picks, snuffers and so on. In 1830 Hutton established his son as a plater on steel in Sheffield, registering his mark of four shields – *Hutton* in script, the triangle, *Sheffield* in script and a repeat of the triangle. The *Sheffield Directory*, 1833, contains the entry: 'William Carr Hutton, 35 Pinstone Street, plater on steel and manufacturer of dessert and fruit knives, spoons, snuffers, etc., in British plate, 58 Eyre St.' This was accompanied by a display advertisement: 'W. C. HUTTON, Plater on steel and general manufacturer, 35 Pinstone Street, Sheffield. Plated on steel:—Table and dessert forks; table, dessert and tea spoons; ladles, etc., with or without the improved silver edges and points; dessert knives and forks, and butter knives with or without handles; fish slicers, skewers; knife rests, nut-crackers, toast racks, snuffers, spurs and other articles.' A third mark was registered by W. Hutton in 1837, also composed of four shields: *Hutton* in script, an orb in reverse, and these duplicated. The address used was now Norfolk Street. A fourth Hutton mark was registered in 1839 – *H & S* with the 1807 triangle symbol reversed. The *Sheffield Directory*, 1839, shows that the firm was then trading as W. Hutton & Son at 50 South Street, Sheffield, and also at 130 Great Charles Street, Birmingham, removing to 27 High Street in about 1845.

By this time there was no compulsion to register marks at the Assay Office. Hutton's final mark, dating from 1849, consisted of *W H & S* with the original triangle symbol. In 1857 W. Hutton & Son registered their mark as silversmiths: *W H* in an oval, superseded in 1866 by *R H* in an oval. Later the Hutton firm became electroplaters: this ware bears the mark of four arrows crossing four arrows formerly used on plated wares by T. & J. Creswick.

Below are the names of five platers on steel, with the years in which their marks were first used, and goods upon which they have been noted.

Stanley and Thomas Howard, London, were the only London close platers to register a mark, entered in 1809. The punch contained the name *Howard* in script, divided into two parts with the device of four links of a chain placed vertically. Found on many dessert knives and forks.

B. Stot, Duke Street, Sheffield, in 1811 registered a two-shield mark composed of *Stot* in script and the device of a capital *R* conjoined with a similar letter in reverse. Found on decorated snuffers and small pickle forks.

J. Gilbert, Legge Street, Birmingham, in 1812 registered three marks each containing the name *Gilbert* broken centrally, in script. Noted on threaded and shell pattern forks and meat skewers.

J. Turton, 8 Church Street, Birmingham, in 1820 registered two marks each including his surname. Found on spoons, sugar tongs and cheese scoops.

J. Prime, Birmingham, from 1839 used four marks but these are usually wrongly attributed to a much earlier period. Found on spoons and forks with scroll ornament on the handles.

# 2. The discovery of Sheffield plate

As indicated in the previous chapter, close plating was a slow, laborious way of imitating solid silver. Simpler, and of far wider application, Sheffield plate proved so spectacularly successful that in 1798 the London silversmiths complained to the Court of the Goldsmiths' Company that 'plated manufacturers have been enabled to produce articles of the highest elegance and fashion, many of which are now made with solid silver – borders, shields, ornaments, finished in exact resemblance to real plate – and which do material injury to the sale of wrought plate.' They asked for a duty of threepence an ounce to be placed on fused plate goods.

Today the characteristic very faintly bluish lustre radiating from Sheffield plate made by fusing silver over copper is preferred by many collectors to the white brilliance of solid sterling silver. Sheffield plate consists of a thin layer of silver over a thicker core of copper so manipulated that only silver is visible until wear reveals an underlying gleam of red. The two metals are fused while still in ingot form, subsequent flattening into plate having no effect upon the ratio; in the same way silver fused upon copper can be extruded into Sheffield plate 'wire'. Thus the craftsman works in the combined material throughout the construction processes, an important point differentiating Sheffield plate not only from French plating and close plating but also from the electro-plating that eventually supplanted it.

It must be emphasized that greater skill and more time were required for fashioning Sheffield plate into attractive shapes than for producing comparable pieces in solid silver. But the tax of sixpence an ounce imposed upon manufactured silver plate from 1784 meant that Sheffield plate could be sold at one-third the price of silver, creating a great demand. The silver tax was increased to one shilling an ounce in 1797, 1s 3d in 1804 and 1s 6d in 1815. During this period Sheffield platers brought their craft to a very high standard, the material being considered worthy of immense elaboration of form and careful finish. The platers at no time were called upon to pay duty on the ornaments, borders and other enrichments of sterling silver finished exactly as real plate.

Although always directly rivalling and imitating table wares and ornaments in silver the basic designs in Sheffield plate tended to remain in production over long periods because of the high cost of essential tools. For more definite dating the collector must have at least an outline knowledge of the processes involved.

The craft may be claimed as wholly English in origin, evolved by a Sheffield cutler Thomas Bolsover (1704–88) although production was soon shared with Birmingham and to a lesser degree with Edinburgh. The long-sustained romantic story of its accidental discovery while following his trade in his garret workshop in Tudor House, Sheffield, during 1742 can no longer be accepted. Bolsover was a scale-maker, scales being the pieces of horn attached to the sides of knife handles. The story credited him with using a copper penny to protect a silver knife handle he was fixing in a cramp and with carelessly overheating the metals which thereupon became inseparably attached to each other. Copper pennies were introduced no earlier than 1797. But however he may have arrived at his discovery Bolsover had the example of the French close platers to prompt him to experiment in fusing thinly beaten sterling silver leaf upon rolled copper plate.

With Joseph Wilson as partner and £170 of borrowed capital he started a factory at Baker Hill, Sheffield, manufacturing silver-plated buttons and buckles. Bolsover sold his buttons at a guinea a dozen, the silver costing him three shillings. The venture was immediately successful and within a year he had repaid the loan and interest. It may be noted in passing that buttons were among the last articles to be made in quantity in Sheffield plate in the late nineteenth century.

The spelling of the inventor's name as Bolsover, contrary to the usual Boulsover, has been confirmed with me by a descendant, Mr J. A. Mitchell-Withers. He kindly searched the family papers and found the name invariably spelled Bolsover. A 14-inch waiter in his possession is inscribed on the reverse: 'Presented by Thomas Bolsover of Whiteley Wood, the Inventor of Plating with Silver, to his eldest daughter Mary, on her marriage with Mr. Joseph Mitchell of Sheffield, Feby 14th 1760.'

Joseph Wilson soon competed on his own account at Highfield, Sheffield, and is entered in *Sketchley's Sheffield Directory*, 1774, as 'silversmith, plater, saw maker, tobacco and snuff manufacturer'.

Bolsover continued experimenting and by 1745 he had made the important advance of fusing silver to copper before passing the copper ingot through a pressure rolling machine. Continued rolling reduced the composite metals to any desired thickness yet retained their relative proportions.

1  Old Sheffield plate. (*top left*) Coffee pot, 1780s. (*top right*) Inkstand, *c.* 1790. (*below*)
Soup tureen, *c.* 1820

3 Close plating. Knife blades and fork prongs

2 Knives and forks with handles of stamped Sheffield plate

5 Eccentric steel snuffers, 1807

4 Close plating. Knife, dessert knife and fork

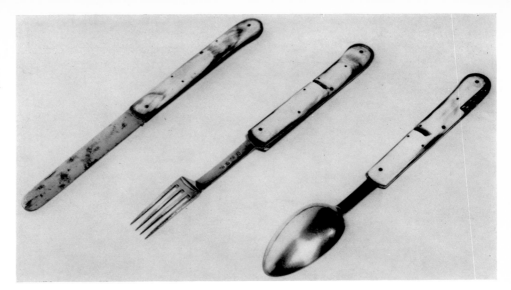

6 Close plating. Folding knife, fork and spoon set, 1807

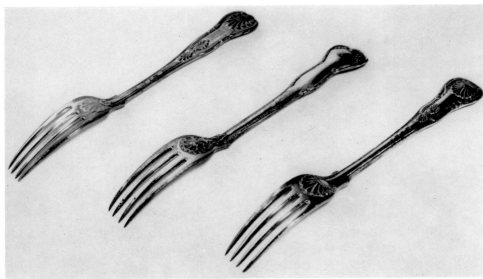

7 Close plating. Four-pronged table forks with stamped handles, *c.* 1812–15

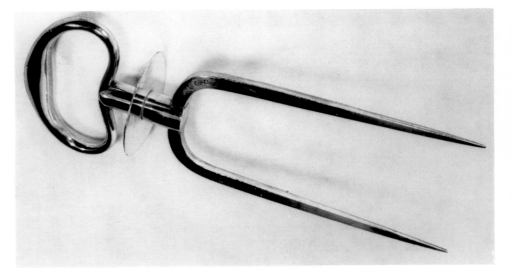

8 Close plating. Two-pronged skewer, 1807

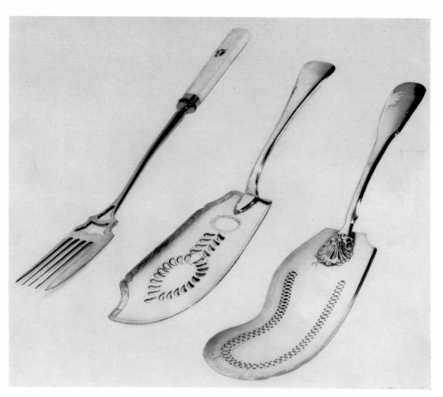

9  Fork for serving and
   cutting fish, *c.* 1820; fish
   slice, after 1807; fish slice,
   1829–35

10  Asparagus server,
    *c.* 1820; lobster crack;
    cheese scoop, 1810

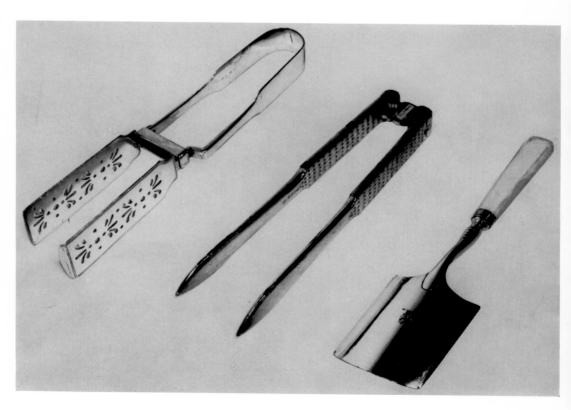

11 Sauce boat and sauce tureen

12 Teapots

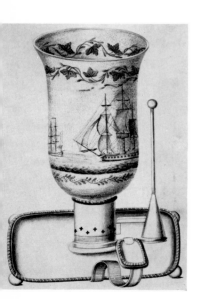

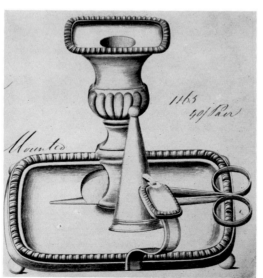

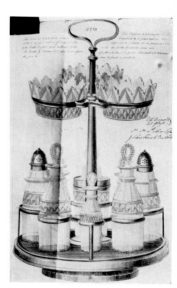

13 Draught-proof
chamber candlestick

14 Chamber candlestick

15 Cruet

16 Salt-cellars in late eighteenth-
century designs

17 Salt-cellars fashionable from the
late 1790s

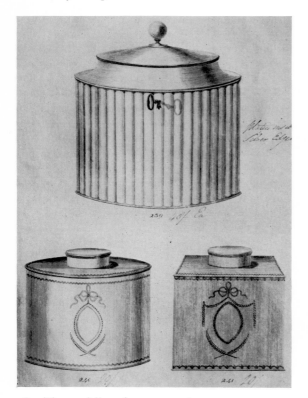

18 Tea caddies, from a catalogue *c.* 1795

19 Beaker, tankard, mug and chamber
candlestick, from a catalogue *c.* 1795

20 Salt-cellars, chamber candlestick and fish server, catalogue of 1792

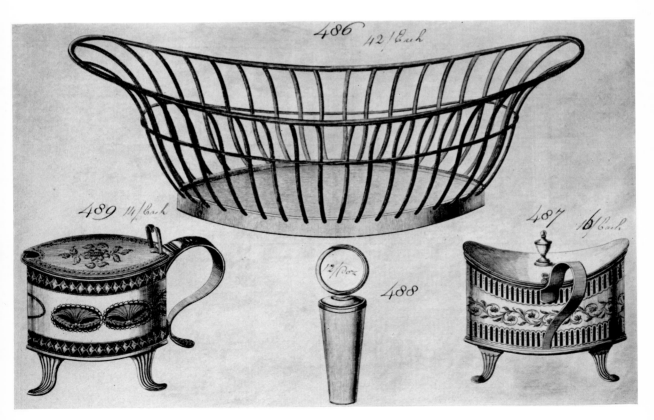

21 Fruit-basket, mustard pots and ringed-and-washered cork

22  Urn-shaped wine cooler      23  Teapot in British plate      24  British plate jug

25  Candelabrum, 1830s–1840s      26  Pair of rococo candlesticks in British plate

27  Teapot, sugar basin
and cream jug in
British plate

28  Tray in British
plate, *c.* 1840

29  Matching teapot,
cream jug and sugar
basin in British plate,
together with coffee
pot, also *c.* 1840

30    Square-based candlesticks in designs of Adam influence, *c.* 1780

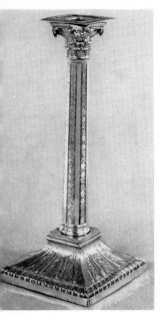

Table candlestick,
*c.* 1760

32  Table candlestick,
*c.* 1780

33  Table candlestick,
*c.* 1780

34  Table candlestick
*c.* 1780

5  Table candlestick, *c.* 1780

36  Table candlesticks: (*left*) 1760s; (*right*) late 1750s

37  Table candlestick with swivel arm, *c.* 1815

38  Dwarf candlestick and table candlestick

39  Pair of candlesticks and coffee pot, 1760s

40  Single-slide,
    c. 1800

41  Double telescopic pillar, c. 1800

42  Five-slide

TELESCOPIC CANDLESTICKS

43  Traveller's candlestick, c. 1805

44  Double-slide,
    c. 1800

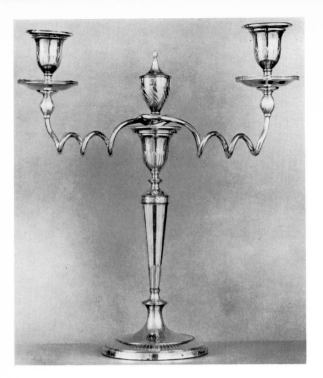

45  Candelabrum, 1790s

46  Candelabrum, 1780s

47  Pair of library candelabra with adjustable branches, *c.* 1810

48 Two-light candela-
brum, late eighteenth
century

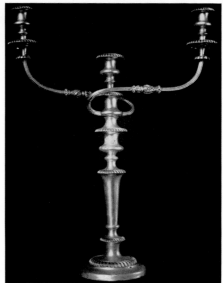

49 Three-light candelabrum,
*c.* 1820

51 Candlesticks and candelabra, *c.* 1830

50 Sheffield plate din-
ing table suite; one of
the three-light
candelabra is convert-
ible to a single five-
light candelabrum,
*c.* 1812

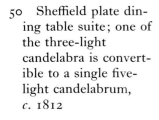

52   Pair of chamber candlesticks

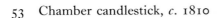

53   Chamber candlestick, *c.* 1810

54   Set of four chamber candlesticks

Bolsover named his new production 'copper rolled plate'. Plated goods were advertised in the *London Chronicle*, 5 January 1768, by Thomas Jeffery, a silver-smith of Cockspur Street, Charing Cross, London. The term Sheffield plate was not used until about 1770: in the following year an advertisement in *Felix Farley's Journal*, Bristol, referred to 'Sheffield Plate Candlesticks'. The usual term, however, was still 'fused silver plate'. In addition to buttons Bolsover now made small circular and oval boxes with pull-off lids and bases embossed in relief. Bradbury describes such boxes: 'the lids are clipped round and fastened to the upper surface of the boxes by lapping over the sides to secure them firmly. To make them more serviceable a loose sheet of unplated copper is secured beneath the lids. The bottoms are fastened in by the same methods, the sides swaged in strips and soldered together, the seams being clearly visible.' It is interesting to note that even such early work shows the meticulous finish characteristic of good Sheffield plate. Not only was the lid tight-fitting but inner linings, sometimes of tortoiseshell, were fitted to base and lid. The sides shaped by swaging were strengthened by concave–convex corrugations and the whole interior might be gilded (see Chapter 5).

The manufacture of boxes for the pocket had long been a profitable craft in Sheffield: the records of the Cutlers' Company show that tobacco, snuff and money boxes in brass and iron were made in large numbers from the 1660s.

Bolsover's range of production was severely limited by the fact that he could not conceal the streak of red copper visible when the plated metal was sheared. This defect was overcome by his former apprentice Joseph Hancock who evolved the single-lapped copper edge in 1758 (Chapter 6). Establishing himself as Bolsover's first considerable competitor, he installed horse power, so that his pressure roller could reduce thicker ingots than formerly into silvered plates of greater superficial area.

Bradbury quotes from a manuscript by Charles Dixon (1776–1852), a candle-stick maker of Sheffield: 'The first articles made by Mr. Joseph Hancock were saucepans plated inside . . . put together in two parts and soldered.' Dixon also observed that Bolsover saved the floor sweepings and sent them 'to Mr. Read's refinery in Green Lane, and in a little time they sent him back £100 worth of silver'. Sweep-washing was an important subsidiary of the silver-smiths', platers', gold beaters' and jewellers' trades by which dust and rubbish was collected from the floors of all workshops. This was known as sweep and sold to sweep-washers who treated it with mercury; mercury amalgamated with the atoms of precious metal which were recovered from the amalgam by a simple process.

Joseph Hancock, a well-established cutler – he was Master Cutler in 1763 – entered the plating trade in about 1751 and made a wide range of domestic table ware, copying and adapting designs formerly obtainable only from silversmiths.

These were intended for the rising middle classes envious of the silver plate seen in the homes of the gentry.

Bolsover himself, now wealthy, felt unable to compete successfully in the manufacture of table ware and in 1762 Hancock acquired his plant. So far each plater had made his own sheets by hand-rolling. Bolsover then concentrated on the rolling and plating of copper, using horse power, for sale to the several newly established manufacturers. These included such pioneers as John Hoyland, his former traveller, Nathaniel Smith, Thomas Law, Henry Tudor, Thomas Leader, Matthew Fenton and others. He also made steel tools, saws and fenders.

Water power was first used by Joseph Hancock from 1787 and a year or so later by John Hoyland & Co., who transferred their factory to Cooper Wheel on the River Sheaf and commenced rolling plate, a process they continued for more than a century. The standard charge was fourpence a pound weight, the copper ingots already silvered being supplied by the customer and rolled to any speci-fied thickness and dimensions. The process of making silvered copper plate continued with little alteration throughout the collector's period but the range of silver ware that could be copied successfully was vastly increased when both faces of the copper were silvered, leaving only the edges to be masked.

Pieces of hollow-ware such as teapots, coffee pots, urns and so on were made from single plated copper and tinned inside. Even when plate silvered on both faces came into general use in the late 1760s this practice continued for lidded hollow-ware. This meant economizing on silver and also proved practical as the interior could be re-tinned frequently when heavy use required this. When pieces of flat ware were subject to scrutiny on both faces the early Sheffield plater might apply two sheets of his material with the copper faces together, but this cumbersome method was gladly abandoned. Within ten years the whole range of articles currently fashioned in silver was to be found in silver-plated copper, the platers having captured a substantial part of the silversmiths' trade.

Horace Walpole writing to his friend George Montagu on 1 September 1760 recorded a glimpse of Sheffield 200 years ago: 'As I went to Lord Strafford's I passed through Sheffield which is one of the foulest towns in England, in the most charming situation, where there are 22,000 inhabitants making knives and scissors. They remit £11,000 worth of goods a week to London. One man there has discovered the art of plating copper with silver. I bought a pair of candle-sticks for two guineas that are quite pretty.'

The *Directory of Sheffield*, 1774, describes the Sheffield platers as

> 'ingenious workmen who make a great variety of Articles', and continued with a list of table ware then in production: 'argyles, bottle-stands, bread and sugar baskets, bottle labels, branches, candlesticks, canisters, chocolate-pots, coffee-pots, cream-jugs, cream-pails, cruet-frames, dish crosses, cups,

dish-rims, epergnes, goblets, jugs, knife and fork handles, ladles, lemon strainers, mustard pots, salts, round and oval, sauce-pans, scallop shells, skewers, snuff-boxes, snuffer stands and dishes, spoons, stew-pans, tankards and measures of all sizes, tea-trays and waiters, tea urns, tumblers, tureens, water plates and dishes, wine funnels, writing stands and equipment.'

Teapots were inadvertently omitted as were bridle bits, buckles, buttons for saddles, spurs and stirrups.

Samuel Roberts in his autobiography recorded that workmen capable of making goods in Sheffield plate were obtained from London, Birmingham, York and Newcastle. The majority were bad characters and ' during the first 20 years of the plating trade journeyman platers were most unsteady, depraved and idle. The masters could neither do without them nor obtain better. They were forced to give them high wages and to wink at their irregularities. From this cause the masters were continually enticing the workmen from each other's houses, giving them money to hire with them, and letting them get into debt as a kind of security. [Imprisonment for debt for unlimited periods was legal at this period.] There were in consequence frequent disputes between masters and workmen and between masters and masters about them; so that they almost occupied the time of the patient Mr. Wilkinson and the impatient Mr. Apthorpe during one day in the week, in the little justice-room at the Cutlers' Hall.' The workmen first employed in the plating workshops were copper braziers and silversmiths.

In a large manufacturing establishment there would be four main workshops for stamping, brazing, piercing and candlestick making, employing about 100 people, men, women and children. Hours were seven a.m. to seven p.m. with one hour for breakfast and dinner and half an hour for tea: on Saturday when wages were paid work ceased at five p.m. Piece-workers earned 50–55s a week and day workers 22–40s.

Charles Dixon, quoted by Bradbury, noted the important development of plated drawn wire (see Chapter 27).

' Fresh ideas sprang up and then began the making of caster frames, liquor frames, toast racks, etc. . . . The trade was greatly obligated to the Wedgwood and other china manufacturers for many of their most beautiful patterns. The study of ancient ornamental drawings was another source of patterns and I have known a person when in London go on purpose to Westminster Abbey there to find out something that might take the attention of customers when made up into tea urns, vases, ice pails, etc . . . When the trade was first begun workmen were obtained from the silversmiths' shops in London as foremen or managers and a great number of copper braziers were employed to raise and hammer the parts of some of the articles.'

This was confirmed in the *Birmingham Directory*, 1839, which added that Dixon manufactured silver plated upon copper on a very extensive scale and applied it to a great variety of articles such as 'urns, teapots, coffee-pots, candlesticks, trays, cups and most of the old decorations of the sideboard which hitherto had been made solely of wrought silver'. The *Directory* article then gave a few facts regarding contemporaneous manufactures, stating that the 'Sheffield ware equals the most richly embossed plate, in the elegance of its designs and the splendour of its ornaments; and of this material, dinner and dessert services have been manufactured from fifty to three hundred guineas, and breakfast sets from ten to two hundred guineas as sold on the spot.'

Associated though it is with Sheffield, the craft had become established in Birmingham within a few years of Bolsover's discovery. By about 1756 John Taylor was making buttons, boxes and similar light articles. The famous Matthew Boulton had established plating workshops at Soho, Birmingham, with John Fothergill as partner by 1762. *Swinney's Directory*, 1774, commented regarding the Soho factory, trading as Matthew Boulton & Plate Company, manufacturers of plated goods: 'they avail themselves of a number of ingenious mechanical Contrivances, by the means of Water Mills, which much facilitate their work and saves a great portion of Time and Labour. The Plated-Work has an appearance of solid Silver, more especially when compared with that of any other Manufactory.'

Before the end of the century there were nearly 100 platers in the town. For convenience collectors refer to their productions as Sheffield plate. It must be emphasized that during the period under review the Birmingham platers, with the exception of Matthew Boulton, catered largely for a less expensive trade than that of Sheffield.

The trade appears to have been captured almost entirely by Birmingham during the 1830s, for the trade directories of 1839 list 24 plated ware manufacturers, 47 silver platers and 20 german silver platers in Birmingham. Sheffield then supported only ten silver platers, one plate manufacturer and one german silver plater.

Two Sheffield platers displayed examples of their work at the Great Exhibition, 1851: Thomas Bradbury & Son, and James Dixon & Son. Their catalogue entries were as follows.

Bradbury: 'Coffee and tea services, consisting of coffee pot, teapot, sugar basin and cream ewer, with kettles and stands for the same. In various patterns. Kettles and pitchers, plated and engraved. Plateau, scroll pattern. Tea urn, fluted antique pattern. Double dish and warmer with pierced and chased border. Antique bread basket, engraved and pierced, with antique massive mountings. Waiter and liquor frame for same. Liquor and cruet frames, various patterns. Chamber candlesticks, Elizabethan. Ink stands, pierced and engraved. Bottle stand, pierced, antique. Cake basket, engraved, French pattern. Candelabrum.' Dixon: 'Best Sheffield plate. Dish cover, melon pattern, registered. Soup tureen and stand, coffee tray, corner dish, tea urn of the Stowe pattern, antique style.'

# 3. Identifying Sheffield plate

The colour and texture of the film of silver fused over the copper plate are accurate guides in differentiating Sheffield plate from imitations. These include British plate made from 1835 (see Chapter 8) in which a coating of silver was fused over german silver, a method tried on a smaller scale on Britannia metal from the early 1820s; electro-plated copper from the early 1840s; Edwardian and later copies. There are also the fakes – that is, reproductions worked on after leaving the factory until they may be mistaken for antiques. The expert experiences little difficulty in detecting such deceptive pieces; those less experienced will find that there are several tests to ascertain that the plate is indeed antique.

*Colour.* Seen in bright daylight and not by artificial light, Sheffield plate has a very faint bluish tint. This may be due to the presence of alloys in both the silver and the copper or the effect of the various industrial processes through which they pass, such as the hardening of the silver over the annealed copper.

*Electro-plating.* This cheaper process was patented in 1840 by George and Henry Elkington, Birmingham, who exhibited at the Société d'Encouragement des Arts, Paris, 1841. The ware has a staring white surface after polishing. In the electro-plating process minute particles of silver are deposited on the shaped copper, producing a coating of pure, unalloyed silver which has to be bright-hammered all over to close the pores and produce an even surface, making the article longer lasting. It is then burnished. It is, in fact, frosted with minute particles of silver, which the electric current has torn from a sheet of pure silver hung in the electric bath and has deposited upon the surface of the copper placed ready to receive them. A patent of 1847 improved the method but the silver has undergone a process of transmutation and no later treatment can give it the colour and texture of fused plate. Heavy electro-plating after a long period of daily use and cleaning, however, will acquire a closely similar lustre. Sheffield plate repaired by electro-plating is not burnished, as such brilliance suggests recent work. So far no method has been discovered of toning this down to the lustre displayed by antique Sheffield plate.

*The acid test* makes it possible when in doubt to distinguish between the two types of plating. The silver used by the Sheffield platers was of sterling quality – that is, 925 parts of silver to 75 parts of copper. The electro-platers used pure silver. A simple chemical test given by Henley's *Book of Processes*, 1922, will permit recognition. First clean the surface of the plate with methylated spirits. Then, with a glass rod, apply a single drop of solution made from potassium bichromate, 1 part; nitric acid of 1·2 specific gravity, 6 parts; water, 2 parts. This drop will, in one minute, change colour to dark red if the silver is sterling quality, and when removed with water a brown spot will remain. In the case of electro-plated silver the spot of test liquid will change to a bright blood-red. When this is removed with water a greyish-white spot remains. The method advocated by Frederick Bradbury is simpler. Apply to the silver a spot of nitric acid slightly diluted with distilled water. If this changes colour to blue the silver is of sterling quality; if it remains clear the silver is pure and therefore the object has been electro-plated.

*Replating* was common during the third quarter of the nineteenth century, when large quantities of worn plate existed and owners were indifferent regarding the mode of plating and often preferred the electro-plater's brilliance. Small advertisements appeared in newspapers and elsewhere from 1849 offering to replate worn Sheffield plate. It is simple to detect replated articles. If mounts and angles show signs of wear and the plating is unrubbed with no visible trace of copper, the piece has certainly been replated. The original seams are difficult to detect beneath replating. Blemishes on some worn Sheffield plate have been concealed beneath silver leaf applied by the close-plating process before appearing as antiques. The replated defects, however, soon re-emerge.

*The seam test* is a reliable method by which early Sheffield plate may be identified. This was usually assembled from separate units, hammered or soldered together. The butt joint was often used, the ends of the plated copper being soldered on the flat without fold or overlap. After burnishing such joints were virtually invisible and have to be sought carefully but they may be detected with the aid of a magnifying glass. Hollow units such as vase-shaped vessels shaped by hand-raising, stamping or spinning were the only seamless parts. Otherwise, if no seams are discovered, it is reasonable to assume that the piece has been electro-plated, thus concealing joins and seams beneath the film of silver as paint may cover cracks in wood. When a piece of Sheffield plate, other than a raised, stamped or spun unit, displays considerable elaboration of form, yet possesses a smooth unbroken surface from top to base, then it should be regarded with suspicion.

*Hinges* such as were used on teapots, coffee pots, hot-water jugs and the like have two leaves and were known to the trade as book hinges. These need inspection. They were so fiddling to make in plated copper that many platers found it cheaper to use sterling silver plate. In plated hinges the ends of the joint pins and bare ends of the lugs were concealed beneath tiny ornamental silver caps. Early hinges almost invariably show some looseness after a century and a half of wear: reproductions omit this feature.

*Filing* is a disfigurement never found on an exposed part of antique Sheffield plate. Lack of care in the manufacture of reproductions during the Edwardian period and later was responsible for many file marks around hinges and around the soldering of wire-work.

*Edges and mounts.* Periods of manufacture may be attributed by examining these. Grouped into ten classes dating between 1743 and the decline of the plating trade during the mid-nineteenth century these are detailed in Chapter 6. If pre-1790 Sheffield plate reveals, either to the eye or to the thumbnail, a fine line where the upper layer of silver has been drawn over the edge and laid back upon the lower layer of silver, then the piece is very probably genuine. If an applied beading or reeding has obviously been soldered over the edge, the same is true. This fact also will usually be apparent to eye or nail. Should the edges show a polished, unbroken surface then the piece is probably electro-plate. Edges and mounts with blurred relief work betray the use of worn tools. During the period of keen competition between silver and Sheffield plate these would have been taken out of use.

*Marks* very closely resembling those entered by the old platers at the Sheffield Assay Office appear on some reproductions. These imitations so nearly resemble originals that very careful inspection is essential. Also, according to H. N. Veitch, a leading dealer in Sheffield plate writing in 1908, successors of original firms were then using, as they were fully entitled to do, marks registered before 1835.

Several authorities declare that the manufacture of Sheffield plate is obsolete. This is not so: many original tools have been unearthed in warehouses and are still in use and one firm has advertised this. Such tools are generally used in association with carelessly constructed table ware in ill-proportioned shapes.

Collectors should always have their purchases of Sheffield plate fully invoiced with a guarantee that they are indeed antique, in any case pre-dating 1835. It is an offence in Britain to describe as Sheffield plate any ware that has not been manufactured by actually fusing silver upon copper (see Chapter 7). Should a salesman prove evasive in replying to questions regarding authenticity it is advisable to abandon any idea of a purchase.

# 4. Manufacturing processes

In the early days of Sheffield plate the same factories rolled and plated the copper and fashioned the finished ware. But plating quickly became a specialist trade, the silvered plate being stocked in three standard qualities varying with the thickness of the silver and the gauge of the copper. These plates were sold to the plate workers for fabrication.

The standard method of making silvered copper plate required pure copper alloyed with one-fifth its weight in brass to give it the necessary rigidity. This alloy was melted in black lead crucibles in an air furnace with an extremely quick draught. The molten metal was cast in two-piece moulds, each cavity measuring three inches wide, $1\frac{1}{2}$ inches thick and from nine to 18 inches long. An elevated mouth-piece or gate – known to the trade as a 'get' – gave pressure to the molten alloy and ensured that no air bubbles were enclosed in the ingot. The mould was heated until the grease smeared over its interior emitted fumes but did not burn. The metal was ready for casting after taking on a bluish tinge.

After solidification, but whilst the metal was still very hot, the mould was opened. One or both faces of the eight-pound ingot were then dressed with a file, cleaned and polished. From about 1820 filing was superseded by steam-driven machine-planing. A plate of rolled sterling silver was similarly prepared: this measured slightly less in superficial area and was of a thickness in accordance with the quality of the final rolled plate. Its normal thickness was one-fortieth that of the ingot: 10–12 ounces of silver to eight pounds of copper was standard. In second-quality plate made from about 1815 the ingot measured $1\frac{1}{4}$ inches thick and the silver was reduced to eight ounces for every eight pounds of copper. Deep cut engraving required at least 24 ounces of silver to eight pounds of copper. It was essential that the coating of silver was more than a mere film to resist discoloration under the heat of the soldering iron.

The prepared surfaces of the silver and the copper were placed together. The silver was covered with a flat-faced iron block for protection against the sledge-hammer blows rained upon it to ensure complete contact between them. From about 1815 the sledgehammer was replaced by the drop hammer, and the iron block by one of steel or copper, whitened to prevent accidental fusion with the silver. Copper, silver and protecting metal were then bound together with iron wires. The edges were fluxed by brushing with a saturated solution of burnt borax. This melted at a low temperature, excluding air which would tend to oxidize the copper and prevent union of the metals.

This prepared ingot was then ready for the plating furnace, which was fitted with an iron door provided with a small peephole. The furnace fuel was charcoal, later coke, laid upon a grating level with the lower edge of the door. A number of ingots were placed upon the charcoal and the door closed. The plater watched through the peephole for the instant when the soldering temperature was reached. During the union of the silver with the copper, the surface of the silver was observed to be flushed around the edges and drawn into intimate contact with the copper. Known to the trade as riveting, this was the signal for removing the ingots from the surface of the charcoal, carefully holding them level whilst the silver set. If permitted to remain even a little longer, the silver became alloyed with the copper and the plating spoiled. The adhesion was brought about by the formation of a film of true silver solder at the surface of contact. Accurate union of the metal required great skill and judgment on the part of the worker.

The ingot was cleaned and rolled to plate thickness by passing it repeatedly between pressure rollers set at 'a great pinch'. This process expanded the copper into a plate measuring four by two feet. Frequent annealing was necessary at a small reverberatory hearth to lessen the vivid red hue of the copper which, if not reduced, affected the hue of the silver. From about 1815 the copper might be slightly alloyed with zinc and lead to lighten its colour and make it more easily workable. After the final annealing the sheets were immersed in hot dilute sulphuric acid and scoured with fine Calais sand and water. The copper and silver were now inseparably joined and the plate ready for fabrication.

The silvered copper plate could be shaped by any of the hand-raising processes customary in silversmithing; by the use of swages; by stamping or pressing; and by spinning.

The hand-raising of Sheffield plate was the work of braziers, the largest group of craftsmen employed in the trade. They shaped hollow-ware such as bowls and urns from the flat plate with no other aids than a steel stake, a wooden mallet and a steel-faced hammer. The sheet, resting on top of the stake, was gradually rounded into hollow form by repeated blows with the mallet.

Cylindrical hollow-ware, such as a coffee pot or jug was shaped by bending the plate and joining the ends with either dove-tail or butt joints. The joint was made by soldering two ends of plated copper on the flat without fold or overlap. Hammering such joints made them virtually invisible but some trace will be detected by careful inspection with a glass. The cylinder was brought to its final shape by hand hammering and a circular base was inserted and soldered into position.

Before decoration the surface of the ware was given a high polish by burnishing, which also assisted in concealing joints. The plate was cleaned and then rubbed with soap. A light steel burnisher, dipped into soap-suds from time to time, was pressed backwards and forwards on the metal. This process closed the pores of the silver and resulted in a hard, bright, but not brilliant, surface as the coarse texture of Georgian steel caused dragging. Finishing with a bloodstone produced a brilliant surface, slow to tarnish.

From the early 1770s lids and spouts, known as noses by the platers, were shaped by drop hammer, a device patented in 1769 by Richard Ford, Birmingham. The plate was laid upon a striking block fitted with a die sunk with a model of the shape required. The die sinker used small, hard chisels for chipping out entirely by hand the various details for his pattern. Above this was a hammer that was lifted by means of a rope between two vertical rods, its face raised with a shape exactly corresponding to the sunken die. When the hammer fell upon the striking block it forced the metal into the desired shape. Such ware required plate of less than one-third the gauge of the metal required for similar products in battery copper. By 1783 two Birmingham stampers were engaged solely in this work. The stamped units were joined together by solder melted by heat from a blowpipe.

Until the mid-1790s most Sheffield plate shaped by the drop hammer lacked clear sharp definition because the tools quickly became blunted. The hard cast steel made at Sheffield in the new large crucibles from about 1793 overcame this defect (see Chapter 5).

From about 1815 complete units might be shaped in this way. A pair of dies might be used to stamp parts for more than one article: a snuffer dish stamping, for instance, might equally well be utilized in a standish.

The shaping and raising of the rims of shallow objects such as trays, waiters, dishes, meat and soup plates, dish warmers and the like were accomplished with the aid of a device known as a swage block, a tool invented in 1762. It consisted of a pair of hinged jaws about an inch wide and measuring eight to ten inches long. This was placed in a vice. The lower surface of the upper jaw was cut with curves and grooves raised in relief, and the fixed lower part held in the vice and known as the face was sunk with corresponding curves (in intaglio).

To protect the fused silver from damage the jaw was covered with a piece of leather. A piece of hard, polished copper was also used for keeping the edges of the article smooth during the swaging process. The edge of the silvered plate was placed between these jaws and held firmly by a cord to which a heavy drop weight was attached. The upper jaw was then struck lightly with a hammer or, if the metal was very thin, pressed down by hand. The plate was then pushed forward a little and the upper jaw struck again. This process was continued time after time around the entire rim until the repeated pressure raised the border to the required outline.

Spinning in the lathe was used to raise hollow-ware, replacing earlier hand raising when the number of pieces required did not warrant the cutting of expensive dies. A special copper of a finer, softer quality than that normally used, yet suitable for the fusing process, was evolved for spinning. The form of the unit to be spun was first turned in a block of hard wood which was fixed in a lathe. Discs of plated copper were cut of a size to take the convex or hemi-spherical form required. The disc of metal was held against the wooden form by means of a short rod extending to the back centre of the lathe. The spinner then greased the centre of the metal and with a long shaft of hardwood pressed the metal as it revolved in a fast-running lathe, forcing it closely to the wooden form. The shaft was held by one hand and under the arm, gradually working it further down until the plate was shaped as the form. For unplated ware the shape was obtained by means of a steel tool or burnisher. Puckering was prevented by manipulation of a wooden block held in the spinner's left hand.

Compression made the metal hard so that it required softening by frequent annealing during the spinning process. This was accomplished by holding the plated copper over a lamp and then placing it in a hot oven until the carbon burned away. The spinning of the softened metal was then continued. When this shaping was complete the spinner lapped over the edge of the rim. Careful inspection of a spun piece will often reveal faint concentric circles although these might be removed by pressure from a steel burnisher. A bloodstone burnisher was used to remove ridges and unevenness and obtain a smooth surface. Some of the largest articles ever made in Sheffield plate, dating between about 1820 and the late-1830s, were worked up from spun units.

Collectors of Sheffield plate should be aware that during the 1820s and 1830s large quantities of cheap, thin-gauge, poorly plated ware were imported from France. This copper, which was quickly spun and required no annealing, was of a redder tinge than its English counterpart, and imparted a faintly pinkish hue to the thin film of silver.

# 5. Decoration and finishing techniques

Surface ornament on Sheffield plate conformed as closely as possible to the designs of the fashionable London silversmiths employing hand-craftsmen and later to patterns devised by the factory silversmiths of Sheffield and Birmingham, being built from units produced by speedy mechanical processes. But the Sheffield platers, of course, laboured under a hazard unknown to members of the Goldsmiths' Company. The silver-plated surface was always liable to crack under their heavy-handed methods, leading eventually to flaking that would reveal the underlying copper. Grace of line and proportion rather than elaborations of ornament became the platers' goal and brought them notable success.

*Pierced Decoration* on Sheffield plate dates no earlier than the introduction of double-sided plating in the late 1760s. It was used on such articles as cake and sweetmeat baskets, epergnes, dish rings, coasters, sugar baskets, mustard pots and salt cellars – some of them fitted with blue glass liners – mazarines, fish slices and so on.

Saw-cutting was impossible as it exposed the underlying core of copper in a way that could not be remedied. Instead, hand-operated fly presses were fitted with steel tools with hardened tips forged to the shape and size of the required perforations. Jewellers had been using such presses for a full quarter of a century. The tool was aligned above a steel bed sunk with a perforation of identical shape. The impact of the heavily weighted rotating arm of the press forced the tool downward through the Sheffield plate into the bed. The tool was so designed that it dragged a layer of silver from the face of the plate, causing it to protrude slightly beyond the sheared copper. The silver was then lapped over to conceal the telltale red metal and the laps burnished until invisible. A bedding tool below prevented mis-shaping of the lower edges. At first each motif was pressed individually, the tool and steel bed necessarily being changed for perforations of various shapes and sizes. By the mid-1790s, after the development of a much harder cast steel, perforations were pressed in small groups, thus doing the work more expeditiously. It is easy to distinguish between the two methods of piercing. After about 1820 steam-operated presses were used. Piercing is often found associated with embossing and flat-chasing.

*Embossing*, known also as high relief chasing or repoussé work, was worked up from the back before finishing upon the front of the plate. It was in considerable use until about 1780 and again from 1820, to decorate hollow-ware such as tea services, jugs, bowls, and so on. The shaped article was lightly sketched with the design in red chalk or, when a number of identical patterns were needed, worked out with pounced tracing paper as used by engravers. As embossed ornament projected from the surface, the plate was held upon a bag of sand and the design hammered from the interior by means of a raising stake or snarling iron held in a vice. The end of the iron nearer to the vice was struck with a hammer, the rebound on the further end being sufficient to raise the minute curves required upon the article. Repeated strokes of the hammer upon the iron raised a pattern of small embossed details that could be worked into flowers, foliage and scroll-work. When complete the vessel was filled with a composition of pitch and crushed ashes from the grate and rested upon the bag of sand whilst the exterior was finished. This consisted of chasing with hammer and punches to clarify the detail but in early work this modification of the contours was minimal. In the nineteenth century deeply cut steel dies produced similar embossed effects.

Embossing in high relief could be carried out only on copper fused with a thicker than standard layer of silver to avoid the hazard of flaking when the silver was stretched, thus exposing the copper. In 1822 William Mitchell, a silversmith of Glasgow, patented a press with which flowers and other motifs could be pressed upon waiters and other flat ware in simulation of chasing. This machine was adapted from Bramah's water press. The specification states that this was suited for decorating 'gold, silver plate, plated or other ductile metals' and that 'the impression required is completed by a single operation of the press and without having recourse to annealing or softening of the metal'. Sir Edward Thomason installed one of these machines in his Birmingham factory immediately the patent had been filed and in his *Diary* stated that impressions of wreaths of flowers, figures and ornaments were made with but one concussion.

*Chasing* decorated Sheffield plate continually from the 1780s. The centres of flat-ware might be ornamented in this way as well as much hollow-ware. Flat-ware was embedded in hot pitch laid on a board which had a hemispherical underpiece resting in a cavity on the work bench so that it could easily be turned about by the chaser. The design was traced upon the metal and then indented with hammer blows upon a range of differently shaped punches. This eventually gave an effect of slight relief to the untouched plain parts. A matted ground was made by punching tiny circles and this also contributed to the relief effect. Such chasing was carried out entirely on the front of the article, the back remaining untouched.

After completion of the chasing the edges were dressed and mounts soldered into position and the piece was boiled in a lixivium of pearl ashes to remove the remains of the pitch. The relief work was then dry brushed with a mixture of rouge and whiting and finally burnished. Hollow-ware was similarly treated except that the vessel was first filled with pitch.

*Flat chasing*. To the silversmith the form of ornament described above might be regarded as flat chasing but to the Sheffield plate decorator the term was given to a process confined almost entirely to his trade, being required as a substitute for engraving. This was used from about 1780 on teapots, coffee pots, sugar basins, tea urns, tea canisters, coasters, salt cellars, muffineers and mustard pots, often in association with piercing. The pattern was transferred to the plated surface in the usual way with powdered chalk and perforated tracing paper and the dotted lines thus formed emphasized lightly with a steel point. The craftsmen worked the lines with tiny punches of various shapes, using a hammer to 'dent in' the pattern. The plate was held against a steel stake as the design was worked upon its surface but the indentations are usually to be detected upon the reverse. Shading and stippling effects were added later.

*Fluting and reeding* decorated Sheffield plate throughout its period, the parallel channels or convexities being either straight or in a slanting, spiral arrangement. Early examples display flat fluting: the indentations are less conspicuous than in the later reedings as the surface of the vessel remained flat. The rounded convex reeding, sometimes called full-fluting, was popular from about 1790. Combinations of fluting and reeding are found on some early nineteenth-century plate. There was a fashion for bat's-wing fluting to encircle hollow-ware. In this graduated flutes radiating from the base of a vessel ended in a series of dipping arcs: the more usual alternative, petal fluting – and petal reeding – ended each channel with a tiny arch.

Reeding and the raised divisions between the flutes constituted a form of embossing which had to be worked from the underside or inside of the article and finished with surface chasing. The interior of the vessel was placed against the face of a raising stake fixed in a vice. The craftsman struck the stake near to the vice, creating a rebound which indented the plate. After the circuit of flutes had been raised the vessel was filled with hot pitch and placed on a sand cushion so that the workman could clarify his outlines with chasing tools.

*Die stamping* was a highly skilled branch of the Sheffield plate trade. At about the same time that Bolsover first fused silver to copper plate, Benjamin Huntsman (1704–76) invented cast steel, thus revolutionizing both the steel and the plating industries. Huntsman, a Quaker working as a clockmaker at Doncaster during the 1730s, disappointed with the lack of uniformity in texture of English and imported steels, evolved a more efficient process by which hard steel of uniform texture was produced. His primary difficulty was to find a source of refractory clay for making crucibles capable of withstanding great heat. Deposits of suitable clay, already being used by the local glasshouses for their melting pots, were found at Handsworth, Sheffield. Here he set up his furnaces and conducted long, arduous experiments until he produced a flawless, homogeneous cast steel combining hardness and toughness with ductility.

A contemporaneous report recorded that Huntsman's steel was so hard that it would 'cut glass, and endure arduous work as a Turning Tool for any kind of metal without undergoing those frequent [maintenance] repairs necessary to tools made of any other kind of steel. It also takes on the highest polish: therefore, for Burnishing Tools, or plated, to heat or roll any kind of metal to a fine surface; and, as to Dies [for stamps] there is no steel that can be made into a face of equal hardness or durability. In Buckles, Buttons and other articles of the steel kind, to which great superficial brilliancy is requisite, there is no other steel so completely adequate. For Mirrors it is particularly suitable.'

The *London Chronicle*, 14 July 1761, noted the recent invention of the drop hammer from which small objects could be stamped, using Huntsman's crucible steel, adding the comment, 'these ingenious dies strike excellent pieces . . . thus it is that sword hilts, watch chains, buttons, snuff boxes, dial plates and many other branches of small manufacture are executed with so much exactness and facility, as enables us to spread our commerce in those articles into every part of the world.'

The almost simultaneous invention of Huntsman's cast steel in Sheffield made it possible for dies to be sunk so skilfully that they could impress the surface of plated copper in long runs, producing clearly-defined patterns that closely resembled embossed work. At first small units were stamped such as feet, handles and knobs struck in two halves, soldered together and burnished to conceal the joint. Before attachment they were made solid by filling with lead-tin alloy. Strip dies were later used for shaping short lengths such as gadrooned and beaded edges. By 1780 lids and spouts were stamped, and from the 1790s flat work such as waiters and trays. As many as 50 strokes of the stamp might be required, the work then being covered by protective plates. Matthew Linwood, Great Charles Street, Birmingham, a silversmith and plater, was first to specialize in the use of such dies for Sheffield plate.

Stamping dies from about 1815 were made from cast iron that had undergone a process of chilling. This gave the metal a very fine close texture reflected in the greater sharpness of outline to embossments. Die work did not finish the decoration which required to be completed by hand with chasing tools. This hand finishing is simple to detect by the irregularity of the fluting and variations of minute curves. Dies were used largely for candlestick units: Bradbury calcu-

57   Cylindrical bougie box

5   Horizontal wax jack,
    *c.* 1800

56   Horizontal wax
     jack, 1780s

58   Vertical wax
     jack, late eight-
     eenth century

59   Bougie boxes, 1790s and *c.* 1820; wax jack, 1780s

60  Snuffers, *c.* 1830; pair of candlestick sconces; taper box, *c.* 1800; snuffer tray, *c.* 1800

62   Pair of two-candle wall lights

63   Lantern, *c.* 1795

64   Shaving mirror
     with oil lamp and
     font, 1798

65  Plain wine cooler, *c.* 1800

66  Wine cooler, *c.* 1800

67  Wine cooler, 1820

68  Wine cooler, *c.* 1800

69   Wine cooler,
     1825

70   Wine cooler, 1820

71   Grecian urn
     wine cooler, *c.* 1810

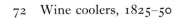

72   Wine coolers, 1825–50

73  Double decanter stands with wire couplings containing rings for the stoppers, 1800

74  Four coasters or decanter stands with turned mahogany bases

75 Decanter wagon in the form of a naval 'jolly boat', *c.* 1825

76 Wine wagon, early nineteenth century

77 Wine wagon containing loose coasters, *c.* 1830

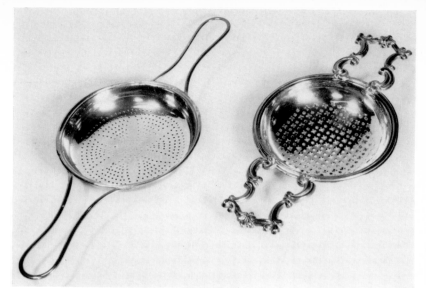

78 Orange and lemon strainers, 1770s and 1780s

79 Orange and lemon strainer for use with punch bowl, silver, 1749, extensively copied in Sheffield plate

80 Orange and lemon strainer, 1778

81 Combined orange and wine strainer, early nineteenth century

82 Early Victorian three-part wine funnel

83 Combined orange strainer and wine funnel, early nineteenth century

84 Orange and lemon strainer fitted to Sheffield plate funnel, c. 1810

85 Octagonal teapot, late eighteenth century

86 Octagonal teapot, late eighteenth century

87 Octagonal teapot, late eighteenth century

88 Oval teapot, early nineteenth century

9   Teapot in 'revived rococo' style

90   Teapot, 1795

1   Teapot, *c.* 1800

92   Three-piece set for tea tray, early nineteenth century

93　Four-piece tea and coffee service with matching tray, *c.* 1810

94 Five-piece tea and coffee service, nineteenth century

95 Three-piece tea service, together with coffee biggin with stand and spirit lamp

96   Three-piece tea set, early 1800s

97   Tea service, 1820s

98   Tea and coffee service, 1811

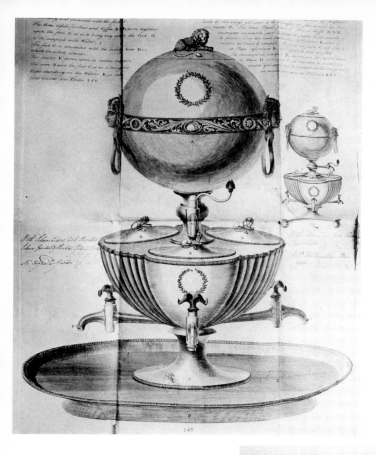

99  Tea and coffee machine, 1797

100  Tea and coffee machine with
spirit lamp

101 Tea and coffee machine, *c.* 1800

102 Tea and coffee machine, early
nineteenth century

lated that the cost of a complete set of candlestick dies could be as much as £50. Manufacturers hired dies and other tools to each other: thus identical articles may be found bearing different marks.

*Silver shields* upon which a coat of arms, crest, monogram, date or other inscription could be engraved, appeared on trays and waiters, tea and coffee services, dishes and their covers, ice pails and many other articles of Sheffield plate, the more nearly to complete their resemblance to silver plate but chiefly for identification purposes. It was essential for the engraving to be carried out on a thick layer of silver as otherwise streaks of the underlying copper would be revealed. During the early years this was done by using plates heavily coated with silver. Then, as mentioned above, there was a vogue for encircling hollow ware with a silver band engraved with ornament, including a shield-shaped reserve for an armorial emblem.

From about 1790 a separate soldered-in-shield was used. This was accomplished by cutting a piece of metal clean out of the plate and inserting either a piece of silver or a section of plate of similar size and gauge heavily silvered to be capable of accepting the burin without showing any red metal. The scarcely perceptible join was masked by an engraved cartouche or a wavy border. Examination of the reverse will reveal if this method has been used. By about 1800 a shield of silver might be soldered directly to the surface of the fused plate without any insertion. A new technique had been developed by 1810. A circle or rectangle of four-gauge silver leaf hand-beaten from pure metal of appropriate size with its edge very slightly tapered off, was 'sweated on' or 'rubbed in' over the silver on the area to be engraved. Such is the powerful cohesion between pure and sterling silver that the union was perfect when well managed, and the two parts when finished and burnished showed no line of demarcation. The plate with the extra layer pinned temporarily into the required position, was heated over a clear charcoal fire until red hot. The silver was then rubbed vigorously with a steel burnisher until it adhered to the plated surface, care being taken that no air remained between the two layers. The burnisher, which was worked outward, became hot with the friction and was kept cool by frequent dipping into cold water. Finally the shield was planished.

The presence of a sweated-in shield is not necessarily indicative of fine-quality plate, for the film of sterling silver fused to the copper plate tended to become thinner during the early nineteenth century. The join may be detected by warming the piece, when the sweated-in silver will display a lighter hue than the surrounding metal. Also, when a piece of Sheffield plate becomes oxidized, a difference in colour between the two qualities of silver will be immediately visible. A microscopic dot was always made in the centre of such shields by which the engraver could identify his central point. The presence of a silver shield is an indication that the piece is genuine Sheffield plate. The shields on goods sold by manufacturers and merchants were plain, to be engraved subsequently to the commission of the final purchaser, but the majority have remained plain.

*Flat hammering* was perhaps the most skilled of all the processes associated with the manufacture of Sheffield plate. This operation was essential to obtain a perfectly smooth mirror-like surface particularly on plate where the engraver's shield had been rubbed in. The metal around this shield stretched and became distorted by heat and hammering. These flaws were removed and the plate made rigid and firm by the use of the 'flat hammer', a tool weighing about four pounds, with a pair of slightly convex faces measuring $2\frac{1}{2}$ inches in diameter. The hardest stroke that can be given by such a hammer will leave an impression no larger than one inch in diameter. The hammer was used on the back of the plated object, its face resting on the smooth, slightly domed top of a highly polished steel stake set into a heavy wooden base. The hammering had to be so controlled that every blow merged with the previous one and an absolutely smooth surface resulted, needing only burnishing and hand polishing to finish.

*Engraving and bright-cutting.* In the ordinary sense engraving is impossible on Sheffield plate as the burin would pierce the silver and reveal the red copper beneath. In the 1770s the London silversmiths were decorating fashionable silver with bright-cut engraving, soon to become highly developed by the Birmingham factory silversmiths. The Sheffield platers had added bright-cutting to their decorative techniques by 1780. The lines of such engraving displayed a delicate faceted effect. Bright-cutting found corresponding expression in the fine diamond-cutting on glass decanters of the 1790s and the tiny inlaid checks found on contemporaneous furniture.

In order to compete, Sheffield plate manufacturers at first introduced the ornament on bands of solid silver which were carefully soldered into position. The band might be as much as one inch wide and was already decorated with bright-cutting. Tea-urns were often encircled in this way. These silver bands, considered to be a desirable ornamental feature, were necessarily raised slightly above the surface of the fused plate.

Bright-cutting carried out directly on the surface of the plate necessitated a deeper layer of silver than was usual: 24 ounces of silver to eight pounds of copper. In this form of engraving the tool employed, in various sizes, was a gouge, sharpened chisel-wise, bevelled from corner to adjacent corner and having two cutting points. Edge and point were used as required to produce what was really a kind of chip carving, outlining patterns of flowers, ribbons and so on by cutting narrow channels with variously slanting sides to produce the faceted effect.

*Gilding* the interiors of sugar basins, salt cellars, cream jugs, mustard pots, egg cups and the like was essential as a precaution against staining by the foods they served which tended to corrode silver and produce black spots difficult to eradicate. Glass linings, although less costly, were clumsy substitutes. Occasionally examples of Sheffield plate, such as dessert stands, epergnes, candelabra, punch bowls and monteiths are to be found with their entire interiors gilded. Because the gilding process was carried out at a temperature more than sufficient to melt off soldered units such as feet and handles these were applied after gilding.

Gilding was carried out by the mercurial process known as fire gilding. This was virtually the method described by Benvenuto Cellini in his treatise on goldsmithing published in 1568. The method used by the Sheffield platers was described fully in *Dictionarium Polygraphicum*, 1735.

> 'Take leaf gold beaten very thin and cut into little bits what quantity you please. Put into a galley-pot or an iron ladle coated with whiting and water and then dried, and put to it so much quicksilver as will just cover it. Stir them with a stick and make an amalgam, and when you have done, strain them through a piece of shammy leather, squeezing the leather hard with your hand. That which remains behind in the leather, and looks like silver, is the gold amalgamated, and that which is to be used in this work.'

I have seen this process used for the gilding of naval officers' buttons, despite the fact that, because of the health hazards involved, gilding in this way has been illegal in workshops for nearly 50 years.

The plated article was first cleaned by scrubbing with a wire brush and water. It was then coated with nitrate of mercury made by mixing a quart of strong nitric acid with a tablespoonful of mercury. This was applied with a rag until the plating became bright. Amalgamated gold of the consistency of stiff clay was then spread evenly over the whole piece and heated, gilded side uppermost, over a fire of court charcoal (coke was used later). This caused the mercury to evaporate leaving a film of dull yellow gold securely fixed to the metal ready for burnishing. The amalgam was generally applied directly to the copper of single-sided plate. Such gilding, although costly, was durable.

No evidence exists that gold might be fused to copper plate. A booklet, *Old Sheffield Plate*, issued by the Sheffield City Museum, states that 'the only pieces ever submitted to this Museum as gold plate were clearly modern counterfeits'.

*Burnishing* was the final process in the manufacture of Sheffield plate. This gave a highly polished surface to the silver and at the same time assisted in the concealment of joins. It was solely the work of women using tools of steel, agate and bloodstone cut with faces into almost every shape and ranging in size from $\frac{1}{4}$ inch to an inch, and pointed to facilitate polishing crevices and corners. These burnishers were cemented into ferrules attached to wooden hafts. The part to be burnished was cleaned thoroughly and smeared with soft soap. It was then rubbed with white Calais sand and water until all traces of greasiness had been removed. Grease would prevent the tool from making contact with the surface. Scratches were removed with a rough agate burnisher passed rapidly backwards and forwards over the metal, considerable pressure being used and each stroke made as long as possible. To prevent dragging the burnisher was dipped frequently into soap suds. The pores of the silver were now closed by using a steel burnisher which also produced a bright but not brilliant surface as the coarse texture of the Georgian steel tended to cause dragging which resulted in streaks. A leather strap sprinkled with burnishing oil hung nearby for the worker to keep her tools smooth and bright. A burnisher of middle-quality agate was then used: this effectively removed all marks left by the steel tool. Final burnishing was accomplished with a bloodstone: this produced a surface difficult to tarnish. The silver surface was then hand-polished with wet rouge and dried with soft old linen. This resulted in a mirror-like finish.

*Tinning* the interiors of hollow-ware such as tea urns, teapots, coffee pots, hot water jugs, dish covers and so on was essential to combat the hazards, real or imaginary, commonly associated with the action of liquids on copper. A tin lining was preferred to double-plated metal, as the molten tin covered all impurities and assisted in keeping the article clean, tin being much more easily cleaned than silver and longer lasting. Pattern books as late as the 1820s describe certain flat articles such as waiters, trays, snuffer dishes and other flat ware with a smooth surface on the reverse as having either 'plated' or 'tinned' backs. Tinned backs were highly polished and when new closely resembled the silver upper surface.

Several patents were granted in the late eighteenth century for 'tinning and lining of all utensils or vessels made of copper', but the processes proved too complicated for commercial exploitation. The method of tinning used by the platers was simple and effective. The surface to be tinned was cleaned thoroughly by scraping and the outer surface protected with a glue-whiting mixture against accidental spilling of molten tin. The surface to be tinned was then sprinkled with a solution of sal ammoniac and the vessel gently heated. Molten tin was then poured over the entire copper surface, being allowed to flow quickly until the copper was concealed beneath a thick coating of tin. Hot surplus tin was immediately wiped off with a linen cloth.

Pure grained tin, costing tenpence per pound in the late eighteenth century was applied thickly. The effect of constant service was that the vessel required re-tinning from time to time. The standard cost was '2d an inch diameter measuring the longest way within the rim'. A method was discovered early in the nineteenth century which made tinning long-lasting, its brilliance resembling sterling silver. Tinning was a dangerous process liable to cause lead or arsenic poisoning. Not until 1909 was it made compulsory by law for tinning to be done under an efficient fume extractor, and for no young persons to be employed.

# 6. Edges and mounts

All makers of articles in Sheffield plate were faced with the problem of concealing the underlying copper. Even when both faces of the copper were plated every edge showed a thin line of the reddish tone. Bolsover and other early craftsmen had also to conceal the underside of the plate. This could be done by tinning but neither this nor silver solder had sufficient wear-resistance for lasting service on edges and rims. Sometimes an early piece was turned back on itself at the edges. But step by step craftsmen introduced, and sometimes patented, better ways of meeting this problem and at the same time strengthening the edges and rims where wear was heaviest. These consisted of adding narrow bands of metal, usually known as mounts. Collectors distinguish between the early period when the mount consisted of some form of the silver-plated copper, and the later period, from about 1775, when the platers largely accepted the need to use more substantial silver. Under close scrutiny it is possible to distinguish ten forms of edge and mount treatment though their periods of use overlap considerably.

*Sheared edge* (1743–58). At first the dark reddish copper edges, exposed when the silvered metal was sheared, were concealed beneath a film of silver solder or tin. This ineffectual method severely limited the range of productions.

*Single-lapped copper edge* (1758–80s) introduced by Joseph Hancock. The silver-plated copper was cut with a blunt tool so designed that the layer of silver, thicker than formerly, was extended beyond the edge of the copper to lap over and conceal the raw edge but offered no lasting wear-resistance.

*Double-lapped copper edge* (1768–early nineteenth century). This was the earliest method of adding separately formed concealment to sheared edges. It was derived from patent no. 905 granted to George Whateley, 8 November 1768. The specification is given in Chapter 27, including a method of plating silver upon copper wire and then drawing it into a fine thread that could be flattened into a narrow paper-thin flat ribbon, wholly silver-covered. This was soldered to the edge of the silvered plate, protruding sufficiently to allow it to be lapped over the raw edge and lie flat against the underside. So skilfully was this done that after burnishing it was difficult to detect the join. This was the first and most obvious way of coping with the edge on Sheffield plate silvered on both faces, but quickly suffered in use and cleaning.

*Silver-lapped edge* (1775–c. 1815). The advance was to a U-shaped or double-lapped wire of sterling silver. This was formed from a narrow ribbon of paper-thin silver, which might measure as little as $\frac{1}{16}$ inch wide. When passed through a hole in a draw-plate this took the shape of a fine-bore tube. The seam was then opened throughout its length to suit the gauge of the plate upon which it was to be mounted. This was accomplished by fixing in a vice a steel plate of the same gauge, inserting it into the seam of the tube and drawing the silver along. The resultant U-shaped silver wire was fitted over the plated edge of the plate and soldered to both surfaces. The joins on both surfaces were burnished until invisible. Silver wire $\frac{1}{22}$ inch in diameter, might be soldered beneath a rim that was to be given a silver lapped edge.

*Drawn silver or plated wire for joints* (1785–1820). Silver wires may also be detected where they have been applied to strengthen the joints of plated articles. For this purpose wires were required in various curved and angled sections: a process for producing them was patented by Valentine Rawle, patent no. 1472, 16 April 1785. The wire might be of pure silver or alloyed with brass but better than sterling, or might be heavily plated. The specification states that 'mitres, angles, and joints of plated wares are covered with stronger plated metal or solid silver [drawn wires] as the nature of the wares may require and which invention is likewise applicable to wires made round, oval, etc. These wires were drawn into a range of cross-sections – flat, half-round, hollow-U, sharp-L, and other angles and curves. These were filled with lead-tin solder and shaped by hand to fit as required.

*Solid silver cast mounts* (c. 1780–1830). The next obvious advance was to use applied silver mounts as a decorative feature of plated ware. Most lavishly and with permanent wear-resistance these might be cast in sterling silver, their ornament finished by hand chasing. Such enrichment is found only on the best Sheffield plate. They were soldered into position and are sometimes difficult to distinguish from the later stamped mounts when these, too, have been finished by chasing. The most handsome in design and workmanship among solid silver mounts were those made by Matthew Boulton & Plate Company who usually impressed them with the inscription SILVER BORDERS. Those made by the platers in Sheffield were stamped SILVER : EDGED.

*Silver stamped mounts* (from the early 1790s). The obvious development from costly castings was the application of ornamental mounts in silver that could be patterned in relief by die-stamping. Ribbons of silver were struck with patterned steel dies in strips of four or five inches at a time. The last part of the impression was so arranged that it fitted into the first detail of the next impression, thus securing a continuous pattern. Such mounts were rendered heavy and wear-resistant by filling with lead-tin alloy. This filling process was described by Frederick Bradbury: 'After brushing the outside edges with a mixture of glue and whitening, the mount was laid in a plaster mould or bed of Calais sand. Into the mount the solder was then poured in a molten state with the aid of a small ladle. A hot, wide-edged soldering iron was gently rubbed over the surface of the molten solder, powdered resin being requisitioned with the object of making the mount 'tin' more readily and causing the solder to flux. Whilst the solder was in a molten condition, a round piece of wood dipped in oil was used for gently rubbing over the surface of the solder, so as to ensure it having a perfectly flat surface and this enabling the edges of the mount, which had been left on by the stamper, to be more easily removed.' Usually, however, this outer edge of silver was lapped over to hide the raw copper, obviating the need for separately soldered-on silver threaded edges. Underseams were burnished until invisible but the divisions between mounts of differing designs may be detected.

The earliest stamped silver mounts were simple bead and thread patterns and the period's straight and slanting gadroons, but early in the nineteenth century technical improvements permitted the scope of design to be widened to include festoon and bead, leaf and scroll, egg and dart, scallop shell, laurel leaf, scrolls and other simple motifs. Technical improvements from about 1800 produced more elaborate designs: scallop shells, dolphins and oak leaves were interspersed with small motifs. The silver was either pure metal or alloyed with brass. Sterling silver resulted in finer work, as regards both colour and durability, but wear on the tools was much harder, considerably reducing their useful life. Pure silver mounts were used on common ware as this could be rolled much thinner for stamping without the hazard of splitting in the tools. Common-quality plate may be recognized by the bevelled edge clearly seen at the back of the mount, where the solder may be distinctly visible.

In the early 1820s designs became more elaborate, including fruit and flowers, fruiting vines and bouquets stamped in very high relief. This heavy ornament was fashionably superseded from about 1830 by arabesque and entwined scroll mounts with an occasional leaf or tendril. This eventually supplanted almost all form of flower ornament.

*Wide silver stamped mounts* (from 1815). These, in ornamental rococo designs were applied to silver-lapped edges. The division between mount and edge is discernible.

*Improved silver stamped mounts* (from 1824). A method was devised for applying rococo mounts so that the junction between the plated surface and the mount was rendered invisible. Samuel Roberts of Sheffield was granted a patent, no. 5057, for this invention in 1824. Briefly, the method was to solder drawn silver wire over the bare edge of the copper. This was flattened with a hammer until it extended a little beyond the ornamental stamped mount. The projecting part of the soldered silver edge was then filed off. The abridged specification describes the process as 'a new method of preparing for and putting on the ornamented silver edges upon those plated articles on which such edges are introduced. After filing the edge of the article to nearly the shape (but somewhat less) of the ornamented indented silver edging to hard-solder a silver thread of the required strength upon the said edge, and then to flat it with a hammer upon a metal strike to the breadth and strength required, and so as that the outer edge will extend a little beyond the ornamented silver edge which is then to be soft soldered in the usual way. The projecting part of the hard-soldered silver edge which extends beyond the ornamented silver edge is then to be filed off, and the two edges burnished together till the joinings disappear.'

*Electro-type mounts* (from the mid-1840s). These mounts were made by Elkington's electro-deposit process used for electro-plating. They may be recognized by being slightly lighter in hue than the sterling silver fused to copper plate and different in surface texture when compared with mounts cast or stamped in sterling silver (see page 80).

# 7. Makers' marks

There was never a legal obligation to strike Sheffield plate with identifying trade marks. During the early years a few makers and retailers struck marks resembling contemporaneous hallmarks on sterling silver. These were intended to suggest to the ill-informed that they were acquiring goods made of the precious metal. Without close inspection it was virtually impossible for a layman to distinguish between the genuine marks and the imitations struck chiefly on tankards, loving cups and covers, coffee pots, candlesticks, small waiters and oval meat dishes made earlier than 1773. The fraud became so widespread that on 8 March of that year a petition was presented to the House of Commons by the silversmiths of Sheffield and Birmingham demanding that assay offices should be established in those towns. This was the result of seven years' vigorous action on the part of Matthew Boulton of Birmingham. Details of commonplace frauds were laid before the Parliamentary Committee. The Goldsmiths' Company of London opposed the application.

The Committee eventually reported that 'the Artificers of Sheffield and Birmingham are now arrived at so great a perfection in plating with Silver the Goods made of base Metal that they very closely resemble solid silver; and if the Practice which has been introduced, of putting Marks upon them somewhat resembling those used at the Assay Offices, shall not be restrained, many more Frauds and Impositions will be committed upon the Public.' The result was that an Act of Parliament was enacted empowering the establishment of Assay Offices in both towns.

The text of the Act so far as plating is concerned reads:

> Persons counterfeiting Marks or Stamps used by the said Companies, or transposing Stamps from one piece to another and exposing such to Sale, or who shall transpose or remove or cause to be transposed or removed, from one piece of wrought Plate to another, or to any Plated Vessel, or to any

vessel of Base Metal, any Mark Stamp or impression made or to be made by or with any Mark or Stamp used or to be used as aforesaid by the said Companies respectively or by any Maker or Worker of Silver Plate, or any or either of them or shall sell, exchange or expose to Sale or export out of this Kingdom any Silver wrought Plate or any Vessel of Base Metal with such forged or Counterfeit Mark Stamp or impression thereon every such person offending and lawfully convicted shall by order of the Court before whom such an offender shall be convicted be transported to some of His Majesty's Colonies or Plantations in America for the Term of 14 years.

And be it further enacted by the Authority aforesaid, that if any working Silversmith or Dealer in Wrought Plate, or any Worker or Dealer in any other Metal plated or covered with Silver, shall strike or cause to be struck any Letter or Letters upon any vessel or other Thing made of metal plated or covered with Silver or upon any Metal Vessel or other Thing made to look like Silver, such Person or Persons so offending shall forfeit the Sum of 100 Pounds.

The text of this Act was shoddily constructed and included ambiguities. This made it essential for an amended Act to be passed in 1784 in which the position of plate manufacturers regarding marks was clearly defined. The alterations read as follows:

If any working Silversmith or Dealer in Wrought Plate, or any Worker or Dealer in any other Metal plated or covered with silver, shall strike or cause to be struck a Letter or Letters, upon any Vessel or other Thing made of Metal plated or covered with Silver, or upon any metal Vessel or other Thing made to look like Silver, such Person or Persons so offending shall be subject to the Penalty mentioned [in the above clause]: and Doubts have arisen whether a Manufacturer of Goods plated with Silver can or may strike his Name upon such Goods without incurring the said Penalty: and by reason of such Doubts the Manufacturers of Goods plated with Silver have been deterred from striking their Names upon plated Goods, whereby a proper Distinction betwixt plated Goods of the different Manufacturers is prevented, and all emulation in that Branch of Business is destroyed, to the manifest prejudice of the said Manufactory: For obviating such doubts be it further enacted That it shall be lawful for any Manufacturer of Goods plated with Silver within the said Town of *Sheffield*, or within one Hundred Miles thereof, to strike or cause to be struck upon any metal Vessel or Thing plated or covered with Silver, his or her Surname or in case of any Partnership the Name or Firm of such Partnership, and also some Mark, Figure or Device to be struck at the end of such Surname, or other Name or Firm: such Mark, Figure or Device not being the same or in Imitation of any Mark made use of by any Assay Office established by Law for Assaying of Wrought Plate, without being subject to any Penalty or Forfeiture for so doing.

Provided that every such Surname or Name or Firm shall be in plain and legible Characters and struck with one Punch only: and every such Mark, Figure or Device shall before the same is made use of be submitted to the Examination of the said Company of Guardians of the said Sheffield Assay Office, and be approved by them and registered in a Book to be kept for that Purpose: for which Registry there shall be lawfully demanded and taken from any Manufacturer of Plated Goods on whose account such Registry shall be made the Sum of two Shillings and six Pence and no more.

And be it further enacted That in case any Manufacturer or Manufacturers of Plated Goods within the said Town of Sheffield, or within 100 miles thereof, shall at any Time hereafter strike any Name, Mark, Figure or Device upon his Plated Goods, which shall not have been previously registered at the said Assay Office for the said Town of Sheffield, or which shall have been previously registered at the said Office by any other Manufacturer of Plated Goods, every Person so offending shall for every such Offence, forfeit or pay to the said Wardens the sum of 100 Pounds, to be recovered in like manner as any Penalty or Forfeiture is authorized or directed to be recovered and to be applied as any Money is herein-before directed to be applied.

Under the Act from which the above sections have been quoted, the Birmingham platers were required to register their marks at Sheffield. The Assay Office drew considerable sums from Birmingham in fines. In 1824 the Birmingham Assay Office applied to Parliament for a new Act which would give them power to register platers' marks. This was unsuccessful. Registration continued until 1836, but between 1824 and 1836 only four Sheffield marks were registered and none from Birmingham. The total number of marks registered was Sheffield 55 and Birmingham 77.

Marks were recorded in the Assay Office Register by 'smoking the face of the punch and then impressing it upon the page' against the plater's name and address and the date. 'The portions of the mark depressed by the punch thus appear in black, the letters being shown in white.' The maker's name in full was rarely used after 1810, the registered device only being used, perhaps with initials. In some instances this was accompanied by the retailer's name and address.

The Act specified that the plater's name and emblem as registered should be struck with one punch only, a requirement which often resulted in a clumsy disfiguring mark which revealed at once to the casual observer that the metal was not in sterling silver, a detail, no doubt, welcomed by the silversmiths. Some marks as recorded in the Register measure as much as $1\frac{1}{2}$ inches in length, necessitating the use of a curved punch on curved surfaces.

After the close of the Napoleonic wars in 1815 a crown might be struck on fine-quality plate. Its purpose was to distinguish Sheffield productions from the tawdry imitations then being imported from France and Austria. The crown was the town mark of the Sheffield Assay Office as incorporated in the sterling silver hallmark struck by this office. It was apparently used without authorization by platers with registered marks. The crown, however, had been used by John Winter from 1765 to 1773.

The quality of the plating varied but at no time were specific standards adopted throughout the trade. Mr H. Raymond Singleton in his booklet, *Old Sheffield Plate*, published by the Sheffield City Museum, gives the following proportions of silver to copper. In the 1760s a proportion of 1 to 10 was usual. This was later improved to a proportion of 1 to 5, a standard that gradually 'deteriorated to about 1 to 15 by the end of the century and this at a time when the silver was generally distributed between the two sides of the copper. Following the introduction of rubbed-in shields in about 1810, the quality dropped still further to about 1 to 20. By the 1840s fused plate was being made, and marked accordingly, in which the proportion of silver to copper was as low as 1 to 50.'

Some platers struck their productions with quality marks such as: BEST SHEFFIELD PLATING 80 DWTS TO 8 LBS; SHEFFIELD PLATING 50 DWTS TO 8 LBS; or SHEFFIELD LIGHT SILVER PLATING 40 DWTS TO 8 LBS. BEST and MEDIUM were terms struck in the 1820s and 1830s. The Matthew Boulton firm struck the words SILVER BORDERS when a solid silver edge had been hard soldered to the edge of the silvered plate. The Sheffield men used the term SILVER: EDGED, often with the final E or D omitted on small articles.

Although the obligation to register marks upon Sheffield plate has never been withdrawn, in about 1836 it was observed that British plate (Chapter 8) with its german silver base instead of copper was technically not Sheffield plate. Manufacturers then began to mark such plate with unregistered devices so closely resembling hallmarks on sterling silver that only an expert could distinguish between them.

In Britain it is an offence to describe as Sheffield plate any ware which has not been produced by actually fusing silver to copper. Among the subterfuges adopted to keep within legal limits is to add the letter 'd' and thus label pieces electrically plated on copper in Sheffield as 'Sheffield Plated'. Collectors should also be aware that successors to some original platers have used the original registered marks of the firms on electro-plating.

# 8. British plate

Georgian makers strove unceasingly to infuse their plate with the cold loveliness of sterling silver. In this respect their greatest success was not with Sheffield plate but with a seldom-named variant advertised at the time as British plate. This is still much in evidence, often regarded by its owners as sterling silver. Its development virtually ended the manufacture of Sheffield plate and it enjoyed a quarter-century of success before itself being eclipsed by electro-plate. In Sheffield plate the thin silver was fused over a core of copper. British plate's triumph lay in the use of a silver-coloured nickel alloy instead of the copper. This alloy was known as german silver but contained no silver at all.

British plate possessed the attributes of Sheffield plate including sterling silver mounts and in addition was harder, more durable, virtually the colour of sterling silver with a similar lustre and did not show pink when worn. An additional advantage was the fact that units could be assembled with hard solder which fuses only at a very high temperature. This saved much of the labour cost of hand-working the seams and overcame the hazard of seams opening under ordinary heat. Yet another cost-reducing factor was the amount of silver used for plating. On copper the silver tended to tinge unless a coating of substantial thickness was applied and might even discolour in the heat from a soldering iron.

German silver, first made at Hildburghausen in Saxe-Meinengen, was an alloy of copper, zinc and nickel, the proportions varying according to purpose. It was introduced to Sheffield in 1820 by one Guitike of Berlin. It was a hard but malleable alloy which could be drawn into wire 1/50 inch in diameter or rolled into plates 1/500 inch thick. The British plate masters of Birmingham and Sheffield imported much of their german silver in ingots from the Isabellenhutte Smelting Works, near Dillenburg, Germany: the composition was eight parts copper, three nickel, $3\frac{1}{2}$ zinc. When used as a substitute for silver the alloy was composed of ten parts copper, five nickel and five zinc. This was known as 'argentan' (not argentine as usually stated) or 'Berlin metal' and the wide range of unplated goods made from this alloy were so advertised from 1835 by Sheffield and Birmingham manufacturers. It is frequently but wrongly stated that argentan metal is another name for plated german silver. Typically an advertisement by W. Hutton & Co., Sheffield, distinguished between goods in plated german silver and in argentan plate.

British plate was preceded for a few years by Roberts plate in which a basis of copper was still retained but was doubly masked, being fused first with german silver and then with sterling silver. This was made under a patent (no. 5963) granted in July 1830 to Samuel Roberts, Sheffield. The preamble to the specification stated that

> 'a layer of german silver or other white or light-coloured metal was introduced between the silver and copper usually constituting plated metal. By this means, whenever the silver is partially or wholly worn off, the defect will scarcely be perceptible. This may be done either by first plating the copper ingot with the white metal, in the same manner that it is usually plated with silver, and then afterwards laying a coating of silver, in the same way, upon the white metal: or the white metal and the silver upon it may at one process be both united to the copper.'

The process is discussed fully in *Register of Arts and Sciences*, vol. 5, new series, 1831. Articles plated in this way are usually mistaken by collectors for Sheffield plate. Large numbers were made, for Roberts licensed his process to makers of fused copper plate. Because the alloy was too brittle manufacturing difficulties had to be contended with and little of this ware is known.

This method of plating was superseded by the method covered by the patent (no. 7018) granted in March 1836 to Anthony Merry, a Birmingham metal dealer. In this specification the copper was omitted and the silver plated direct to a foundation of improved-quality german silver. Under the new formula the metal was whiter than formerly and less liable to split under the hammer. The specification describes in detail the method of making the plate, no different from that already well-known to the platers on copper.

The patent application reads as follows:

> The Application of Certain White Metal, Plated, to Certain Manufactures of what are commonly called Plated Goods to which it has not been hitherto Applied: In order to plate the aforesaid alloys with fine silver I melt, say, twenty or thirty pounds weight of the softest and best German silver I can find in a casting pot, throwing in a handful of charcoal broken into small pieces, and this metal, when melted, I run into ingots of about one inch thick, three inches wide, and eight or nine inches long, or any other size I may want, more or less; I then cut or saw off the end or get [projection] plane or file the

surface flat and clean: I then fine file, scrape or otherwise smooth the surface to be plated, taking care that every part intended to be plated is clean, and free from oxidization or discolouration; I then take fine silver and roll it to the proper size or thickness I may want; I then scrape or otherwise clean the silver on one side clean and bright; I then cut the rolled silver to one-twentieth of an inch, or thereabouts, less than the metal to be plated, and place the scraped or clean side upon the bright or filed metal: I then put the metal with the silver so placed on an anvil, or any other solid foundation, and place a thick piece of iron or steel with a flat face upon the silver, strike it with a sledge hammer until I find the silver quite flat and bedded to the metal, that is, by striking it until the surface of the metal and silver touch all over; I then take a piece of flat copper, cut the size of the silver, and about one-sixteenth of an inch thick: I then get some whitening, mix it into a paste with water, and with a brush spread it over one side of the plate, and when dry I put the whitened side of this plate upon the silver, bind all three together with five or six bands of about seventeen gauge iron wire, twisting each band tight; I then take a little burnt borax ground into a paste with water, and apply it lightly around the edge of the silver, then place the metal flat in the fire of a common plating stove heated with coke, until you see the silver flush around the edge, then with great care remove it from the fire, and hold it out of the fire until the silver is set, minding at the same time to keep the metal when removed from the fire as flat as possible; I then pass it through rollers, giving it the first time a great pinch, and after this roll it in the usual way of plated metals to the width and thickness required for the article to be manufactured with it, whatever that article may be.

When Merry carried samples of his plated german silver to the Sheffield platers he was astounded to discover that his patented process had already been anticipated and fully tested by Thomas Nicholson of Gainsford & Nicholson. Although this had not been marketed, Merry's patent was invalidated and the process made available to the trade in general.

The majority of the British plate trade was secured by Birmingham. No more than three years after Merry's application for a patent the number of Sheffield platers had become drastically reduced. Robson's *Birmingham and Sheffield Directory*, 1839, lists in Birmingham 18 makers of german silver, three platers and rollers of german silver, three german silver polishers and 20 manufacturers of goods: in Sheffield there were three platers and four manufacturers. The directory shows too that Birmingham also scooped the trade in non-plated german silver.

The goods made in British plate covered the same range as Sheffield plate, the same tools being used in many instances. One firm, later to become the celebrated makers of stainless steel, Thomas Firth & Son, Sheffield, catalogued in 1839 'tea services in seventeen elegant patterns consisting of tea pot, coffee pot, sugar basin gilt inside, cream jug gilt inside; epergnes; celery stands; tea urns; corner dishes, oblong shape; corner dishes, melon pattern; corner dishes, with warmers for hot water; kettles plain or chased with stand, and lamp for spirits; bread baskets; cake baskets; cruet frames, for from four to eight glasses; egg frames with gilt cups; pickle frames, for two or three glasses; liquor frames; table candlesticks, from 8 to 12 inches high; branches to match ditto; waiters, shaped pattern, from 8 to 20 inches; chamber candlesticks; muffin plates; mustard pots; salts, gilt; ditto with rich cut glass saucers; table snuffers; chamber snuffers; knife rests; decanter stands; toast racks; wine funnels.' Another firm, David Cope & Son, Birmingham, advertised 'British Plate Wares, spoons, soup and punch ladles, asparagus tongs, sugar tongs, decanter corks and ladles, caddy shells, sugar crushers, spoons, forks &c.'

Other advertisements of the period extol the advantages of British plate. One firm announced that it was 'the nearest resemblance to Sterling Silver of any metal hitherto discovered, and warranted the power of resisting the severest acids' (a defect of Sheffield plate) and concluded with a reference to 'its most beautiful style and workmanship'.

The shapes of British plate were stereotyped for most of the units from which a piece was assembled were stamped by the drop hammer. A coffee pot, for instance, required seven sets of stamping dies for shaping the units to be soldered to the body, itself turned up from sheets of metal.

Two types of silver mounts were used. At first they were stamped from paper-thin sheets of sterling silver applied in such a way that the junction between plate and mount was invisible. The back hollows were made solid by filling with tin-lead alloy. The edge of the piece to be ornamented was first shaped and then drawn silver wire was hard soldered over the bare german-silver edges. The projecting part of the soldered silver edge was then filed off. Burnishing made the join invisible, even to the enquiring fingernail.

Mounts from the mid-1840s were made by the electro-type method. Models of the mounts were prepared in wax or plaster of paris and saturated with wax or tallow and rubbed over with plumbago, an excellent conductor of electricity. These were placed in an electric apparatus which deposited upon them a thin film of compact, unalloyed silver. The resulting silver shells, filled at the back with tin-lead alloy, were slightly lighter in tone than the sterling silver fused to the german silver.

The *Report of the Juries of the Great Exhibition*, 1851, has only one entry regarding plated ware. This was the British plate made by Thomas, James and Nathaniel Creswick, Sheffield. The report states that 'they exhibit articles important in size and of good taste. They are of plated silver, plated by the old process of uniting the metals by heat: the edges and mountings are of silver. The Jury have remarked some plain candelabra, one of them of antique form, one in the style of Louis XIV, and another in the style of Louis XV. The workmanship of their dish-covers, teapots and trays is as carefully executed as the style requires and perfectly adapted for long use. The Jury award Messrs Creswick the Gold Prize Medal.'

The Catalogue entry states that the entire exhibit is 'plated by fire on german silver and have silver mountings' and include 'bread basket with silver handle, cruet frame with silver handle, embossed tea kettle with teapot, sugar basin and cream ewer, ice pails, double shell salt cellars gilt inside and with silver feet, bottle stand with a silver shield, waiters, centre stand and plateau, fruit stand and flower stand.'

British plate was usually struck with devices designed to resemble so closely the hall-marks on silver plate that only the knowledgeable could distinguish between them. There is no evidence that such marks were applied to British plate by the makers: more reasonably they were struck by the merchants. Registration of makers' marks on plated ware had been compulsory from 1772, but the practice appears to have been abandoned in 1836, the year of Merry's patent. This was in direct contravention of statutes of 1772 and 1819 which explicitly laid down that it was illegal to stamp any marks on plated silver other than those registered at the Sheffield assay office. The penalty was £100 for each offence.

British plate makers appear somehow to have over-ridden the law and struck their ware with convenient devices, most of them being punch marks resembling hall-marks in size, design and placement. The presence of what appeared to be a row of clearly struck hall-marks was calculated to convince an envious guest that here was sterling silver. Obviously silversmiths must have suffered from this deception and it seems strange that the law was not invoked.

Many pseudo hall-marks have been brought to my notice on British plate, usually because their present-day owners believe they possess sterling silver and require the marks deciphering. The following example is typical, bearing a cunning resemblance to the London hall-mark: the leopard's head crowned; the lion *passant gardant*; a letter; a maker's mark; a head in profile.

When this mark is analysed it is found that no part of it was incorporated in hall-marks during the British plate period. The leopard's head on sterling silver appeared without a crown from 1822 onwards when also the lion on silver changed to the position known as *passant* (looking straight ahead); the date letter bears no resemblance to any date letter found on London sterling silver; the maker's mark cannot be associated with any mark registered at the Sheffield assay office; the head in profile intended to resemble the monarch's head duty mark is in reverse.

Some candlesticks, teapots and other domestic ware in British plate copied Queen Anne and early-Georgian designs in silver and it will be noticed that such pieces may show only four punch marks, omitting the head in profile. The monarch's head duty mark on silver was first used in 1784, and this confirms that the deceit was deliberate, a retail practice making it possible for British plate to be sold to the unwary as silver.

The demand for British plate continued for at least 20 years, even after Elkington's invention of electro-plating in 1840. For several years the coating of electro-plated silver tended to peel off or become blistered in use. Generally, however, the collector can distinguish at a glance between any form of fused plate and electro-plated ware from the fundamental difference in construction. As already stated, in Sheffield and British plate the fusion under heat preceded all stages of manufacture. In electro-plated ware the covering of silver was the final operation, masking all the constructional detail that intrigues a collector. It became customary to advertise British plate as 'plated by fire' to emphasize its superiority over electro-plating.

# 9. Domestic lighting, I

*Table candlesticks; candelabra; telescopic candlesticks;
dwarf candlesticks; chamber candlesticks*

Fashionable Georgian rooms were large and, to be enjoyed in their full splendour, required illumination by many wax candles. On important occasions the several hanging chandeliers might be augmented by candlesticks bearing more than 500 costly candles of English beeswax emitting a pleasant perfume. Always the dining and dessert tables gleamed in pools of mellow light from table or pillar candlesticks and branched candelabra. The formal dinner table in a well-to-do household displayed as many as 24 candlesticks and several two- or three-light candelabra which, from the 1790s, would flank a taller four- or five-branched candelabrum, all in Sheffield plate. These spectacular sets, ranging from early plain patterns to elaborate Victorian rococo, have usually been despoiled by family division in later years.

The candles throughout the house, private apartments excepted, were attended by a liveried waiter who carried 'basins wherein to bestow the snuffings'. This was a responsible duty, for an Act of Parliament of Queen Anne's reign decreed that 'if any servants, of what degree so ever, shall through negligence set fire to any dwelling-house, out-house, &c., they are liable to a penalty of One Hundred Pounds; and if they are not able to pay that sum, they are to be sent to the House of Correction for eighteen months to hard labour.' This was emphasized by an advertisement in *The London Chronicle*, 2 February 1768.

The Sheffield City Museum possesses one of the earliest table candlesticks made in Sheffield plate (fig. 36). The edge of its square base is impressed HANCOCK showing it to have been made by Joseph Hancock, Union Street, Sheffield, the first plater to make domestic hollow-ware. His original trade was cutler and later he was elected Master of the Cutlers' Company. Its ornament is an adaptation of the gadroon pattern fashionable in sterling silver from the time of George I and continued in Sheffield plate until the 1880s, usually catalogued as Queen Anne pattern.

A chronological sequence of such table candlesticks illustrates admirably the

changing methods of construction and improvements in the quality of craftsmanship. Hancock's candlestick is crudely but clearly constructed, obviously
during the experimental period of the late-1750s before his men were fully
skilled in the use of fused plate, silvered on one side only. It is 10 inches in
height and faintly visible seams show it to consist of 60 individual units, including an iron strengthening rod passing through the centre from base to socket,
with a tinned iron plate beneath the four-stepped square plinth. The plinth
incorporates 37 units, each step being built from eight pieces of flat plate with
gadrooning decorating the angle between the first and second steps. The stem is
based on the inverted baluster form, its square shoulder expanded to become a
field for ornament, often in shell pattern, but in this instance die-struck and
hand chased with spiral fluting. Similar ornament decorates the flaring nozzle
and the cone-shaped foot rising from the plinth, which in this style may have
two, three or four shallow steps.

The pillar may be smooth-surfaced or vertically fluted. The socket is vase-
shaped and the shoulder may be encircled with gadrooning. Such a candlestick
bearing one of Hancock's later marks, JOS^H HANCOCK or I.H. SHEFFIELD consists of six stamped units soldered together. In some instances the base is circular
or lobed, with scroll or cartouche designs matching similar ornament on the
loose nozzle.

Charles Dixon, a candlestick maker, writing in the nineteenth century,
recorded that Hancock's Corinthian candlestick was 'very neat, care being taken
to preserve the Order in its construction. They used to have the nozzle of the
candlestick, which holds the candle, stamped and put together in two parts, they
at that time not knowing how to plate the metal on both sides, this they called
the cow and calf.' The copper was attached back to back and the upper edge of
the outer layer turned over to conceal the bare copper. The manufacture of
candlesticks was a distinct branch of the Sheffield platers' trade: some platers
made nothing else and there were outworkers who concentrated only on nozzles.
An important general plater would operate a candlestick garret on the top floor
as the work was not heavy.

Table candlesticks were built in six sections: the pedestal and foot; pillar
and capital; candle socket; bizzle (the inner tube of the capital into which the
hoop slides); hoop (the tube fixed to the pan to secure the nozzle within the
capital); nozzle, the spreading loose pan intended to catch drops of melted wax.
Sets of the original dies used for stamping these units nearly two centuries ago
are still in existence.

In fitting together the units of a table candlestick all superfluous edging caused
by stamping was trimmed by filing. The sections composing the base were
joined by soft solder, but in many late examples the base was stamped as a single
unit. The pillar might be a rolled and vertically seamed tube which was generally

first decorated in relief, the pattern being die struck on the flat plate, silvered on one side only.

Die stamping was consistently used. Until the early 1790s much of this work was touched up by hand chasing, especially on bases and nozzles: fluting then became irregular and may be confused with the earlier hand raised fluting. Ribbed pillars were shaped with dies, but a similar effect has been noted on examples dating from the 1770s achieved by the less costly method of using long hair pins of drawn wire in half-round section soldered to a plain rolled tube. The base, plinth and foot in a single unit – the largest and heaviest part – would be struck with a cast iron block faced with a detachable steel tool sunk with the desired pattern, sometimes to a depth of several inches. Such a block might weigh as much as half a hundredweight.

The pillar in the form of a caryatid was an early feature of Sheffield plate candlestick design. This is a female figure or demi-figure in the round carrying the candle socket with its lower portion resting upon a short baluster or knop stem rising from a circular base. This graceful pattern was derived from silver candlesticks fashionable nearly half a century earlier. The Sheffield plate version was constructed from stamped units soldered together and burnished in such a manner that joints are invisible. The base of an unmarked example (fig. 36) in the Sheffield City Museum is decorated with rococo scrollwork in bold relief. A similar example has been noted struck with the mark ⟦IR⟧ which was registered at the Sheffield Office in 1776 by the silver cutlers, John Rowbotham & Co., Norfolk Street, Sheffield. This mark has been noted on close plated cutlery dated to 1768. The caryatid design was revived early in the nineteenth century with the draped body tapering to feet standing on the base.

Candlesticks with pillars adapted from the shapes of classical architectural columns on square pedestals were made in Sheffield plate from the early 1760s. These dominated fashionable candlestick design until about 1780 but they were made until the end of the century. The vertical units were stamped by cast steel dies, without the use of the swaging block. These were plain Tuscan and Doric pillars and Corinthian columns with decorative capitals containing recessed sockets and loose nozzles. Pillars were usually fluted in the Ionic or Roman styles.

The column might rise from a high four-sided inward-curving pyramidal foot supported by a square-faced stepped plinth. The faces of the foot were usually ornamented in low relief with floral swags or, more ambitiously, with motifs such as classical vases and rams' masks, festooned with flower and laurel swags. An example in the Sheffield City Museum with two rams' heads below the socket shows the join down the centre of each, continuing downward into the pillar. More usually the curved faces of the pyramid were ornamented with acanthus leaves and bordered top and bottom by beading. Other well-known relief decorations include: bas-relief figure of Hercules with festoons; vases and swags of foliage; borders of leaves and foliage. Each angle of the foot might be decorated with a single flowing acanthus leaf.

Pillars included the cluster column design with foliage capital and square pedestal used by Thomas Chippendale for table and chair legs in the 1760s. These were made in Sheffield by Thomas Law during the late 1760s and the 1770s. A similar and contemporaneous design made by John Hoyland & Co. has each angle of the foot filled with gadrooning and the faces decorated with all-over scrollwork pattern finished at the top with gadrooning.

Most of the Sheffield platers made composite architectural pillars from the early 1770s, the lower section reeded as on the Corinthian form, the upper part cylindrical and decorated in low relief with entwined leaves, oak and laurel being the most popular. Plain columns were common, on feet simply decorated with bead mounts. These candlesticks were costly because of the time spent in their production.

Other neo-classic designs in Sheffield plate candlesticks were introduced during the 1760s. One pattern fashionable during the 1770s and 1780s was the slender four-sided, shouldered and downward-tapering pillar supporting a socket in the shape of a stemmed and footed Grecian urn. The four flat faces of the pillar might be decorated in low relief with lions' masks, rams' heads and hoofs, festoons of flowers or drapery, lotus, and other neo-classic ornament. The pillar usually rose from a pyramidal foot, its four incurving surfaces chased with floral swags. Square pedestals were usual, with elliptical and circular shapes as more costly alternatives.

Fashionable Sheffield plate candlesticks of the 1780s and 1790s were made with circular pillars tapering downward to circular domed and spreading feet. Such pillars might be fluted vertically in a series of well-defined patterns: at first the fluting was repeated on vase-shaped sockets but these later became a field for ornamental motifs. Spiral fluting was a feature of pillars and feet during the 1780s.

Motifs derived from ancient Egypt, such as lotus flowers, decorated a series of round pillars during the final decade of the century. Nozzles, shoulders and feet were enriched with silver mounts.

At about this time appeared the first of a long series of candlesticks with baluster stems, elliptical in section, on elliptical feet, smoothly plain all over with the exception of threaded borders measuring between $\frac{1}{4}$ and $\frac{1}{2}$ inch in width, varying according to height. Under candlelight it is still difficult to distinguish them from sterling silver.

Eighteenth-century patterns continued far into the following century, chiefly because of the vast accumulation of costly steel dies for the essential stamping. New designs consisted mainly of adaptations of Georgian rococo styles. A pattern book compiled between 1788 and 1815 illustrated 1,190 patterns associated with the candlestick trade, including 219 candlesticks; 95 swage top candlesticks; branches for, 324; 111 chamber candlesticks; 182 patent candlesticks; 56 wax winders.

The pillar formed by four termed figures was a familiar Regency design, the heads supporting the socket and the draped bodies tapering plainly to end in feet resting upon a circular base with uprising centre.

From the early 1790s candlesticks were decorated with stamped silver mounts such as bead, thread and a variety of gadroon patterns. Mounts became increasingly elaborate including festoon and bead, leaf and scroll, laurel leaf, egg and dart, scallop shell and scroll and others. Some very ornate patterns appeared between 1810 and the 1820s, their bases, pillars and sockets becoming grounds for extravagant ornament.

Between 1815 and the early 1830s it was found profitable to stamp candlestick units in paper-thin silver and fill them with lead-tin alloy, plated copper being used only for the hoops, pans and bizzles of the nozzles. These were not assayed as the silver did not conform with either sterling or britannia standard.

When, during the Napoleonic wars, there was a national shortage of silver and copper, Sheffield plate was rolled thinner than formerly. This was used only for the lower-priced articles. Candlesticks in continual use quickly lost their silvery brilliance and became shabby. A pair seen in a Canterbury antique dealer's display window in 1968 was virtually devoid of silver: pillars, bases and nozzles showed only the bright red of copper and the bare mounts were seen to have been close plated. They were, of course, unmarked. The pillars distinctly showed the seams to have been straight and not dovetailed. Such seams, virtually invisible until the silver is worn, can be felt when twisting the pillar in the hand.

Sheffield plate candlesticks made from hollow units required weighting by filling or loading to give additional strength and stability. After fitting an iron rod through the length of the candlestick pillar from the base of the socket to the upper part of the foot to prevent breakage at the most vulnerable parts it was filled with molten pitch or resin mixed with loom, the latter being finely crushed wood ashes. When cold this became a hard, solid mass. The base was filled with small lumps of a pitch and pumice mixture. Some candlesticks will be found filled with a cream-coloured substance – a mixture of plaster of paris and loom. This was used to weight candlesticks exported to hot climates where resin and pitch loading tended to melt.

The loaded base was originally sealed by fitting a turned disc of fine boxwood or mahogany. Later, in a cheap candlestick, a seal of tinned iron plate was used and covered with green baize to prevent scratching of furniture. From about 1830 the base was sealed with single-plated copper.

The variety of designs in candlesticks of Sheffield plate is beyond computation. The majority were inspired by the silversmiths, but they lack the individualistic charm of the sterling silver. Contemporaneous pattern books of Sheffield plate in the Victoria and Albert Museum show that in the 1790s the average price of the 12-inch table candlestick was 40s a pair; seven inches, half that amount. Branches for converting candlesticks into candelabra were sold separately. A pair of square-based candelabra with festoon decoration cost 40s and branches to match 48s extra.

Candelabra or branch candlesticks were made throughout the periods of Sheffield plate and British plate. The branches were removable, enabling the pillar to be used as a candlestick. Chambers' *Cyclopaedia*, 1753, records that 'large candlesticks contrived for holding a number of candles are called *branches* or *Girandoles*'. The Sheffield plate pattern books seen invariably refer to them as branches. Present-day collectors term them candelabra, a name first used in this connection from 1792 when it appeared in *The Times*.

A candelabrum was composed of a table candlestick with an expansive base weighty enough to balance a tall ornamental finial supporting two or more curved branches placed equidistantly, each terminating in a candle socket. This branching unit fitted tightly into the candlestick socket by means of a solid cylindrical peg. Wax candles for table candlesticks and candelabra were standardized to a diameter of one inch. Sockets were similarly standardized and deep enough to hold such candles vertically and firmly without sideways play. They were usually fitted with loose nozzles. Branches were stocked by retailers in numerous patterns and being interchangeable could be bought separately from the pillar at a later date. A height of about 21 inches was most favoured, but by the 1790s 30 inches was not unusual.

Early branches were plain, usually displaying re-curving arms springing from the base of the finial, each terminating in a candle socket matching that of the pillar.

Branches were strengthened by filling the Sheffield plate tube with soft solder. Many branches were smooth throughout their length but these would not withstand harsh treatment from servants during cleaning and tended to bend, which in turn led to denting when they were straightened. In another and more common series the branch was made from two sections of tube, the joint being concealed beneath a plainly spun collet. Alternatively, to the end of the branch emerging from the pillar might be soldered a length of ornamental relief work, often foliate, stamped from sterling silver. Other branches were reeded throughout their length. Those octagonal in section were usually associated with faceted pillars.

Twin branches were more common than threes or fours and from the 1770s might scroll or twist around the central finial which might be a replica of the urn-shaped socket below. In many instances this was given a decorative lift-off cover enabling the piece to be used for three lights if required. Scrolled branches, curving upward from the stem finial might extend to a height of 24 inches above the table. The demand for branches to convert table candlesticks into candelabra became so great that some Sheffield platers specialized in this work. Patterns, however, were laboured, lacking the individualistic charm associated with branches made by platers with an extensive range of productions. By 1800 the branches might rise with a high upward sweep from the central socket, the two arms forming a semi-circle. Twin branches were always the most common. Candelabra dating from the 1820s may have spreading lobed feet, baluster pillars and spiral branches with vase-shaped sockets, all chased with elaborate flowers and foliage. The Bradbury pattern books, 1788 to 1815, illustrate 324 designs for 'Branches for Candlesticks'.

The single elaborately designed candelabrum became fashionable as a dining-table centrepiece from early in the nineteenth century. This burned five or more lights and might measure as much as 36 inches in height. Around it, in the form of a rectangle, were arranged four table candlesticks. Sometimes the central urn of the candelabrum was shaped differently from the surrounding candle sockets, with straight sides and a loose cover. This was used as a pastille burner. Such candelabra might also be placed on gilt or japanned stands or gueridons.

Five-, six- and seven-light candelabra were numerous and elaborately designed, often with cut glass nozzles from 1815. A five-light example, 33 inches in height, might display four spiral branches springing from sheaths of foliage with a lift-off flame finial to the central candle socket. The circular foot was chased with shells and gadrooning. A six-light example might have a square domed base, pierced and decorated with wave ornament and foliage scrolls, a central socket and five scroll foliate branches with vase-shaped sockets. A seven-light candelabrum might rise from a triangular plinth with incurved sides and three paw feet, a stem in the form of three caryatids and hexagonal sockets. Another type had two tiers of three branches each and a central light. By the late 1840s the fashionable candelabrum reflected eighteenth-century French patterns, such as those in the silversmith's styles of Louis XIV and Louis XV made by T. J. & N. Creswick and shown at the Great Exhibition, 1851.

Folding bracket candelabra for library use were made by J. Green & Co. from about 1805. The position of two of the three lights could be adjusted by extending the arms or closing them on the 'lazy susan' system or by folding three hinged sections. The branches on the pair illustrated (fig. 47) extend from 10 to $18\frac{1}{2}$ inches.

Sheffield plate candelabra were usually sold in fitted cases of fine leather, shagreen or exotic wood.

Telescopic candlesticks were introduced in the 1790s. For nearly half a century they did duty in the drawing-room at the embroidery stand, needlework table, writing desk, music stand, spinet and piano. One stood on each side of the user, the height of the flame being adjustable to suit personal convenience, thus avoiding the annoyance of cast shadows. Extensive matching sets are still to be found – as many as a dozen – although pairs are more common.

Known contemporaneously as sliding candlesticks, several types were evolved during the 1790s. In all the pillar stem was a plain cylinder containing one to five adjustable slides rising from a loaded base either circular, square or, from about 1810, lobe-shaped. The majority were made in Sheffield plate, but examples are to be found in sterling silver and in brass.

The earliest and most efficient telescopic candlestick, operating on the principle of the Archimedean screw, was introduced during the early-1790s. The device was based on the water raising instrument evolved about 2,000 years earlier by the celebrated Syracusan mathematician, Archimedes. This was a tube spiralled around a long inclined cylinder, its lower end placed in water. When the cylinder was revolved on its axis water was lifted from bend to bend until it flowed from the top of the tube.

A miniature adaptation of this contrivance fitted into the round pillar of a telescopic candlestick enabled the inner slide with its candle socket to be raised or lowered merely by turning the pillar. The base of the socket of such a candlestick was fitted with a small spike.

A less costly telescopic candlestick was patented on 26 October 1796 by A. J. Eckhardt and Richard Morton. These were manufactured by Morton, Handley, Sykes & Co., Brinsworth Orchard, Sheffield until 1809 when the firm traded as Richard Morton & Co., production continuing under this name until the 1820s. The patentees spent £120 on legal fees in contesting a successful effort to upset their monopoly by Morton's former partner from 1787 to 1793, a Mr Warris of Norfolk Street, Sheffield. He contested the validity of the patent on the grounds that such candlesticks had been made and sold during the period of his partnership with Morton, which was dissolved two years before the Eckhardt–Morton patent was granted.

The cylindrical pillar of this patent candlestick contained a slide with slits on either side. Adjustable brass collets pressing against the slide permitted it to be raised or lowered within the pillar as required. The interior of the pillar was lined with textile, obviating metal-to-metal binding during adjustment and ensuring that the slide fitted closely and firmly within the pillar. Quite as important, it prevented scratching on the outer surface of the extended slide. Until 1809 such candlesticks were stamped on the foot rim ECKHARDTS PATENT within two punches: from that year the mark, stamped with a single punch, was MORTONS PATENT or merely PATENT.

Rarely a third mark is found. The firm was established in 1765 by Richard Morton, who traded as Richard Morton & Co. until 1780, becoming one of the most prolific platers of the period, specializing in lighting ware, but also producing other domestic articles. His mark, registered at the Sheffield Assay Office in 1785, was MORTON & CO accompanied by a cock struck with a single punch. This continued to be used throughout the firm's existence.

A more popular telescopic candlestick was invented by Samuel Roberts, partner in the firm of Roberts, Cadman & Co., Cheney Street, Sheffield. A patent, no. 2210, was granted to Roberts on 23 January 1798 and production continued for about a quarter of a century. The interior mechanism was based on the 'notch and catch' principle. The patent specification describes this invention as 'working, adjusting, supporting a slide in table candlesticks of silver, silver plated or other metal'. A Sheffield plate catalogue issued by Roberts, Cadman & Co. in 1800, now in the Victoria and Albert Museum, illustrates these patent candlesticks with round pillar stems, pricing the 12-inch size at 48s a pair and the 10-inch at 37s a pair. The foot rim was usually struck with the mark R.C. & CO in a single punch. The mark registered at the Sheffield Assay Office by Roberts, Cadman & Co. in 1785 was a bell in an oval cartouche, but this was rarely used until about 1810, the firm then trading in Eyre Street, Sheffield. Many telescopic candlesticks are to be found bearing this mark, some of them obvious forgeries. Samuel Roberts was granted several other patents including one in 1798 for making candlestick nozzles, and another in 1807 for folding toast racks.

Early in the nineteenth century an improved form of the Eckhardt patent was marketed. The slide was operated by unscrewing it slightly and then, with the fingers, expanding the inner pillar until it pressed more securely against the outer pillar. This was simple to accomplish as the end of the tube was slit into two divisions.

Telescopic candlesticks were made from copper plated on one side only. The pillars, necessarily cylindrical and plain, were rolled from flat plate and invisibly seamed. Edges were usually double-reeded but might be decorated in relief with a swaging tool. The sliding sections were similarly made with the upper edge of each encircled by mountings.

The pillar of the telescopic candlestick rose from a base heavily loaded with lumps of resin-loom sealed beneath with a disc of tinned iron covered with green baize. The base was commonly circular but might be square or, from about 1810, lobed. It was usually composed of three units invisibly joined: a vertical outer rim; a narrow concave or step unit; a wide spool-shaped or trumpet-shaped support rising directly to meet the pillar. From about 1810 this support might be fluted and from 1815 decorated with ornamental chasing, its upper edge encircled with a silver mount.

The telescopic pillar might consist of as many as five slides each topped by simple ornament matching that on the nozzle. A 12-inch five-slide telescopic candlestick extended to 21 inches. In many early examples, particularly those in which the pillar was textile-lined, the slides became loose under long wear and the candlestick was discarded.

The early socket was cylindrical and plain, a style that continued throughout the period. From about 1805 it might be urn- or vase-shaped with the rim expanded into a grease pan for candle drippings. By about 1810 the lower part might be encircled with gadrooning or simple chased ornament such as shell and foliage motifs. Detachable nozzles with wide concave rims if not edged with swaged reeding were edged with silver mounts such as gadrooning, shell and scroll work, ovolo, flower and foliage patterns matching similar ornament on the pillar and slide rim.

Telescopic candelabra using these techniques were made throughout the first quarter of the nineteenth century. The pillar contained two or three slides, the lowest descending into the tall pedestal foot, the second sliding into this and supporting an urn-shaped socket into which fitted a two-armed branch, each arm terminating in a wide grease-pan supporting an urn-shaped socket with a loose nozzle above. The cylindrical pillar might rise from a circular or square plinth supporting a tall trumpet-shaped unit with long, curved flutes on the instep, similar flutes decorating the sockets. The base would be a square or circular plinth.

Three-light candelabra with gadrooned bases were more common and usually sold in pairs. They are to be found stamped on the foot rim ECKHARDTS PATENT with two punches and from 1807 MORTON & CO accompanied by a cock. These, closed, measured 16 inches in height and 21½ inches when elongated. The two scroll branches might be reeded and with foliage decoration, but more usually were plain with urn-shaped sockets and beaded wax pans.

The telescopic principle was incorporated into travellers' candlesticks devised by Samuel Roberts in about 1800. These were carried in Georgian coaching days to provide additional illumination in taverns and inns where lighting was normally no more than a pair of rushlights for which a charge of twopence was imposed. A pair of these chamber candlesticks could be dismantled by removing the telescopic pillars from their deep saucer-shaped bases. The bases were screwed together at the rims forming a receptacle capacious enough to contain extinguishers, pillars and candle-sockets. The complete set was enclosed in a shagreen or leather case.

Dwarf candlesticks were made throughout the Sheffield plate period. These were catalogued in 1792 as toilet candlesticks. But they had other uses too. For example, they might illuminate music scores on the piano as illustrated in James

Gillray's 'Playing in Parts', a print of a musical evening in 1801. They might be carried by the houseboy, too, when he preceded his master or mistress along unlit passages carrying a dwarf candlestick in each hand, a duty illustrated in early nineteenth-century cartoons by John Doyle. They were, in fact, all-purpose candlesticks measuring from five to seven inches in height.

Until about 1800 the usual design had a square pedestal supporting an in-curved pyramidal foot. For the most part the pillar was plainly cylindrical, but with narrow ribbing or fluting: occasional examples are to be found entwined with swags of flowers and foliage. A plain capital was used as a socket, its depth about half the diameter of the column. The pillar was of a length and diameter suitable for gripping in the fist and made from die stamped units. A catalogue attributed to the early 1790s gives a cost of about 20$s$ at the works. In the nineteenth century entirely plain examples on circular feet were very much cheaper.

A plain dwarf candlestick of this type in the Mitcheson collection is six inches in height with a base diameter of four inches. All units are made from single-plated copper. The cylindrical pillar is rolled and seamed, swaged at each end with double reeding in which, also, the seam is visible. The candle socket is $\frac{5}{8}$ inch deep with an everted rim, the nozzle attached to this has a swaged edge and concave rim and is tin lined. The base is composed of five units and, with the pillar, is weighted from beneath with resin-loom mixture. The base is sealed with a tinned iron disc and covered with green baize. The lower edge of the foot is sheared, revealing the copper and the iron sealing disc is soldered to this. The whole consists of 16 hand-worked and spun units.

Chamber candlesticks were intended for carrying from room to room, for lighting the way upstairs, for use in private apartments and bedrooms, and on most occasions where individual or temporary illumination was required. In the well-ordered home a side-table in the hall was set out with a plentitude of chamber candlesticks. Each person lit his own candle from a master taper kept burning for the purpose. A supply of candles for replenishment was kept in a horizontal candlebox hanging near at hand or placed towards the back of the table.

Originally known as a low-footed candlestick and later catalogued as a 'flat candlestick', the chamber candlestick measures about $3\frac{1}{2}$ inches in height and is light in weight, its conspicuous feature being its base shaped as a shallow saucer about six inches in diameter. A scroll bow or ring handle, soldered beneath the base, curves outward and upward, its terminal $1\frac{1}{2}$ to two inches above the rim. The upper curve of the bow may be shaped into a substantial thumb-rest, or a thumb-rest may have been added as a separate unit. A small socket fixed to the terminal of the handle fits the hook attached to a cone-shaped extinguisher which is often a particularly attractive detail, its finial shaped as a cone, acorn, pineapple, vase, flame or ball. The tip of the extinguisher is usually level with the rim of the candle socket.

Some early Sheffield plate chamber candlesticks followed a popular pattern made by silversmiths during the second quarter of the eighteenth century and later. The socket was fitted with a detachable nozzle, its rim widely expanded to catch drops of melted grease. This and the rims of the extinguisher and the base were edged with matching mounts, usually reeded. The chamber candlestick with a rectangular tray dates from the 1780s and was usually raised on four ball feet, its rim broader than formerly and decorated with gadrooned, beaded or reeded mounts. The socket was vase-shaped, but rectangular on plan.

From about 1800 the nozzle might be dispensed with and the socket rim extended and encircled with mounting, round gadrooning being common from 1810. The extinguisher might then be hooked to an attachment on the socket soldered immediately opposite the handle. By about 1815 the socket might be cylindrical with a sliding thumbpiece for forcing up the candle end. Octagonal trays date from about 1820 with mountings fluted and scalloped: square outlines had become common by the early 1830s. Late mountings included a wide border of foliage with the socket similarly ornamented. Until about 1815 chamber candlesticks were usually sold in matching pairs, fours, sixes and dozens.

The chamber candlestick incorporating a pair of snuffers into its design was made in Sheffield plate from the early 1770s. The candle socket was raised on a vertical slotted support, its opening placed at right angles to the candlestick handle. Into this was placed the box of the snuffers, the finger loops extending beyond the tray rim to facilitate removal for use. When hard stearic candles with plaited and twisted wicks were invented in the early 1840s, snuffers were rendered superfluous and provision was no longer made for them on the chamber candlestick.

On careful examination a chamber candlestick in the Mitcheson collection was found to consist of 18 separate units. The centre of the dish with a plainly swaged rim was raised to form a low rectangular platform for supporting the slot for the snuffers. This was composed of a pair of waisted hollow uprights weighted with pitch-loom. These were soldered to the platform which, beneath the dish, appeared as a rectangular depression also weighted and covered with fused plate. The slot uprights supported a short spool-shaped stem, its lower end sealed with fused plate. On this a rectangular vase-shaped socket held the loose nozzle. The encircling edge of the socket shows the bare copper of the fused plate. The upright handle was shaped from thick plate to which a flat thumbpiece had been attached, pierced with a square hole for the extinguisher hook.

Chamber candlesticks with two sockets are found occasionally. Rising from the centre of the circular tray is a slot for snuffers surmounted by a pair of scrolling branches each terminating in a candle socket and each with a conical extinguisher hooked to the side. Sockets and pans are edged with matching mounts.

Victorian chamber candlesticks continued the earlier plain patterns, but the fashionable type was usually circular with a shaped outline, the socket soldered directly to the domed centre of the tray. The extinguisher rested vertically upon a stem rising from the tray and might be in ogee form. A popular pattern of the 1850s and 1860s was in the shape of an expansive leaf, the stalk curving upward and over to form a handle, its socket shaped as the corresponding flower such as an open lotus flower: convolvulus, regina lily, nasturtium and other flowers were similarly treated. A spray of oak leaves might terminate in an acorn cup to receive the candle, and an ivy leaf in a bunch of ivy berries from which the socket emerged. These lacked nozzles and extinguishers.

Because of the fire hazard caused by draughts and billowing curtains and bed hangings, a pattern in chamber candlesticks was designed with protection for the flame. The socket with its candle was contained in a spherical, cylindrical or bell-shaped flint-glass shade which might be ornamentally engraved. This fitted tightly into a circular clip pierced with air-vents such as a double row of crosses or circles. The cone-shaped extinguisher was provided with a slender rod rising from its tip, long enough to extend to the candle flame and extinguish it without the fingers coming into contact with the hot glass. These candlesticks were made in variations until the 1840s, including a less costly type in which a simple wire frame in Sheffield plate, composed of four uprights and two rings, was soldered to the tray around the socket. This held a cylindrical glass chimney, lifted slightly above tray level by four knops to permit a free flow of air.

# 10. Domestic lighting, II

*Tapersticks; wax jacks and bougie boxes;*
*snuffer-trays*

Slender wax tapers burning in miniature candlesticks of silver were long used as accessible sources of flame in the houses of the rich. They were particularly in demand during the summer months when fireplaces were screened. They were never intended for illumination purposes and gave considerably less light than the more costly wax candles. The taperstick measured between four and six inches in height with a deep, narrow socket for the slender taper, its end wrapped in paper to facilitate removal of the stub.

For more than 100 years it was used by smokers for lighting the tobacco in their clay pipes, and as such was known as a tobacco candlestick. Complete with burning taper the stick was lifted to the pipe bowl, hence the necessity for a deep socket to prevent the taper from falling out. To prevent contamination of the tobacco, non-odorous tapers were burned, made from spermaceti wax. These seldom required snuffing and could therefore be left unattended without fear of guttering. The fumes of spermaceti candles contained arsenic and their use for domestic purposes was discouraged but the single small flame was not considered harmful. The wax was prepared from a white, brittle fatty substance found in a solution in the head of the sperm whale.

Tobacco tapersticks were plain and smooth-surfaced, never fitted with loose nozzles or bordered with extraneous grease-catching ornament. Basic shapes followed those of contemporaneous candlesticks. They continued in use until superseded towards the end of the eighteenth century by 'instantaneous light contrivances' and eventually in the 1830s by friction matches.

More decorative tapersticks came into use during the 1740s and continued fashionable in silver and Sheffield plate. They were required on the tea-table for a ceremony which might take place three times a day between main meals but was associated particularly with the evening. These tapersticks, known as tea-candlesticks, held tapers of English beeswax, burned for their sweetness rather than for practical purposes. English beeswax was pure enough to burn without

103   Tea urn, *c.* 1800

104   Tea urn, 1790s

105   Rectangular tea urn, late
eighteenth century

106   Tea urn by Matthew Boulton

108 Beehive tea urn, *c.* 1815

107 Tea urn, 1760s

109 Tea urn, early
nineteenth century

110 Tea urn, *c.* 1790

111 Tea urn, 1780s

112 Tea urn, 1770s

113   Pair of helmet cream jugs, catalogued
      *c.* 1780

114   Hot-water jug,
      1780s

115   Hot-water jug,
      1780s

116   Adam-style jug, 1770s; coffee pot, 1770s; hot-water jug, 1780s

(*left*) Hot-water jug, *c.* 1770. (*right*) Hot-water jug, te 1750s

118 Interchangeable coffee pot and teapot on stand, 1790s

119 Coffee biggin with stand and spirit lamp, 1790s

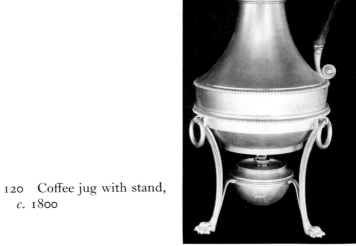

120 Coffee jug with stand, *c.* 1800

121  Tea canister, 1760s

122  Sugar pail, c. 1780

123  Sugar basket, c. 1800

124  Sugar basket, late eighteenth century

125–9   Sheffield plate tea caddies

130   Coffee biggin, *c.* 1800        131   Coffee pot, 1760s        132   Coffee pot, *c.* 1760

133    Coffee pots: 1760s; 1810; 1810; 1770; and 1775

134 Interchange-
able epergne and
three-light candel-
abrum, 1812

135 Epergne, *c*. 1820

136  Epergne, late eighteenth century

137  Epergne, 1760s

138  Sweetmeat epergne, early nineteenth century

139  Epergne, late eighteenth century

40   Four-division supper dish, *c.* 1815

41   (*behind*) Wirework sugar basket; pair of second-course dishes with warmers; argyle.
(*front*) Two entrée dishes; loving cup; wirework cake basket. All late Georgian

142   Set of four George IV entrée dishes

143    Soup tureen, *c.* 1820

144    Vegetable dish, *c.* 1810;
       Soup tureen, *c.* 1810

145    Soup tureen, 1790s

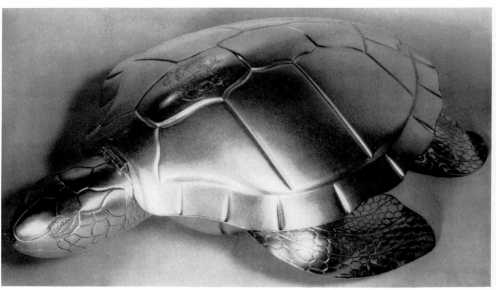

146   Entrée dish; wine cooler; tea caddy; second-course dish and warmer. All *c.* 1815

147   Entrée dish, early nineteenth century. Soup tureen, *c.* 1820

148   Pair of steak and vegetable dishes, 1820s. (*centre*) Soup tureen

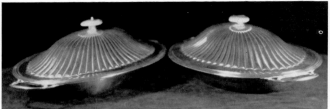

149    Pair of entrée dishes, *c.* 1790

150    Entrée dish and warmer, *c.* 1820

151    Covered dish, *c.* 1820

152    Entrée dish, *c.* 1795

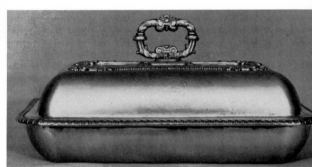

153    Entrée dish, *c.* 1800

154    Entrée dish, *c.* 1800

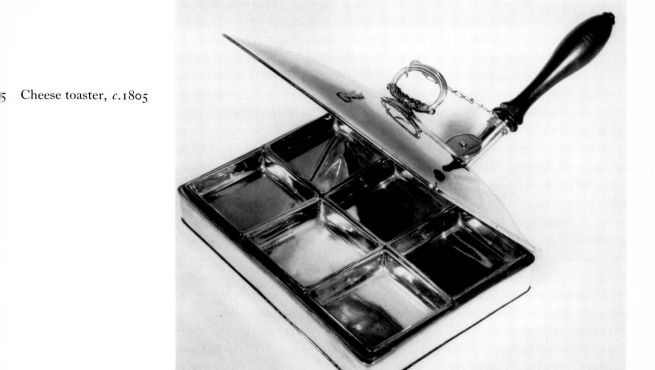

155   Cheese toaster, *c.*1805

156   Cheese toaster,
    *c.* 1800

157   Dish cover on meat dish, *c.* 1820

158   Bread tray, 1820s

being bleached and in consequence emitted a delightful fragrance. They were also brighter burning than tapers made from imported beeswax. Tea tapersticks followed the form of contemporaneous table candlesticks and might be made *en suite*. The majority were in architectural column patterns with square plinths. A detachable nozzle with spreading up-curving rim was essential to catch drips of hot wax which would be difficult to remove from the ribbed pillar. This was of similar outline to the base and was similarly ornamented. Some examples were gilded. Height might be as much as six inches.

The tea-candlestick in the form of a caryatid, adapted from the silversmith's version, was made in Sheffield plate, but is now rare. There was a fashion revival for these early in the nineteenth century and also a vogue for chamber tapersticks with suitably small sockets, detachable nozzles and extinguishers. These might be gilt with shell and foliage rims and handles.

Contemporaneously the term taperstick was applied to the much smaller type that accompanied the standish or inkstand. This burned a smokeless taper specially prepared for melting sealing wax.

Thin, flexible wax tapers also had their place among household equipment throughout Georgian days. These could provide a glimmer of light for carrying around the house with comparative safety and convenience. They were quickly forgotten by the Victorians but are remembered with pleasure by collectors today because of their small holders known as wax jacks and bougie boxes. The taper in its holder could be carried from room to room and used for lighting the way upstairs: it supplied a steady fumeless light for needlework or reading, required no snuffing and when made from beeswax it freshened the room with its fragrance. The hazard of sprinkling grease spots was negligible and if set down for a moment and forgotten its flame quickly burnt itself out.

The wax jack consisted of an open frame supporting the taper coiled upon a reel or spindle; the bougie housed the coil inside a lidded box. Both designs required long, slender tapers that could be coiled without cracking or flaking. Such a taper was made by winding a cotton wick on a drum and leading it beneath a guide roller revolving in a trough of molten wax containing a little turpentine to ensure flexibility. From this it was twisted through a series of holes, progressively smaller, until a considerable length of compact solid taper was obtained. This was wound upon another reel and stored in a vermin-proof box. The coiled tapers from about 1760 were called bougies after the Algerian town which supplied much of the bleached wax. Until the early 1770s these tapers were always coiled. This meant that the layers tended to adhere to each other at warm temperatures, a defect which was lessened by rolling the taper into a loose ball. The wax jack was modified slightly and the result catalogued by the Sheffield platers as a 'wax ball taper holder'. Tapers until the 1790s were always white which tended to yellow with age: thereafter they might be coloured blue, green, red or pink.

As early as the seventeenth century manufacturers had foreseen the convenience of such long-lasting miniature candles and their ingenuity had prompted silversmiths to design the wax jack as an article of desk equipment. The small flame was found especially convenient for melting sealing wax in a day when envelopes were unknown.

The wax jack was inventoried also by such terms as the wax taper stand, holder or winder, names indicating the general nature of the open frame stand supporting the coil of wax taper either horizontally or vertically. The term jack was derived from the frame or jack in which a ship's windlass was turned by a handle.

The early design, made in silver and in brass, was superseded by a more compact, less flamboyant version with a handle for carrying. This has an oval or rectangular frame of strong silver wire, either round in section or shaped by passing through a swage block. The frame is supported on a stemmed foot, circular or oblong and edged with reeding or moulded gadrooning. The stem is usually highly domed or trumpet-shaped, hollowed from the plate by spinning in the lathe. A scroll or ring lifting handle is attached and a small loop extends from the taper spindle for unwinding the taper as required. At the opposite end of the spindle a cone-shaped extinguisher is hooked on a bracket. The top of the frame holds a flat plate of similar outline to the foot, with a central aperture containing a short tube for receiving the taper end. In some instances the burning taper is held in the centre of an expansive, slightly concave wax pan and gripped by a scissor-action clip. The pan's smooth surface is easily cleaned of wax drippings.

The vertical wax jack dates from the same period. This holds the reel of coiled taper on a spindle rising from a rectangular or saucer-shaped foot with a reeded or corded rim and usually mounted on three ball, paw or claw and ball feet. An upward scrolling handle is fitted for carrying.

Sheffield plate pattern books dating from about 1780 illustrate a wide variety of wax jack designs. Prices range from 14*s*. for a wax jack with a plain frame; coiled taper covered with a canopy 17*s*; enclosed in a wire cage 24*s*. The open wire globe captioned as a wax taper ball holder was catalogued by several firms during the 1790s, opening across the centre for insertion of the ball of taper. By this time it was usual for the wax jack frame to be attached directly to a saucer-shaped foot, fitted with a ring handle and a flat, oval thumbpiece.

There were obvious advantages in protecting the wax taper from damage by mice and other pests. Cylindrical box taper holders were devised for this purpose early in the eighteenth century but few examples remain that can be dated earlier than the 1750s: Sheffield plate catalogues referred to them as wax boxes or bougie boxes.

The bougie box measures about three inches in diameter and has a slip-on cover. A fitted tube rising from the centre of the cover contains the tightly fitting nozzle that controls the emerging taper. The cover is usually flat and plain but may be slightly conical: by 1800 the dome shape had appeared.

Like the taper nozzle, the rims of container and cover may be encircled with reeded, beaded or gadrooned moulding. Vase-shaped nozzles date from about 1800. But few bougie boxes are now found with their nozzles intact. John Green's Sheffield plate catalogue issued in 1792 illustrates a plain bougie box with beaded rims priced at half a guinea; in his 1799 catalogue the price has been reduced to seven shillings. A double-scroll or s-shaped handle made from stout flat ribbon is soldered to the side.

The majority of these bougie boxes are undecorated, but late eighteenth-century examples might be encircled with bands of bright-cut engraving, usually swags of flowers or foliage. Between 1790 and the 1820s the sides might be pierced, at first with a single band of ornament encircling the centre of the body and later with vertical pales added above and below. By 1815 the cover too might be pierced. Many pierced bougie boxes contain linings of thin blue or clear flint-glass to protect the contents from inquisitive mice. From early in the nineteenth century bougie boxes might be catalogued as 'with silver shells and mounts', this ornament being pressed from thin sterling silver given weight and solidity by solder filled into the concave back.

The bougie box might be so designed that the flame was sheltered from draughts. The box rim was encircled by a gallery pierced with a double row of ornamental air vents. Into this fitted a cylindrical chimney of flint-glass which might be plain or engraved. In this design the box had a lateral handle and an extinguisher provided with a rod rising from the peak of the cone: this was long enough for the user to insert it inside the chimney and hold it over the flame without moving the glass. A simple cone-shaped extinguisher might be pegged into a loop soldered to the side of the body opposite to the handle. It was attached by a fine hand-made guard chain fixed to a small eye above the rim and to a ring on the cone finial to prevent it from becoming mislaid. The extinguisher finial might be a turned ball, vase, acorn or knop and was usually aligned with the rim of the loose taper nozzle.

A trade catalogue of the 1830s illustrates a bougie box in the pseudo-Gothic style with elaborately cast units – body, handle, cover, urn-shaped nozzle and cone-shaped extinguisher. But a comprehensive catalogue of sterling silver and electro-plated goods of the early 1850s includes neither wax jacks nor bougie boxes: the whole notion had been outmoded by the revolutionary improvement in candle wick design introduced in the early 1840s.

Scissor-like candle snuffers share the long history of the candle. The loosely plaited wicks of Turkey cotton used until the early 1830s required constant attention to ensure a bright, steady flame. Otherwise the long, grease-soaked wick would curl over until its hot charred end dipped into the gutter of melted wax on the candle top. Cutting off or pinching off the snuff or unconsumed burnt part of the candlewick was known as candle-sniting. The snuff was dropped into a metal dish to lessen the hazard of molten wax or the fragments of red-hot wick damaging clothes, carpet or table cloth. Samuel Pepys in his *Diary*, 1667, recorded that 'this night comes home my new silver snuff dish which I do give myself for my closet'. The *London Gazette* in 1676 reported the theft of 'a Silver Snuffer-dish and Snuffer chain'd'.

Snuffer-dishes until the mid-eighteenth century, in silver, pewter, copper or brass, were flat-based and rectangular, often with clipped corners, with applied moulded edges deep enough to contain the pair of snuffers and dead snuff with safety. In some instances the dish was raised on four scroll feet. A wide, lateral up-curling handle was soldered to the centre of one side with a finger ring beneath, succeeded in about 1720 by the pear-shaped or vase-shaped lifting handle without a finger ring. By the mid 1740s snuffer-dishes of waisted or hour-glass shape had become fashionable although made earlier, and by 1750 the rising scroll handle capped by a flat thumbpiece was in vogue.

An immense amount of ingenuity now began to be lavished upon the decoration of snuffer handles, every conceivable device being exploited to enrich handles and bows. Nevertheless, as working instruments, candle-snuffers continued to suffer from one great defect that the charred end of the wick fell from the container as the blades were opened. After each candle was snuffed the container had to be emptied. Some assistance in conveying the snuff to the receptacle was provided by a patent device of 1749 introduced by Benjamin Cartwright of the Strand, London. This was a spring that controlled the movement of the blades and obviated unintentional opening which might scatter the charred waxy wick. The pivoting joint of the snuffer was covered by a boss concealing a coiled spring so arranged that it closed, and kept closed, the snuffer after use.

This invention was directly responsible for snuffer-dishes being superseded by shallower snuffer-trays. Cartwright's snuffers contained a coiled spring to control the movement of the flat press into the snuffer box, thus extinguishing the smouldering snuff and preventing fragments of hot wick from flying. The snuffers tray, requiring only a very low rim, was decorated in styles associated with the more important waiter. The pair of snuffers was fitted with three very short feet, usually turned in baluster form, one beneath each finger loop, the other beneath the prick-wick. These lifted the tool a little above the edge of the rim making it easy to grasp for removal from the tray. The hour-glass shape continued and became more popular.

Snuffer trays were immediately put into production by the newly established platers in Sheffield and Birmingham and their manufacture eventually became a distinct branch of the trade. An early specialist was Samuel Evans, St Paul's Square, Birmingham. The sunken central part of the tray was stamped by means of the same dies that were used by the factory silversmiths, so that similar sizes and shapes are to be found in both silver and Sheffield plate.

Beaded, corded and gadrooned rims were characteristic, encircling shallow, hand-sunk plates, at first plated only on the upper surface and tinned beneath. In some instances the sides of the tray and the ends were slightly incurved. This pattern has been attributed to Tudor & Leader as early as 1768, but an example on ball feet by John Cage is hallmarked 1764. Vertical rims pierced with pales, ovals, crosses, rosettes and other devices and fitted with handle and feet were introduced to snuffer trays at this time by R. Morton & Co., Sheffield, and quickly copied by others. By 1770 the incurved gadrooned rim with shell corners and a scroll handle at each end had become fashionable, often with shell or claw feet. The flat base of the tray might be chased with a pattern incorporating formal flowers, oak leaves and scrollwork in a feather-edged border. The centre of the design contained a shield engraved with a crest or cypher.

The elongated oval and canoe-shaped snuffer-tray with beaded or reed rims and scroll ends became fashionable in Sheffield plate during the mid-1780s. Others were ornamented at the ends with a pair of masks of filled silver. Octagonal and rectangular snuffer-trays with silver mounts date from the mid-1790s often with a D-handle at each end, often corded: later this shape might have silver mounted scroll ends. The four-lobed snuffer-tray designed to accommodate snuffers and a pair of cone-shaped extinguishers was first made in Sheffield plate by D. Holy, Wilkinson & Co. in about 1800. Heavy borders were introduced in about 1810, adapted from the eighteenth-century rococo but with clumsy effect.

Large snuffers date from about 1815 with matching snuffer-trays enlarged to conform and often a foot in length. Known as table snuffers, these lay conveniently between a pair of table candlesticks. Formerly snuffers and trays had been in matching pairs. Standard-size candle snuffers were now catalogued as chamber snuffers and were used in association with chamber candlesticks (see Chapter 9).

Snuffer-trays in Sheffield plate were made in a tremendous variety of patterns. The Watson & Bradbury pattern books illustrate 165 designs between 1788 and 1815. A catalogue page of about 1790 in the Victoria and Albert Museum illustrates and prices six snuffer-trays. One, canoe-shaped with scroll ends and wavy sides, edged with fine silver wire, cost 20s. The next three, oblong hexagonal with flat fluting at the base and ends; shallow oval with pierced and flat-chased ends; oblong hexagonal but plain – all edged with fine silver wire, 18s each and without silver threads, 15s each. A similar but smaller example with a perfectly plain edge, 10s 6d; plain, oval canoe-shaped with plain edge, 10s 6d.

Snuffer-trays from about 1820 onward were laden with wide florid mounts of silver, shellwork and foliage being especially favoured. Plates were chased mechanically with flower and shell patterns around rubbed-in silver shields.

From the mid-1830s snuffer-trays might be in British plate (Chapter 8) ornamented with elaborate silver-filled mounts. A popular series of table snuffer-trays at this period, catalogued contemporaneously as Queen Anne pattern, were derived from the smaller version fashionable in silver from about 1720 to the mid-century. In this design a lateral lifting handle extended from the centre of one of the incurved sides. This was most commonly pear- or vase-shaped.

Candle-snuffers might be in sterling silver, but the great majority were in steel, their manufacture being counted as part of the steel toy trade. At first they were hand-forged and finished by filing: in the nineteenth century the units were stamped. Snuffers with cutting blades and box of steel might be fitted with handles, bows and prick-wick of silver or close plating (Chapter 1). Sir Edward Thomason recorded in 1810 that steel snuffers might be close plated all over, the whole instrument then resembling silver. This was satisfactory with his own improved close plating but otherwise tended to fall away if held in the candle flame for more than the moment needed for snuffing. In 1839 Birmingham supported 30 makers of steel candle-snuffers and one specialist close plater – Charles Banister, 16 Moland Street.

When the non-guttering candlewick was devised in the 1830s, together with the introduction of palm wax candles, snuffers and their trays became superfluous to those who could afford the increased cost. But manufacture continued for many years, particularly of snuffer-trays of electro-plate from the mid-1840s. Palm wax candles were advertised from 1839 by the makers, Blundell, Spence & Co., Hull, as 'superior to Bees'-wax Candles and are only half the price. They are perfectly free from Arsenic and DO NOT REQUIRE ANY SNUFFING. They maintain their Solidity at a very high temperature: hence, are admirably adapted for burning in crowded Apartments'. Wax candles were more than four times as costly as candles normally used in the home.

# 11. The service of wine, I

*Wine coolers; bottle stands; decanter stands;
wine wagons*

In days of arduous coach travel, evening hospitality called for lavish preparations in the homes of the gentry, manufacturers and prospering merchants. In the living chambers dried lavender would be tossed on the blazing pine logs and wax candles set alight in every wall sconce and candelabrum. The heat must often have been well-nigh unendurable but at least the wine was kept cool. The usual arrangement was for the bottles to stand in a cumbersome cistern of iced water placed beneath a side table: for service each bottle was transferred to an individual, one-bottle wine cooler of silver or Sheffield plate containing iced water and lumps of ice.

The table wine cooler in Sheffield plate was a vessel of circular or octagonal form measuring seven to 12 inches in height, slightly tapering towards a flat, rimless base. This contained a detachable inner vessel or liner with a diameter rather greater than that of the wine bottle which it held in a nearly upright position. The space between the liner and outer vessel was filled with iced water or finely crushed ice. An encircling collar projecting from the liner's rim rested upon the brim of the cooler concealing the icy water. Thus the bottle of wine could be lifted out, cold but dry, when required. If was eventually realized that the ice was more easily inserted when the collar was separate from the liner which might be placed loosely inside the cooler.

The early Sheffield plate wine cooler was pail-shaped, straight-sided, tapering to a flat base and encircled by four applied flat bands or hoops, including one each at rim and base. During the late 1780s and early 1790s the hoops encircling bucket-shaped coolers became a ground for ornament and were customarily decorated with bright-cut scrollwork: later they were often reeded.

Rising from the rim diametrically opposite to each other were a pair of flat vertical ears cut with hand-holds. During the 1790s vertical loop handles of flat plate came into use, being considerably safer and more convenient. From about 1800 four ball feet might be fitted. For such table vessels the names of ice pail and ice bucket were long retained. Contemporaneous invoices and pattern books show that both silversmiths and Sheffield platers used the term ice pail until the early 1840s when the term wine-cooler became fashionable.

At the turn of the century the bucket or pail form gave way to the tub or barrel shape encircled by two or three reeded hoops. Height averaged nine inches. By 1805 collar, rim and base might be encircled with gadrooned or beaded silver mounts. At first the vessel was given slender, out-curving loop handles, the ends secured in shell-shaped bosses and the loops rising high above the rim. These were followed from about 1810 by loose drop-ring handles swinging from substantial lion masks.

In that glitter-loving age claret, burgundy and other red wines were served from diamond-cut decanters set in wine coasters: white wines from the continent to be served cold were tabled in wine coolers of silver, Sheffield plate or porcelain. Matching sets of four, six or a dozen delighted the rich, and at important banquets this number was greatly exceeded by hiring wine coolers from silversmiths' stocks. Most authorities refer to their importance on contemporaneous sideboards: they were, however, used on the table. In 1801 Sir Edward Thomason recorded the 'new fashion of drawing the corks of wine at the table, the pierced cork being placed in a finger-bowl'. Pairs of wine coolers were usually sold in satin-lined cases covered in morocco leather, shagreen or exotic woods.

The vase-shaped wine cooler on a short stem with a round spreading foot was made in Sheffield plate from the early 1790s. At first the vessel was plainly cup-shaped; then its lower part might be decorated with silver mounts, a calyx of acanthus leaves being fashionable, while the handles rose from a plain encircling rib. Reed-and-tie and gadrooned rim mounts were usual. Shapes were derived from the various phases of neo-classic design in marble, silver designers delighting in the campana or inverted bell-shape.

The impact of the Greco-Roman art revival prompted Regency designers to encircle wine coolers with applied friezes in relief showing scenes from classical mythology. Designs were influenced by sculptors such as John Flaxman, R.A. A design taken direct from a silver original consists of the 'Chariots of Apollo and Diana' in high relief. Infant Bacchantes in compositions of huge beribboned boughs of grapes were introduced by at least two platers in Sheffield.

In 1812 the silversmith Paul Storr made wine coolers in the shape of the celebrated white marble vase then in the grounds of Warwick Castle. This had been excavated at Villa Adriana, Tivoli, Italy, in 1770 and attributed to 325 B.C. It had been brought to England by the Earl of Warwick in 1774. The Sheffield platers were making versions of this 'Warwick vase' by 1815, starting a half-century vogue for this pattern. I. & I. Waterhouse & Co., Sheffield, made such wine coolers from about 1820, their illustrated catalogue of 1830 showing the wholesale price to have been 32 guineas a pair. The engraving was inscribed 'made to the scale of one-fourth of the celebrated Warwick vase'.

The Warwick vase wine cooler followed the shape of the Greek krater, standing upon a plain panelled square pedestal decorated on each face with the owner's coat of arms applied in relief in silver. The body, foot and stem were hand-raised; the handles were in the form of twisted vine branches; egg and tongue borders and various silver units were die struck, the four Bacchus masks each stamped in two halves. The interior was tinned and polished. An example measured was 10 inches in height and a foot wide, but smaller and larger ones are known in similar proportions. Several examples in Sheffield plate were displayed at the Great Exhibition of 1851, including one by Henry Wilkinson & Co., Sheffield, catalogued as 'Ice pail (Warwick vase) with pedestal'.

The economic stresses of the Napoleonic wars eased in 1815 and wine coolers became more elaborate, the main features being bold curves, beaded silver mounts, reeded bands, gadrooning and acanthus mounts. The fruiting vine continued a fashionable decoration mainly in the form of bands of vine leaves with tendrils and bunches of grapes. In the following decade the vessel might be decorated with mounts of laurel festoons, oak leaves and acorns rising from four shell and scroll feet. By the 1820s flower and foliage arrangements virtually supplanted classical motifs. Bowl-shaped and cylindrical vessels, floridly designed and supported by heavy feet, date from the same period.

Wine cooler ostentation was carried further by a few platers who elevated ornate models on equally elaborate stands. Typical was the circular or rectangular stand with a raised centre to support the vessel. This might be fluted or chased with a wide mount, often a composition of shells and scrolling foliage. Other stands were raised on paw feet and decorated with honeysuckle and palm foliage. Others were raised on plain, square plinths.

A Sheffield plate catalogue of about 1800 illustrates a 'fluted wine pail plain above and enriched with a pair of silver lion heads and gadaroon mounting' and prices it at 110s. A very similar design illustrated in 1833 by I. & I. Waterhouse & Co. is priced at 16 guineas a pair – an increase of about 50 per cent over a third of a century – and 20 guineas for a pair in the form of a Grecian vase.

The detachable collar concealing the iced water and supporting the liner vertically within the vessel and equidistant from its walls was also a ground for ornament. At first the plain collar was short and incurved, rising above the body upon which its rim rested. It was edged with simple mounting in silver, sometimes applied vertically. By 1812 its curved outline had deepened and it was bordered with such silver mounts as shell and foliage, scrolling rosettes and the ever-popular gadrooning. The mounts widened as the decade progressed. Sunken collars were usually wide-rimmed, at first plain and then bordered with fruiting vine or guilloche mounts. On an ornate example the edge of the collar was decorated with a wide mount, floridly patterned, with a matching mount on the vessel's everted rim.

Handles on wine coolers were made in many patterns. Until about 1805 the dominating type was an upward and outward curving loop or D emerging from a pair of ornamental bosses. Then came a pair of reeded struts rising from lion or satyr masks and joined by foliage: in some instances masks of Bacchus accompanied struts joined by vine leaves. Masks, highly fashionable, were in silver. Lion mask handles might be fitted with loose lifting rings pendant from the mouths; or the rings might be hinged to the rim with lion or other masks immediately below. Laurel wreath drop ring handles are comparatively rare. Pairs of bearded classical masks rising from the rim and linked by bars of foliage were fashionable between about 1810 and the early 1820s.

Reeded handles might rise from clusters of vine leaves or shells and might be bifurcated. Floral and foliage handles were popular as they gave stability to the grip: these might accompany rims of similar pattern. Serpent handles were fashionable from about 1810 to 1825. Pairs of snakes might be introduced emerging from foliage, rising to grip the rim of the vessel between their jaws, a single snake might curl upward from the base of the cooler and bite its rim. Vertical handles date from shortly before 1820 and might take the form of entwined vine tendrils sprouting from a fruiting vine encircling the upper part of the vessel.

The creative urge was largely lost by the Sheffield platers in the 1830s and designers resorted to more or less slavish copyings of all the earlier styles of wine coolers. Collectors should be aware that unimaginative wine coolers were made in Sheffield plate during the late-Victorian and Edwardian periods: they were also made in electro-plate for use in hotels.

The wine-table accessory known to Georgians variously as a bottle slide, bottle tray, bottle stand, decanter stand and wine wagon is termed by present-day collectors a wine coaster. Yet in this connection the *Oxford English Dictionary* dates the name coaster no earlier than 1887. Wine bottles in the early eighteenth century were made from a comparatively soft, coarse glass, dark in colour. The shape included a high kick in the base producing an encircling rim that quickly became roughened by cellar and pantry use. This became a matter of consequence when the dining table was made of mahogany so splendid that the cloth had to be removed to display it towards the end of the meal. Wine drinkers pushing such bottles from one to another tended to mark the fine wood. This hazard was reduced from the mid-eighteenth century by the introduction of wooden bottle stands, originally known as slides.

Madame du Bocage in her *Diary*, 1750, commented regarding her visit to

London that 'after the dessert the cloth is taken away and the women retire. The table is of fine Indian wood [mahogany] and very smooth, and little round vessels called sliders which are of the same wood serve to hold the bottles and the guests can push them round as they think proper.'

Silversmiths by 1760 had welcomed the opportunity to make this newcomer to the service of wine in their precious metal, but the Sheffield platers are not known to have made them until after the invention of double-plated copper in the late 1760s. Trade cards of the period refer to them as bottle stands, the term used in the price list issued by the Assay Office in 1777 and in Sheffield plate pattern books until early in the nineteenth century.

The collector notes changes in size, necessitated by changes in bottle dimensions due to technical advances in glass manufacture during the late eighteenth century. In shape the stand consisted of a circular plate enclosed by a low vertical gallery known to the Sheffield plating trade as the bar. This was about $1\frac{1}{2}$ inches deep, its rim slightly everted, and edged with narrow beading or reeding. The bar was shaped into a circle and the ends joined invisibly by soldering. For ornament it was often pierced with short vertical pales and sometimes further enriched with applied swags and ornamental medallions, sometimes thinly cast in solid silver of less than sterling quality. The pattern most widely used, because comparatively inexpensive, consisted of four rows of horizontal pales alternating with circular holes.

The undersurface of the early bottle stand was highly burnished so that a slight push would send it gliding smoothly over polished wood. When the bottle was lifted the stand remained on the table, revealing an engraved cartouche enclosing the owner's crest or cypher. This proved unsatisfactory, however, as the high kick of the bottle might create a vacuum: when it was lifted the metal stand was liable to accompany it for an instant, then fall with a clatter and bruise the table. The defect was overcome by replacing the metal base with one of heavy hardwood such as mahogany or boxwood. This was lathe-turned and the surface ornamented with a central boss encircled by three or four concentric rings and polished in the natural colour of the wood. The underside was covered with baize. The weight of the wood gave stability and the turned rings enabled air to reach the kick, so that the bottle was easily lifted from the stand. The centre of the base might be inlaid with a plated boss upon which a crest could be engraved. The lower edge of the bar was folded tightly over the wooden base and held in place by an encircling collet.

Fashionable piercing on bottle stand galleries during the 1780s and 1790s, and later on less costly examples, included groups of ten vertical pales spaced between solid rectangles engraved with classic motifs, and bands of piercing encircling upper and lower edges and bordering a band of bright-cut engraving, which may be recognized by its delicate faceted effect.

Bottle stands with undulating rims date from the early 1780s. From about 1790 a classic motif in silhouette might be pierced beneath each crest of the rim. A double row of horizontal piercing might be press-cut immediately below the rim and the remainder of the gallery sparsely pierced with geometric motifs. Octagonal bottle stands date from the 1790s and were intended for gin bottles. The rare square coasters accompanied spirit bottles.

When the diameter of wine bottles was reduced to about $3\frac{1}{2}$ inches in the 1780s, their height increased proportionately so that capacity was unaltered. The height of the gallery of a bottle stand was then raised to about three inches. Engraved and pierced designs continued. A Sheffield plate pattern book in the Victoria and Albert Museum dated 1792 prices a variety of bottle stands with silver edges at 22s a pair.

By about 1830 the fashionable bottle stand was raised on a spreading foot with a high instep. The height of the gallery now equalled the diameter of the bottle. Decoration consisted of geometrical piercing. These were used for the service of hock and catalogued as hock stands at prices ranging from £3 to £4 a pair.

Sets of bottle stands from the 1780s might be accompanied by tumbler stands with matching but shallower galleries. In these the base was in Sheffield plate and mounted on three low scroll feet. Sheffield plate catalogues illustrate and name these.

Bottle stands are known with narrow-rimmed plated galleries encircling bases of Pontypool japan. Typically decorative motifs were painted on a red ground.

The earliest decanter stands were indistinguishable from bottle stands. When, in the 1780s, they became established as a class of their own they were made with deeper galleries, their diameters ranging from $5\frac{1}{2}$ inches to $6\frac{3}{4}$ inches with six inches the most common. Gale & Martin's *Sheffield Directory*, 1787, differentiated between 'decanter stands' and 'bottle trays' in their list of articles manufactured in Sheffield. Patterns were in the main adapted from the less costly of silver originals. The Sheffield plate catalogue issued in about 1800 by Nathaniel Smith & Co., Wingate, Sheffield, illustrates 20 patterns of galleries, pierced, chased, swaged and in plated wire, prices ranging from 18s to 20s a pair. Another pattern book illustrates 105 designs made between 1788 and 1815.

Until the introduction of silver stamped mounts, decanter stands were unskilfully finished, usually displaying a faintly copper hue. The reason for this was that the fused silver was stretched to its utmost during the piercing of the gallery, the vertical rim of which was inturned slightly to ensure a snug fit for the decanter. The galleries from about 1790 were often of the half-fluted type, that is, the centre of the bar was encircled by a band of convex reeding, with a matching horizontal rim. In others the upper part of the gallery was reeded and rimmed with gadrooning, the lower part pierced. Early in the nineteenth century the positions of reeding and piercing were reversed.

Flamboyant design was required to harmonize with the new-fashioned flint-glass decanters which they carried. These were lavishly cut with diamond patterns in deep relief and each facet scintillating its rainbow colour in candlelight was reflected in the highly burnished horizontal rim of the stand. From about 1800, therefore, the silver rim mountings on decanter stands were wider, relief designs including festoon and bead, leaf and scroll, laurel leaf, egg and dart, shell and scroll. By 1810 silver mounts included shell and foliage, and flower and shell patterns. From this period decanter stands might be enriched with blue glass liners.

Five years later the gallery of a fashionable decanter stand might be shaped in the swage with a slight outward curve, smooth surfaced and often lightly engraved. The silver mount became wider and extended horizontally with a wavy edge. Its surface formed a field for floridly designed and chased ornament in high relief, including pierced vine wreaths, fruiting vine, ivy leaves, pierced festoons. In one little-known series of Regency and George IV decanter stands the gallery was everted and extended at four points, terminating in ornamental scrollwork.

Wire work (see Chapter 27) decanter stands date from about 1790. At first the gallery was composed of a series of overlapping wire semi-circles soldered into and rising from a low foot ring of plate attached to the perimeter of the hardwood base. Less expensively several upright wires supported a reeded rim.

Double decanter stands were devised in the early 1790s. At first two decanter stands were fitted to a slider or platform of hardwood, usually mahogany. The surface and edges of the platform were covered with single-sided Sheffield plate and baize was glued beneath to facilitate pushing over the table top by means of a D-handle or reeded shaft attached to one end. Before long the platform was omitted, the two decanter stands being connected by two pairs of rigid couplings, one pair on each side. These were so shaped that loops were formed to receive the decanter stoppers whilst the decanters were in use. Vertical loop handles were attached to the ends.

Double decanter stands were fashionably superseded by wine wagons, catalogued as decanter carriages from the early 1830s. Each stand was fitted with two axle-mounted wheels and the upper rims of the galleries were joined by a rigid coupling. Beneath one end was hinged a six-inch pushing bar with a loop- or T-handle. A plain example cost £6; with pierced galleries £7.5.0; and with an openwork wire and vine gallery, £7.15.0. Bottle carriages were also made. Collectors should know that wine wagons have been constructed during the present century from pairs of period decanter stands.

The wine carriage in the form of a naval 'jolly boat' fitted with four wheels and measuring a foot in length, was evolved in silver in 1823 by John Anderson, St James's. It appeared in Sheffield plate about two years later. The deck contained two decanter recesses and two smaller depressions for their stoppers. The shaft was made from twisted plated wire and hinged to the axle at the stern. Contemporaneously, a boat-shaped wagon was designed to accommodate a single bottle of wine lying at a slant on its side.

# 12. The service of wine, II

*Bottle tickets and decanter labels;*
*orange strainers and wine funnels*

Early Georgians usually tabled their wines in long-necked French-quart wine bottles of heavy, greenish-black glass. The wine, its colour obscured beneath the glass, might be identified by an engraved silver ticket suspended from a slender chain encircling the shoulder of the bottle. This silver trifle was but replacing the parchment ticket, hand-written with the name of the wine, that had long served the same purpose. Such a ticket was attached to the pack thread that held down the bottle's wax-sealed cork. Several caricatures drawn by James Gillray (1757–1815) illustrate this detail and the same picture may also depict silver or Sheffield plate bottle tickets – usually crescent-shaped – hanging around the shoulders of decanters, carafes and wanded wine bottles.

In 1740 Dean Swift recorded the use of 'silver plates to distinguish bottles of wine by'. The term bottle ticket, however, was current in Swift's day and continued until the end of the century. For instance, *The Daily Advertiser*, 28 February 1756, in announcing the sale of the household effects of Stephen Theodore Janssen, proprietor of the now celebrated Battersea enamel works, referred to 'bottle tickets with chains for all sorts of liquer'. The *London Gazette* invariably used the term bottle ticket in its editorial columns at this period. The newly established Birmingham Assay Office in 1773 entered such wine-table accessories as 'labels for bottles' during a period when it was fashionable to engrave flint-glass decanters with the title of the wine in bold letters. But in 1777 the London Assay Office was using the name 'bottle ticket', and the Marking of Silver Plate Act of 1790 continued the custom.

In what year silversmiths first turned their tools to the dainty bottle ticket has not yet been determined, but hallmarks show that Sandilands Drinkwater & John Harvey, of Gutter Lane, London, were producing them during the 1730s. Early bottle tickets were in three shapes: small, narrow oblong; crescent; escutcheon. These were never entirely outmoded and were illustrated in silver-smiths' catalogues of the 1890s.

Bottle tickets in Sheffield plate date from the 1760s: the first Sheffield trade directory, published in 1774, listed them among the articles then in production. They were made also in close plated steel. Penzer records a narrow oblong example in Sheffield plate with clipped corners and plain edges, struck with the mark of John Prince, Navigation Street, Birmingham. As this mark was not registered at the Sheffield Assay Office, the ticket dates earlier than 1770. More than 300 wines, spirits and sauces have been noted on Sheffield plate bottle tickets out of the 1,500 so far collated, some of them unknown today. The wines most commonly named on the several hundred silver wine labels in the Patrick Sandeman collection are: madeira, half as many again as port; then sherry; then claret.

The coating of silver on the front of a Sheffield plate bottle ticket was necessarily thicker than usual to accept the engraving of the title. The letters, always in upper case type, were outlined in thick lines. Frequently these were filled in with close hatching; in others the title was made easier to decipher by filling the outlines with black enamel.

Sheffield plate wine tickets of the eighteenth century were plain to the point of severity and may be grouped into four classes: oblong, crescent, escutcheon and oval. Those dating earlier than the development of double plated copper in the late 1760s have only the front surface plated, the reverse being tinned or close plated. Such a ticket was given slight convex shaping to ensure that it would hang closely against the bottle.

Narrow oblong bottle tickets were cut from the plate, their dimensions approximating $1\frac{3}{4}$ inches wide and $\frac{1}{2}$ inch deep. In the early 1790s an oblong bottle ticket was catalogued at ninepence plain, one shilling if engraved with the title. The corners might be square, rounded or clipped, the latter sometimes appearing in catalogues as octagonal. They were usually decorated with feather edges. By 1780 the edge was commonly bordered with a single row of fine beading or reeding; less common are double line borders, single plain lines, wavy or zig-zag lines between double straight lines. The upper outline of the oblong might now be arched, with sometimes a matching curve on the lower edge. The arch usually contained engraved ornament and examples have been recorded with crests or monograms in this space, extending downward almost to the title.

At first it was usual to pierce two holes immediately below the upper edge for the rings at the ends of the suspension chain. More commonly later a pair of almost circular eyelets extended from the edge. In some early nineteenth-century bottle tickets the centre of the upper edge was extended in a curve with an eyelet on each side for the chain rings. The delicate link chains on Sheffield plate bottle tickets and decanter labels, and the rings at the ends, were hand-made in silver by women workers, a feature overlooked by the makers of reproductions. An early Victorian plate catalogue illustrated the current fashion for making the chain long enough to double itself round the neck and shoulder of a taper decanter or wine bottle, the label itself positioned a little below the shoulder.

Crescent-shaped bottle tickets appeared concurrently with the oblong form and the shape was used also for decanter labels. The widespread horns, terminating in eyelets for the chain rings, are usually about one inch apart. The edges of early crescents in Sheffield plate lacked decorative borders. Then came the feather edge, double and triple line borders, wavy or zig-zag lines and bright-cut edges. A variant of the crescent dates from 1790. In this the inner arc is divided into two matching curves meeting in a central point. The Watson-Bradbury catalogue, about 1815, illustrates a crescent wine label with the space between the horns filled by fruiting vine and an urn on an elaborate stand.

The plain escutcheon or shield-shape bottle ticket appeared in Sheffield plate from the early 1770s with a feather edge and continued to the end of the century. A series in which the sides were decorated with fluted drapery or festoons appeared early in the nineteenth century. The escutcheon shape was revived after about 1830, edged with elaborate mounts including foliate scrolls. The oval bottle label was made with the usual run of edge decoration. The pointed oval or ellipse was popular by 1790 and often edged with bright cutting.

A Sheffield plate catalogue published in the early 1790s by John Parsons & Co., Sheffield, illustrates 'labels for bottles', oblong, crescent, escutcheon and oval, all with single-line beaded edges. These are titled variously W PORT, R PORT, RUM and HOCK. The 1797 catalogue of Roberts, Cadman & Co., Sheffield, in the Victoria and Albert Museum, describes similar pieces as 'wine bottle labels'.

A catalogue page of the 1790s, illustrated by H. N. Veitch, shows a crescent bottle ticket with draped sides priced at 14*s* a dozen. Veitch, a specialist dealer in Sheffield plate early in the present century, was impressed by 'the almost incredible number of designs to be found in bottle tickets and wine labels'. Duplicates of the oblong, crescent and escutcheon types with single-line beaded edges were catalogued a century later at 27*s* a dozen.

High fashion demanded that bottle tickets from the 1780s should display the owner's crest or cypher usually engraved on a shield-shaped cresting to the ticket. In early examples ticket and cresting were worked from a single piece of plate: in the nineteenth century many were stamped. The tiny shield might rise from the top of an oblong with strengthening supporters, or the horns of a deep crescent might be elongated and rounded sharply to support it.

The simple hoop or bottle ring wine label dates from about 1790. Its flat surface was set at an angle so that it fitted snugly against the sloping neck of a wine bottle or taper decanter: it was unsuitable for deeply shouldered bottles and elaborately cut decanters. Bottle rings were engraved in two places with the name of the wine. From about 1800 a plain ticket might be hinged or looped to a bottle ring. These continued into the early Victorian period. The catalogue of Nathaniel Smith & Son, Sheffield, undated but probably published in about 1810, illustrates a plain neck ring label together with three oblong bottle tickets with clipped corners and plain triple line borders.

Wine tickets and decanter labels with the names of wines cut through the plate in block capitals date from the 1790s. The original intention of cut-out titles was to make the name of the wine easier to decipher by displaying the letters against the dark glass of the bottle with a surround of silvery plate. Engraved titles were often difficult to read. A second series of cut-out titles dates from the mid-1830s. In some instances the name of the wine was enclosed within a light frame: in others the letters were mounted between a pair of bars.

A yet clearer style of bottle ticket had been introduced by 1805. This was in the form of a tall, slightly convex oblong edged with an applied mount and perforated with a single letter. Such tickets were intended for marking wine bottles for individual use such as by club members and in the dining rooms of residential hotels and so on. The letter indicated the name of the owner of the bottle rather than the title of the wine.

Wine tickets shaped as letters, the initials of various wines, date from the mid-1820s and continued until the late nineteenth century. In most instances the letter was suspended by a chain from loops worked into the top edge: in others the loop was placed centrally. These initials, measuring between one and two inches in height, were often shaped in elaborate type forms such as nineteenth-century Gothic with the surface elaborately engraved.

Bottle tickets were always plainly utilitarian. The first suggestion of highly ornamental design appeared not in metal, but in pictorial representations of wine labels, engraved, gilded or enamelled on the surface of 'new-fashioned label decanters' advertised from the early 1750s. The title was enclosed in a spacious reserve with mantlings above, vine leaves and grapes below, the illusion of a suspended wine label being completed by encircling the decanter shoulder with engraving to resemble the chain.

Silversmiths were soon producing expansive, elaborately designed labels to hang around the necks of flint-glass decanters, shortly to be cut with relief diamonds and fluting. There were now two different types of labels, each for a different purpose: the small plain bottle tickets and the larger, more flamboyant decanter labels, and they were so differentiated by their users. The drastic reduction of the excise duty on French wines in 1786 was followed by an immense increase in the consumption of fine wines. These were served from equally expensive cut-glass decanters hung with silver labels. War-time shortage of silver resulted in a demand for decorative labels in Sheffield plate.

In Sheffield plate a few early attempts at elaboration have been noted in hand-worked specimens but little more than the simplest of bottle tickets were made until after the development, in the early 1790s, of a hard tool steel capable of withstanding long runs at the stamp without loss of detail in the die. Formerly, after a very short run clear sharp definition was lost. Relief decorations were being applied to Sheffield plate wine tickets by the 1790s. Die-struck from paper-thin sheets of silver, the stampings were filled with a mixture of molten lead and tin. These mounts were soldered to the face of the plate, an outer strip of silver being left to lap over and conceal the raw copper edge of the Sheffield plate. Such ornament became progressively more ornate as decanter labels became a practical proposition in Sheffield plate.

The Sheffield plate wine label from about 1810 was, normally, an oblong or oval name plate encircled with an ornamental silver mount such as flowers and foliage or scrollwork, stamped and chased. Reeded scrolls in association with shells or grapes are noted, as well as gadroons or thread and shell borders. From about 1815 silver mounts became wider than formerly and the copper tended to be rather thicker: area also increased. Mounts widened still further from the early 1820s.

The wine label shaped in a single piece by stamping from the plated copper appears to date from about 1815. The scallop shell was a fashionable pattern, the suspension chains being attached to the ears with the title enamelled in black on a plain reserve which might be near-oblong or curved ribbon-like and extending across the width of the shell. The 'hinge' of the shell in a later series was decorated with a narrow scroll. Vine leaves, with the occasional addition of tendrils, were fashionable from the same period, synchronizing with the after-war demand for French wines. Dozens of variations of the leaf have been noted, each requiring a separate set of tools: the Birmingham platers charged about 7s 6d each at the factory. They were, of course, hand-finished. Vine leaves in which the title was given the clarity of perforation were introduced in silver by Charles Rawlings in 1824: these were quickly reproduced by the platers. The Victorian vine leaf label harmonized with engraved sprays of fruiting vine encircling many fashionable decanters, often in colour.

Wine labels in Sheffield plate were virtually outmoded by the Licensing Act of 1860 which permitted stores for the first time to sell bottles of wine and spirits for home consumption. It was a legal obligation to label such bottles. But a dark bottle pasted with a paper label was a poor substitute for the flint-glass decanter, cut or engraved and hung with a silver label, and electro-plated silver bottle tickets continued in demand until the 1890s.

Wine bottle corks mounted with Sheffield plate labels date from the 1790s. The specially graduated cork, always of excellent quality, was fitted with a flat, deep-rimmed top of plate. The surface is engraved with the name of the wine and at the centre rose an upright finger loop. A catalogue of the period illustrates an example, pricing them at 12s a dozen. In a less common series the finial was a strong, vertical disc engraved on both sides with the name of the wine or a number. From the late 1820s the plated mount might be flat with the name of the wine inscribed around its rim and an ornamental finial in the centre. These cost 2s 9d each at the factory. Vine leaf and ivy leaf finials were usually in silver.

Orange juice has been a zestful ingredient of drinks for many centuries. Cookery books from the fifteenth century include recipes for preserving the juices of oranges and lemons by a process enabling them to be stored for a year. Sir Hugh Plat in *Delights for Ladies*, 1602, recorded a simple method beginning 'first, expresse their juice and pass it through an Ipocras bag to clarifie it from the impurities and seeds . . .' The Ipocras bag or Hippocrates' sleeve was a conical bag of cotton, linen or flannel strengthened at the rim. By then silver orange strainers were already in use.

When punch became a fashionable drink in the mid-seventeenth century strained orange and lemon juice flavoured the heady compound. Bates in his *Dispensary*, 1694, declared fine punch to be 'a pleasant and grateful drink' made by mixing 'fair water; brandy a quart; choice pure lemon or orange juice, a pint; double refined sugar, 1 lb; and if you please add one nutmeg grated.' This recipe served the directors of the East India Company at their meetings. Another fashionable drink of the period was claret and orange juice. In October 1714 Margaret Adams wrote to Lord Fermanagh: 'we toasted our friends at Claydon in claret and orange.'

The juices were squeezed from the fruit through a strainer but not directly into the liquor. Instead a small vessel was used, of silver, pewter, porcelain or earthenware. When the required quantity had been extracted it was added to the punch or wine. These strainers were small and weighed about two ounces.

Orange juice was imported from Spain in kegs throughout the eighteenth century. John Ashley who established the London Punch House on Ludgate Hill in 1723, advertised in *The London Chronicle*, 1766: 'ORANGE JUICE lately imported from Seville. It will keep a year, and in the Making of Punch equals any Seville Oranges when in their Perfection.'

Orange or lemon juice was added to the punch, hot or cold, through a hemi-spherical silver strainer shaped by raising from the plate. A pair of rests or handles cut from flat plate were soldered diametrically opposite to each other on the rim of the strainer which was encircled with strengthening moulding such as simple reeding or beading. The handles measured about four inches long and $1\frac{1}{4}$ inches broad except where they were expanded to join the strainer rim. They were wavy-edged and perforated with simple motifs such as hearts, trefoils and scrollwork. Usually the expanded surface of one rest was engraved with the owner's crest, cypher, initials or identifying emblem.

The orange strainer bowl had become shallower by the time they were made by the Sheffield platers in the early 1760s and soon its base was almost flat, saw-cut and drilled with fanciful arrangements of perforations. Usually it was fitted with openwork handles of drawn silver wire. At first these had small shell terminals beneath the ends of the loops to prevent the strainer from slipping into the punch bowl.

The Assay Office listed these as orange strainers, charging one penny each for the assay, but when Matthew Boulton submitted such strainers for assay from 1773 he entered them as punch strainers. These he also made in Sheffield plate. They had large deep hemispherical straining bowls fitted with rests long enough to extend across the diameter of a punch bowl, at that time made in sizes ranging from about nine to 24 inches. With these the orange juice was squeezed directly into the punch. The strainer extended downward into the punch and became a receptacle for the unpeeled squeezed oranges, then very much smaller than those of today. They remained in the strainer soaking into the punch and imparting a full-bodied orange flavour until the strainer was lifted from the liquor immediately before serving.

The earliest of these strainers resembled a capacious ladle with a long, hollow handle and with a sturdy hook of flat metal attached to the strainer rim diametrically opposite. This was clipped to the edge of the punch bowl as a safety precaution. The rim was gadrooned and the upper surface of the rests chased with vines, scrolls and shells. The introduction of colanders or strainers *en suite* with porcelain and earthenware punch bowls virtually confined the silver and plated orange strainers to use with punch bowls of silver, Sheffield plate and finely enamelled porcelain.

Because so few orange strainers date later than about 1780 it has been wrongly assumed that oranges were no longer incorporated in punch. There were, in fact, more than 50 orange merchants in London at the turn of the century. But the orange strainer had been superseded fashionably by a combined wine funnel and orange strainer.

Until early in the nineteenth century wines threw a sediment which could be removed by means of a wine funnel or strainer. The earliest known example in silver was made in 1651 and is now in the collection of the Earl Fitzwilliam. The actual straining unit was a Hippocrates' sleeve of muslin fitting inside the tube.

Not until the 1760s did the wine funnel come into widespread use for decanting wines, as a result of the fashion for tabling wines in shouldered decanters of clear flint-glass. Even so, some sediment passed the strainer and sank to the bottom of the decanter. With clear glass this was a disfigurement: hence the introduction of cut flutes around the decanter base to conceal the deposit.

The body of a Georgian wine funnel in Sheffield plate was urn-shaped or ogee in outline, containing a detachable silver strainer fitted into the waist. Many were accompanied by two or three finer strainers in silver and a ring upon which could be mounted a muslin strainer. These required regular and careful cleaning to avoid imparting a mouldy flavour to the wine. The rim was strengthened with applied edging such as gadrooning, beading, reeding or other swaged work: chased basket pattern from 1810; scrollwork from about 1820.

The tapering spout or stem extending from below the centre of the body was curved at the end and the tip sliced vertically so that the opening was at right angles. The flowing wine could then be inspected as it cascaded down the side of the decanter neck: this also reduced aeration of the falling liquid. Attached to the side of the upper part of the spout might be one or two narrow spring clips to prevent it from pressing against the neck of the decanter and causing an air-lock.

Wine funnels and orange strainers were counted among the popular Sheffield plate productions listed in *The Sheffield Directory*, published in 1774. Twenty years or so later the platers had evolved the combined orange strainer and wine funnel. This dual-purpose device consisted of a hemispherical, octagonal or ogee-shaped orange strainer measuring about $3\frac{1}{2}$ inches in diameter. This was shaped by spinning the plate in the lathe: the octagonal shape was hand-hammered at a cost of nearly half as much again as the plain spun type, and with drilled holes covering an area of about $1\frac{1}{2}$ inches in diameter at the base. The rim was fitted with a flat, plain or shell-shaped hook about one inch in length soldered to the rim and to which it might be hinged. The strainer could thus be hung on the rim of a punch bowl. Beneath the strainer was soldered a vertical ring-socket about $1\frac{5}{8}$ inches in diameter and about $\frac{3}{8}$ inch in depth. This contained a spring which secured a detachable wire ring suspending a very finely meshed muslin bag, a derivative of the Hippocrates' sleeve and discarded after a single use. Over this ring was screwed the upper part of the four-inch-long tapering spout, which might be partly fluted or ribbed but was usually smoothly round. This could be removed from the orange strainer in a moment so that the wire funnel slipped loosely into the neck of the decanter. The combined strainer and wine funnel measured about $5\frac{1}{2}$ inches overall, consisting of 11 units soldered together and burnished so that joints were invisible. To prevent corrosion this might be gilded within at a cost of about five shillings extra, but the exterior usually remained ungilded.

Until the 1820s the combined orange-strainer-wine-funnel when not in use rested spout uppermost upon a circular, saucer-like stand, slightly domed at the centre, its rim encircled with moulding matching that on the strainer rim. Stand and funnel might be engraved with the owner's crest or cypher.

By the 1830s the wine funnel might be widely everted, edged with plain moulding and accompanied by a domed cover with an ivory finial. This funnel swung from a bail handle on substantial hinges. Funnels lacking strainers and with straight tapering spouts were used for pouring spirits into square decanters.

# 13. The tea equipage

*Teapots; milk jugs; sugar vases; baskets; canisters; tongs; tea and coffee urns and machines*

The silver or Sheffield plate tea equipage set the tone for the whole elegant tea-time ritual practised by the Georgian hostess. Arranged upon a silver, plated or wooden tea board of handsome proportions were the teapot, a pair of tea canisters, sugar bowl and cream jug, often dominated by a graceful tea-kettle on a tripod stand.

Tea was always freshly made in the drawing room or boudoir. At first it was the custom for the water to be carried in, boiling, by the tea-blender, usually the most presentable house-maid or parlour-maid of the establishment, who had charge of the tea-table equipage, preparing the tea and handing a cup to each guest and member of the family. The teapot itself was mounted over a spirit lamp. Eventually it was realized that the kettle and not the teapot should be mounted over a lamp to ensure a good brew of the costly drink.

The plain incurved teapot design, a version of the pear shape, its curves following a shallow ogee line, had been fashionable in silver during the reign of George II. This was reproduced by the platers in a somewhat ungainly style until it was developed into the urn outline. But in the 1770s the neo-classic vogue for plain surfaces and uninterrupted curves prompted the platers to copy the factory silversmiths with less elaborate designs than the stemmed urn shape. For easy assembly these were vertical-sided and might be circular, oval, rectangular, polygonal or lozenge-shaped on plan with slightly domed lids and flat chased ornament. Some had vertically fluted or corrugated bodies and an attractive series was serpentine on plan composed of a variety of concave and convex curves. In another style the urn-shaped body tapered to a narrow stem rising from a round spreading foot. By about 1790 the cape teapot had become fashionable – a rim or gallery encircling its lid opening. The lozenge-shaped teapot with a pierced gallery encircling the top of the body and a hingeless cover dates from about 1795. The low-placement of the straight tapering spout is characteristic of many Sheffield plate teapot designs which became so diverse that a full description is impossible. An interesting feature in teapots at this period was the increase of length – from spout-tip to handle – in proportion to height, the length frequently being the greater. In the early nineteenth century there was a return to the early Georgian pear shape and the squat, globular 'melon' which might lack a foot ring and was strengthened by lobed ribbing: these were, of course, far more capacious than the early vessels, but to the platers were 'Queen Anne'.

In early examples Sheffield plate teapots had neither foot rim nor feet to lift the broad base, heated by the tea, above the fashionable tea tray of polished wood, which was liable to be disfigured. Consequently a teapot stand of Sheffield plate was introduced. This might be supported by ball or short outcurving feet, or slender claw and ball feet. In the early nineteenth century the pot itself might have ball feet. The stand was encircled with beaded or gadrooned mounts matching those of the teapot itself. The teapot handle might be plainly curved in a single piece from ivory, ebony or hardwood, or shaped from horn, all with a thumbpiece on the apex of the curve. The lid was flush with the body rim and might be either flat or slightly domed.

Catalogues show that teapots were made in sizes of one quart and $1\frac{1}{2}$ pints. Prices of straight-sided examples varied: a teapot serpentine on plan with a flat chased border, swags and flowers, cost 50s, quart size. A plain oval teapot with a pierced gallery sold for 43s.

Like other components of the Sheffield plate tea equipage, the milk jug passed through its own individual phases, reflecting current fashions. As in silver, no attempt was made to match the jug with teapot or sugar bowl until the 1770s. These milk jugs were shaped in an unencumbered flow of Grecian outlines. The body, often octagonal on plan, tapered smoothly from rim to base, a slender stem joining it to the circular or oval concave foot which might be mounted on a four-sided plinth. The handle had a similar simplicity of outline, recurving and sweeping down to the base.

A less easily overturned cream jug was introduced in about 1785, becoming popular about 10 years later. This shapely little pitcher had the high everted spout of the classic design and the classic handle rising vertically from the rim, and then projecting a short distance before flowing smoothly down to the base. But instead of tapering to a stem foot the whole body of the jug was wide and rested flatly on the tray. The rim was strengthened with reeded moulding and the lower body might be ornamented with wide facets below a band of bright-cut engraving. By 1810 this style of milk jug, its lines more graceful than formerly, was raised upon four ball feet. Structurally, the jug body was usually shaped in two halves, the foot made separately, often as a single piece. Decoration when present consisted of body engraving or flat chasing. These were succeeded by the jugs resembling a narrow-necked classical vase with one side of the rim extended into a wide everted spout.

A long series of early nineteenth-century milk jugs was designed in the style of the Roman urn, the lower half of the body gadrooned or reeded. The body-neck junction was concealed beneath applied mounting. Later the body gadrooning became narrower and shallower and a band of mechanically produced embossment encircled the body immediately below the rim and a narrow edging encircled the rim. Such a jug would be supported on a low circular foot and the square-shouldered handle continued in the harp shape.

Reeding gradually became wider and more convex and the tea-table milk jug became taller by the addition of a vertical neck. The lower part of the body might be embossed. The handle became heavily elaborate by the 1820s and a four-footed ring base became fashionable. Towards the close of the Regency period the platers issued a series of smooth-surfaced jugs with a fillet in a raised pattern encircling the body.

In conformity with the design of the accompanying items of the tea-table equipage, the George IV milk jug was generally an ornate vessel embossed in relief, its rim decorated with heavy mounting. It stood upon four short scroll feet moulded in a piece with the shallow base rim. The melon-shaped body with wide reeding or lobes became fashionable at this time. At first the lobes might be smoothly plain, but the majority were handsomely embossed or chased in panels with such motifs as flowers, foliage and fruit. The spout tended to rise in a curve sweeping beyond the body. The handle was shaped in a single graceful curve.

The reign of William IV brought a return of the designs used by the silversmiths before the mid-eighteenth century, such as the pear-shaped jug, fluted, or flat-chased, the handle once more in a scrolling outline, and the rounded base of the body raised above the table on short scroll feet.

A covered sugar bowl, usually hemispherical or octagonal in shape with a moulded foot ring, formed part of the silversmith's early Georgian tea equipage. By the 1730s a fashion had developed for keeping a pair of tea canisters in a casket or 'tea chest' of silver, shagreen or finely figured wood, and in many instances this also contained a matching silver sugar box, slightly squarer and more capacious than the canisters. Whereas the canisters tended to have small circular lid openings, the sugar box's hinged lid covered the whole top of the box. The few examples remaining in Sheffield plate date to the 1760s. By the 1770s, however, the fashionable use of silver and Sheffield plate had been discontinued, the box being replaced by a flint-glass sugar bowl.

Meanwhile, new trends in fashion evolved by the silversmiths and quickly reproduced by the Sheffield platers were beginning to give the English tea-table the stately graces of Grecian ornament and inevitably the sugar bowl had to conform to the neo-classic craze and appear in the shape of classic vases, wide at the shoulder and tapering to a spool-shaped stem above a round foot. The highly domed lid terminated in a vase-shaped finial. At the same time pierced ornament was set off by a liner of blue glass.

The upper portion of the vase body might now be both geometrically pierced and elaborately flat chased with festoons while the lower portion was embossed and flat chased, often with thin leaves radiating vertically from the foot stem. The cover was decorated to match the lower part of the body. Pierced sugar vases continued to be made with round and square feet until about 1815.

Others, from 1775, were of unpierced plate. The classic design of the vase or urn was developed to the full in the wide-brimmed bowl, often elliptical, with a pair of long narrow handles rising from the rim and recurving down to the base of the body. Already by 1770 some sugar vases were being made without covers. This led to the development of an alternative arching handle design, for what was known as a sugar bucket. This was a more homely little vessel, plainly bucket-shaped but displaying the popular pierced decoration of the period over a blue glass liner. Alternatively it might be of open wire work in a neo-classic shape, on a high spreading foot. The swing handle might also be pierced.

Canoe-shaped sugar-baskets date from the mid-1780s. The body might be pierced and fitted with a blue glass liner, or solid and enriched with festoons and medallions in bright-cut engraving. The rim was edged with threadwork ribbon to strengthen the hinges of the basket handle, and a short, spool-shaped stem linked the bowl to a foot in a corresponding outline.

Just as the turn of the century witnessed the re-establishment of a more stolid pitcher design for the milk, so also it approved a low, flat-bottomed sugar bowl, sometimes the oval shape squared up so that on plan the vessel was a round-cornered rectangle. As in the jug, the sides bulged, but a balanced design was achieved with a flat-topped handle at each end, curving from rim to base. By 1800 the sugar bowl might conform with reeding or fluting around the lower part of the body. Some early examples had narrow foot rings.

With the reign of George IV and a general return to rich versions of the rococo in silver, the Sheffield platers made much of the widely ribbed melon-shaped sugar-bowl, often ornately flat chased and with a pair of scroll handles. This had an applied base ring to which were soldered four ornamental feet.

Complete tea equipages were fashionable in Sheffield plate composed of tea-pot, sugar bowl and milk jug *en suite*. The vessels rested squatly on narrow base rims or ball feet: those resting directly on flat bases were usually accompanied by a tea tray.

Early tea canisters were copied from the oriental stoppered tea-jar of porcelain or stoneware, the plain flat sides rising from a rectangular base and curving sharply at the shoulders to terminate in a narrow cylindrical neck fitted with a detachable highly domed cover. This the hostess used for measuring the leaves into the teapot. The corners might be chamfered, resulting in two broad faces at the sides and three narrow ones at each end, shoulders curving steeply up to a flat platform from which rose a cylindrical neck fitted with a domed and knopped cover. Dome and neck tea canisters were made in silver until about 1760 and then in Sheffield plate during the 1760s–70s and again in the second quarter of the nineteenth century when they were catalogued as the Queen Anne style. As with the teapots these were more than twice as capacious as the originals.

Tea canisters in the shape of classic vases and urns were handsome productions of the Sheffield platers during the late eighteenth century. The tapering body was embossed in low relief with classic ornament, flowers or radiating convex reeding around the base, above a narrow stem and high concave foot, sometimes rising from a square plinth on ball feet. The incurving shoulders rose to a domed cover, soon changed to a dished, concave outline. Foot and plinth had become sturdier by the end of the century and reeding might rise more than halfway up the body.

By the turn of the century Sheffield plate tea canisters were being made in a multitude of geometric designs, square, rectangular, hexagonal, oval on plan, their vertical sides being decorated with flat chasing, engraving or bright cutting, usually in narrow borders; some were plain with no more than applied rims of gadrooning. A series of oval tea caddies had corrugated sides. Covers were flat and topped by substantial lifting knops. These were fitted with lock and key. In some instances the top was a fixture with a short cylindrical neck and a close-fitting pull-off cover.

Similar canisters, in pairs or threes, were fitted into plain chests of richly coloured woods such as satinwood but more commonly of the more pedestrian mahogany. A pattern had appeared in Sheffield plate by about 1800 consisting of two separate cube-shaped compartments each with a hinged lid. By 1820 the flamboyance of silver mounts was reflected on square and oblong tea canisters – now termed caddies in the catalogues. These were often handsome pieces but few remain.

Lumps of sugar cracked from the sugar loaf with steel sugar nippers were lifted from the sugar-bowl to tea-cup with the aid of sugar-tongs. In the scissor design the loop handles and scrolled arms terminated in wide scallop-shell sugar-grips, their interior surfaces flat at first and then hollowed. The pivoting joint was concealed in a flat circular box, one side displaying a decorative boss, the other roundly smooth. Sugar-tongs of this type seem to have been made by silversmiths until the 1790s, but few examples in Sheffield plate are known.

The vogue for U-shaped tongs, later advertised as spring tea tongs, began in about 1760. These were fool-proof in action and vast numbers were made in Sheffield plate. Until about 1790 such tongs were constructed by soldering together five units: a U-shaped arch of silvered copper hammered to such a degree that it became springy and, when bent, automatically separated the ends of the arms after removal of pressure. This arched spring was made convex outside and concave within, the outer surface being decorated with any of a wide range of flat-chased or engraved designs, a line border enclosing a flower or scroll ornament being popular. Soldered to each end of the spring was an ornamental arm pierced in designs fashionable at the period. At first the arms and grips were manufactured separately, the grips being stamped from silver and popularly shaped as shells, acorns or leaves, with circular or oval interior depressions.

Sugar tongs made from single strips of double-plated copper had appeared by 1790. The central portion of the strip was hammered until springy; the flat tapering arms were pierced; and the grips shaped with press tools. By 1800 such sugar-tongs were made with unpierced tapering arms and spoon-shaped grips. Until the early 1820s arch and arms were slim, plainly smooth, finely ribbed or with a touch of engraving. In some instances each grip was in the form of a tea leaf to match the accompanying caddy ladle.

From 1805 to about 1815 ornament on sugar-tongs consisted of little more than threaded edges. Arms were then made to match teaspoons with old English or fiddle ends. Sugar-tongs from about 1815 were made from thicker copper plate than formerly and the arms were lengthened to cope with the more massive sugar-bowls of the colourful tea-sets then being made in bone china. Sheffield plate sugar-tongs *en suite* with silver or Sheffield plate sugar-bowls remained slenderly dainty, however, the final touch to that most loved collection of Sheffield plate, the tea equipage.

During the late Regency period tea caddies of tortoiseshell and mother of pearl were accompanied by spring sugar-tongs with arms of the same materials. In a series dating from 1815 to about 1835 the tongs consisted of an arch of Sheffield plate linked by rivets to arms of mother of pearl carved with shell-shaped grips and surface decoration. Others possessed ivory arms, plain and fitted to the spring arch by means of thin slots cut deeply into their ends and held firmly by three silver rivets.

The Sheffield plate tea urn typified late-Georgian hospitality and shared with other table ware the changing vogues of neo-classicism, Regency solemnity and the florid extravagance of post-Regency inventiveness. But basic usefulness always controlled the design. The first indication that the silver tea-kettle was declining in fashionable favour was the modification of design which introduced a tap protruding from the vessel's broad base. This saved the hostess the effort of lifting and tilting the heavy kettle when hot water was required and it quickly evolved into what Cowper called 'the bubbling and loud hissing urn throwing up a steaming column'.

Contrary to popular notion, tea was not made directly in the teapot but in the tea urn, as proved by several contemporaneous conversation pieces, such as James Northcote's 'Dr. Johnson taking tea with Sir Joshua Reynolds', painted in 1783.

Tea urns in Sheffield plate were heated at first with smokeless court charcoal, a method preferred by some platers until the end of the century. In these the body of the urn could be lifted from its broad spool stem, revealing a perforated cylindrical charcoal brazier. Rising from this, and passing through the body into the dome of the lid, was a copper draught tube, gradually diminishing in diameter and terminating in a loose ornamental finial: adjustment of this created a draught which drew hot air through the chimney, heating it and thus the water around it. Another type of urn rested on a cubical box containing a charcoal brazier.

Charcoal heaters began to be superseded from 1774 by the solid cylindrical box iron. This substantial block of cast iron was heated until red in the kitchen fire and inserted into a close-fitting heater case or deep socket of copper plate that fitted vertically inside the vessel, so heating the water around it. John Wadham, a brazier of St George-in-the-East, London, patented this device. The specification, to be seen in the Patent Office, is accompanied by a sketch showing a sectional view of such an urn. Wadham is known to have supplied copper heating cases and cast-iron box irons to Sheffield and Birmingham at five shillings each. He also patented the double compartment tea urn, 'a machine that answers the purpose of teapot and boiler together'. The water was brought to the boil in one compartment, whereupon a valve permitted it to flow upon the tea leaves in the other section which took the place of a teapot.

Surprisingly, it appears that urns mounted over spirit lamp heaters were not sold until about 1790 and were first used in association with tea machines. The lamp font usually matched the shape of the urn above and was supported by a spool-shaped stem rising from a flat plinth. These lamps, usually flat-bottomed and resembling funerary urns, proved more efficient than earlier shapes. The spirits of wine burned without emitting fumes but it was costly and not always available outside London and some industrial centres. Less expensive, non-odorous smokeless fuels, such as camphorine, were not available until the 1830s, when they caused a fashionable reversion to the silver tea-kettle with its lamp and stand.

The earliest design of tea urn in Sheffield plate had a pear- or barrel-shaped body with a bell-shaped cover and a pair of scroll handles at the shoulders insulated with ebony or ivory discs. The flat base fitted upon a thick spool-shaped stem rising either from a square plinth which might be ornamentally pierced, or from a cube-shaped plinth perhaps containing a charcoal brazier.

Tea urns with neo-classic vase-shaped bodies appeared in about 1770 and continued until the 1790s. Narrow and tall, this style of urn was usually severely plain apart from a pair of D-shaped handles and an engraved coat of arms. In a few instances the vessel was encircled with a decorative garter of thin silver plate below the neck. This pattern is illustrated in a Sheffield plater's list of 1774. The bell-shaped cover with a small ventilator at the top was ornamented with an animal head, classic motif or plain knop finial. D-shaped handles were superseded in about 1780 by a pair of slender handles rising above the cover, then recurving to end half-way down the body; later they extended to its base. The vessel's stem, too, was extremely slender in the box-heated design. The square plinth was raised by a foot at each corner.

The spherical urn was hand-raised from the plate in two parts, joined horizontally. The upper section was sliced to form a cover, usually fitted with a ball finial; those made by Roberts, Cadman & Co. are recognized by their seated lion finials. A vase-shaped urn dating from the 1790s had four vertical depressions extending the length of the body, alternating with narrow flat-topped reedings. The plinth was in the same shape on plan and the cover in the form of a slender spool expanding towards the base to fit the body opening. In gallon capacity the works price was £8.10.0 – probably 12 guineas in the shops.

Body fluting or reeding, vertical or spiral, often with very narrow flutes, appeared at about the same time with similar decoration on the foot and on the cover and its finial. Horizontal ribbing is also noted. In 1792 tea urns with fluted bodies enriched with silver mounts and engraved garters were priced: gallon capacity, 160s; three pints, 70s; quart 60s. Plain-bodied urns of similar capacity cost 147s, 64s and 54s each. By 1805 the vessel might be melon-shaped and widely fluted: others were encircled with bands of gadrooning.

In about 1790 appeared a new design in tea urns. Resembling a Roman funerary urn and with a flat bottom, it was supported at the shoulders by four flat reeded columns rising from paw feet soldered to a rectangular plinth, usually with incurved edges and mounted on four ball feet.

The fashion for a wider body created by the introduction of the spirit-heated lamp found happier expression towards 1800 when the urn body resembled a wide-mouthed circular vase or was spherical with little applied decoration apart from a pair of mask-ring handles. The body was supported by a stemmed foot rising from a square plinth with four heavy paw feet. Watson & Bradbury's catalogue published in about 1800 illustrated more than 100 patterns then in production.

After the close of the Napoleonic wars florid mounts were applied to all fashionable shapes. The four upright columns were curved into s-shape with paw feet and topped by heads of animals or birds. Mounts of thin silver stamped with elaborate designs were used, the hollows being filled with hard or silver solder.

The urns were plated on the exterior surface only, the coating being rather thicker than was normal for other tea-ware. Interiors were heavily tinned: with continual wear this required frequent renewal.

The urn tap, projecting horizontally and positioned as low as possible at the vessel's base, was a source of trouble to makers and users. The majority were cast from hard pewter, an alloy mainly composed of tin, and close plated. In others tap and handle were stamped in thin silver plate, filled with pewter and carefully soldered together.

Until about 1790 the tap was fitted with a sturdy T-handle, often in the shape of an escallop shell, fluted, pierced or plain. This detail might be in solid silver of less than sterling quality and therefore not hallmarked, or in ebony, carved or plain, or in ivory, often stained green. Tap design was poor and the metal incapable of long wear. The spout was liable to drip soon after being taken into use because of the difficulty of sealing the plug and the softness of the Sheffield plate which might become warped – hence the necessity for a sliding shelf on the urn stand to support a small drip bowl. Strengthening flanges at the plug-body junction on charcoal heated urns were in cut-card work and might be made from silver plate.

The drip-proof tap was patented in 1786 by Lancelot Palmer, but few date earlier than 1790. Through the brass cock was cut a slot opened or closed by pulling forward or pushing backward a U-shaped lever fitted with a ball finial of ebony or ivory. Strengthening flanges were no longer necessary at the plug-body junction.

The urn tap from the mid-1820s was cast in a single piece from german silver and the surface close plated – electro-plated from the mid-1840s. The handle was usually bow-shaped, rising vertically from the tap and pulled forward to release the liquid. Such taps are found as replacements of worn taps on earlier urns.

The country house breakfast of late eighteenth-century or Regency days was usually a delightful self-service meal, each member of the household rising at a time suited to his personal convenience. Because architects tended to place the bustling kitchen regions well away from the breakfast room, usually positioned to face the morning sun, an array of silver or Sheffield plate entrée dishes containing hot foods was laid out on a massive sideboard or serving table, often measuring as much as 10 feet in length. Here the comforts might include a tea machine. One cupboard of the sideboard was tin-lined and used as a plate warmer. It was fitted with an iron plate rack and a small tripod to support a red-hot ingot of cast iron carried from the kitchen. The so-called tea machine was composed of three near-spherical urns each supported by its own small plinth, usually square or cruciform, and each fitted with a box iron to heat its contents or accompanied by a small hemispherical spirit lamp. The central urn was for hot water and might hold six pints or more and this was flanked by a pair of matching three-pint urns intended for tea and coffee. The hot water urn swivelled on its stem so that water from its tap could be directed into either of the smaller urns without the necessity of moving it. Nevertheless each urn could be lifted from the stand to be used separately from the machine.

The urns were grouped upon a cruciform-shaped platform or galleried stand raised above the sideboard by ball or bracket feet. The stand was sectioned to the right and left of the central urn to fit the plinths of the small urns, while at the front it might be recessed semi-circularly or extended in a bow to take a hemispherical waste bowl. The complete machine approximated 24 inches in height, 20 inches back to front and weighed more than a quarter of a hundredweight.

A typical tea and coffee machine in the Sheffield City Museum following this pattern was made by Daniel Holy, Wilkinson & Co., Mulberry Street, Sheffield, during the 1790s. The mark of this firm, a churchwarden tobacco pipe, was registered at the Sheffield Assay Office in 1784 and continued in use until 1804 when the firm's mark became Daniel Holy/Parker & Co., accompanied by a pineapple. This tea machine shows a feature associated with Daniel Holy, Wilkinson & Co.: each spherical vessel is supported by four flat reeded upright columns, curved into shallow s-shapes and attached by capital finials. Moulded silver claw or paw feet are soldered to these supports, resting on the corners of a flat plinth. The centre of the plinth in this specimen is raised, but might be flat or sunk with a depression to take the spirit lamp. The tray, on six ball feet, is bow-fronted to form a circular platform for the waste bowl.

A detail noted on the tea machine urn was the wide strengthening garter in sterling silver to conceal the roman joint of the upper and lower hemispheres. These encircling bands were elaborately enriched with bright-cut engraving, the motifs including festoons of flowers and foliage, acanthus leaves and scrollwork often interspersed with classical medallions. Alternatively the urns were thickly plated and the joint concealed with a band of light engraving. Well-modelled human or animal masks, usually lions, with solid pendant rings, were fitted at the widest diameter for use as handles.

An illustration of such a machine in a catalogue attributed to 1808 names it 'Tea Equipage Compleat', giving a trade price of £30. The large urn is stated to hold six quarts and the pair of small urns two quarts each. Individual platers

159   Dish ring, 1785

160   Dish ring, *c.* 1800

161 and 162   Adjustable dish
crosses, 1790s

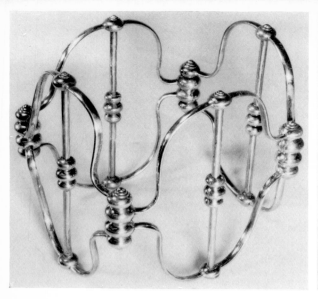

163  Folding dish stand, *c.* 1810

164  (*top right*) Revolving dish stand, 1790s

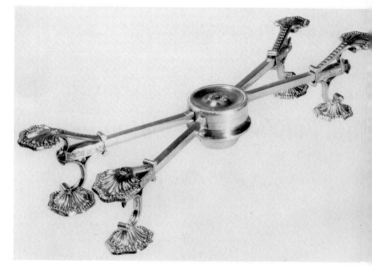

165  Dish cross, 1770s

166  Dish cross, *c.* 1800

167 Sauce boat

68 Pair of sauce boats, late eighteenth century

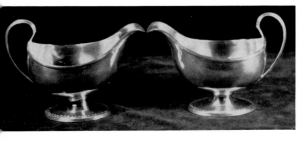

169 (*below*) Sauce boat, *c.* 1820; tea urn; sauce boat, *c.* 1830

170    Set of sauce tureens, early nineteenth century

171    Sauce tureen, late eighteenth century

172    Sauce tureen, late eighteenth century

173    Sauce tureen, 1770s

174    Sauce tureen, 1830s

175  Argyles, *c.* 1790 and 1830s

176  Argyle, 1770s

177  (*below left*) Argyle, 1780s

178  (*below right*) Argyle, late eighteenth century

179 Soy frame, 1800

180 Soy frame, 1790

181 Spirit frame, 1785

182    Epergne and cruet frame, *c.* 1800

183    (*below left*) Epergne and cruet frame, 1790s

184    (*below right*) Combined epergne and cruet
       frame

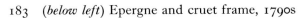
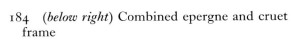

185 Salt-cellar 1780s–90s

186 Salt-cellar

187 Salt-cellar, *c.* 1780

188 Salt-cellar

189 Pair of salt-cellars,
early nineteenth century

190 Salt-cellars

191   The Trafalgar inkstand, from 1806

192   Saucepan, late 1750s

193  (*top left*) Egg-cup stand, *c.* 1790

194  (*top right*) Egg-cup stand, *c.* 1800

195  (*left*) Egg-cup stand, *c.* 1805

196  (*below left*) Egg stand combined with toast rack, *c.* 1810

197  (*below right*) Combined egg-cup and toast rack, 1812

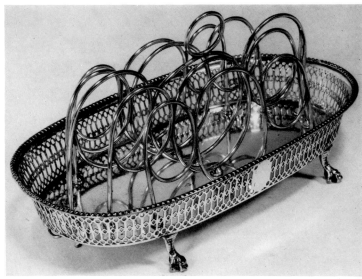

199   Toast rack, 1785

198   Toast rack, early nineteenth century

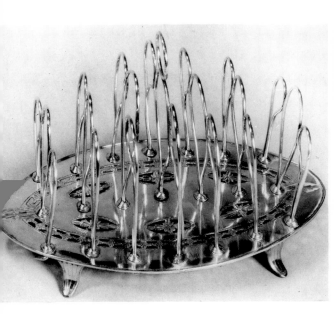

0   Toast rack, *c.* 1800

201   Toast rack, 1790s

202    Fish slices, 1780s–90s

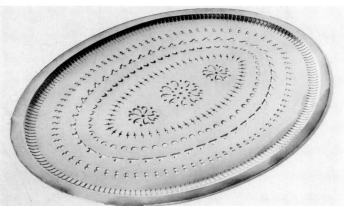

203    Fish plate or mazarine, 1780s

204    Sheffield plate of
    of late eighteenth
    century, including
    asparagus tongs;
    knife and fork voider
    flanked by punch
    ladles; and (below)
    cheese toaster and
    steel knives

205 and 206 (*above right and left*) Tea trays, late eighteenth century

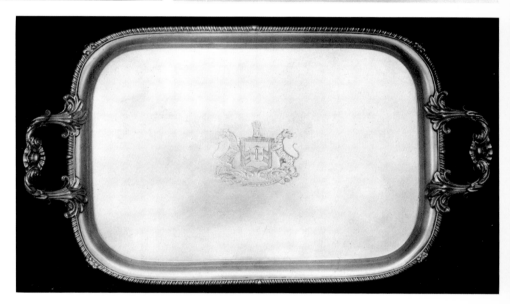

207 Early eighteenth-century tray

208 (*below*) Tea tray, late eighteenth century

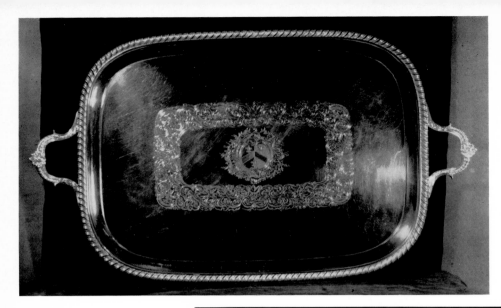

209   Tray, *c.* 1830

210   Tray, 1824–8

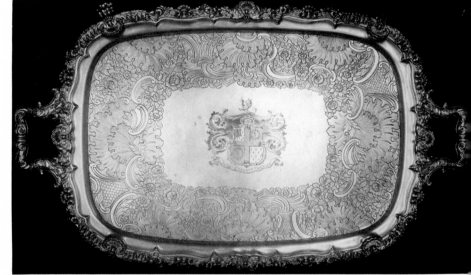

211   Tray, 1824–30

212    Salver, early nineteenth century

213    Tea table, early nineteenth century

214    Waiter

215　Inkstand, late 1760s

216　Inkstand, 1820s

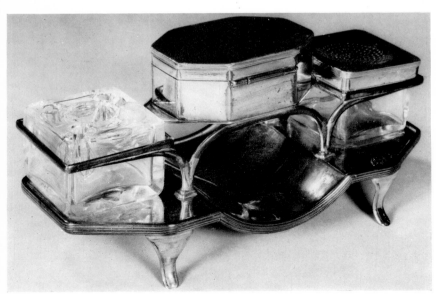

217　Inkstand, *c.* 1785

developed their own designs incorporating refinements from earlier and contemporaneous patterns. Several pattern books published by Sheffield platers in the 1790s and early 1800s illustrated such machines. The catalogue published in 1797 by Roberts, Cadman & Co., Eyre Street, Sheffield, and now in the Victoria and Albert Museum, contains an engraving (fig. 99) of such a machine annotated in handwriting: 'With Silver Edges and Engraved Silver Garters and Shields with Patent Cock £31.10.0. No engraved Garter £28.8.0.' In this example the six-quart urn containing a box heater is raised above the three vessels it is to supply, which are contained within a single bowl that can be revolved around the tall central stem. In this way the vessels for teas and coffee can be placed under the water-urn's tap as required. As a further refinement the tray below also revolves so that cups placed upon it can be moved under the taps projecting from the lower vessels.

A less elaborate version of a similar machine, shown in the same plate, is without a silver garter or rotating tray but is supported on a triangular plinth and each cover has a lion couchant finial. This is priced at £20: a silver-engraved garter cost £2.12.0 extra. These tea machines were struck with the mark of Roberts, Cadman & Co., a bell in an oval, registered at the Sheffield Assay Office in 1785. Few machines of this type have been recorded although it is known that many were sold.

Regency pattern books illustrate less elaborate tea machines, the three urns and footed waste bowl being arranged on a deep-rimmed, footed tray with loop handles.

Sheffield plate catalogues usually specify decoration of tea machines with silver mounts as an extra. These were usually pearl work or gadroons which were stamped in thin silver and the hollows filled with a soft alloy before being soldered to the Sheffield plate. A coat of arms, crest or cypher might be engraved in a reserve on the silver garter immediately above the tap of each urn. From about 1800 there was a vogue for silver shields with chased borders enclosing the arms, made separately and attached to the urns. In 1796 Lancelot Palmer noted that the 'furniture' of tea and coffee machines – cocks with their outer strengthening washers, garters, handles and finials – might be gilt, but the many pattern books inspected make no reference to such enrichment.

Tea and coffee machines were made also in copper: collectors of Sheffield plate should carefully examine items which display all the attributes of hand work of the late eighteenth century but which, nevertheless, may prove to have been electro-plated in recent years. Here a clue to note may be the absence of silver mounts.

# 14. The service of coffee

*Coffee-pots; coffee biggins; chocolate-pots*

Coffee at its most elegant was sipped slowly from tiny cups of Chinese porcelain set on silver or silver-gilt saucers placed on mats of embroidered silk fringed with gold. In the homes of the early Georgian gentry, the hot fragrant liquid was served from a plain, smoothly rounded or octagonal silver coffee-pot and the table illumined and the room perfumed with costly candles of English beeswax burning in silver candlesticks. Such domestic silver is now universally treasured. Humbler folk and the coffee-houses used copper coffee-pots although fashionable taverns served the beverage from silver pots. It was customary to grind coffee beans at table: staff appointments to the royal household included a coffee grinder.

The early Georgian coffee-pot was cylindrical, tapering slightly to the rim, with shallow collet foot, a high, rounded domed lid and a graceful swan-neck spout. They were advertised as 'right and left' and sold in pairs, one with a handle of ebony or black stained hard wood for coffee: the other, for milk, with a handle in ivory or natural-coloured box-wood. The servant was thus able to hold a pot in each hand, pouring coffee and milk into the cup simultaneously. This, it was thought, improved the flavour of the drink. The pear-shaped body was also fashionable with simple gadrooning encircling the rims of cover and foot. These basic shapes with low double-domed covers, usually without ornament, continued until the 1830s in silver, Sheffield plate, copper, japanned iron and earthenware.

Chelsea, Worcester, Bow and other porcelain potteries were making coffee-pots by the 1750s, and by 1760 Joseph Hancock of Sheffield, the first plater to specialize in table ware, was adapting the new process to forms hitherto considered the preserve of the silversmiths. The fashionable coffee-pot by this time had become slender, pear-shaped, long-necked with a spool stem rising from a wide circular foot. Hancock excelled in making richly embossed ware in patterns closely resembling silver, although they were more laborious to produce in Sheffield plate. He obtained skilled silversmiths from London.

A coffee-pot in the Sheffield City Museum attributed to about 1760 has a collet foot struck from a die and hand finished. This was made from two pieces of plate soldered back to back so that silver is displayed both top and bottom. The domed cover was built from three die-struck units soldered together. The spout, handle sockets and pineapple knob were each struck in two halves and silver soldered together before these units were incorporated into the coffee-pot. The right-angled hinge, known to platers as the 'joint', was common on eighteenth-century coffee-pots but was not an invariable feature. One leaf rose vertically from the top of the upper socket to a three-lug joint from which the second leaf extended horizontally on to the rim of the cover. The book-type hinge was also used. This was arranged with one leaf inside the handle socket and the other end fitted between the back-to-back plates of the cover.

The body was made from flat plate bent until the two ends joined. It was shaped with the aid of a raising stake, bellying hammer and sand cushion. The ends were then cut to dovetail accurately into each other, making a tight seam known to the platers as a cramp, but usually termed a roman joint. A straight seam was used on small work. The ends were then soldered and burnished. When fully assembled the interior of the coffee-pot, including the spout, was tinned.

Production was speeded by shaping the units with drop stamps and hand presses. The number of dies required for a plain coffee-pot was two each for the spout, knob, cover, top and bottom sockets. Dies were not used for the body as this was turned up in two vertical halves from copper plated on one side only and the circular base inserted. Alternatively it might be hammered up from the plate, but these are rarely found. The proportion of silver was heavier than standard, shown by the fact that remaining examples are in fine condition after decades of use.

The lower part of the swan-neck spout was enriched with relief decoration such as acanthus foliage and in many instances was further decorated on the upper outer curve at the spout outlet. The junction of the spout with the body was carefully shaped to fit snugly against the curve of the shoulder on the plain pear-shaped coffee-pot. The spout was designed so that its outlet rose until it was in line with the body rim, as did the top curve of the handle.

The handle was carved from a single piece of black-stained hard wood and fitted into a pair of hollow sockets, each end secured with a substantial rivet of sterling silver. If the rivets are of german silver the piece dates later than 1835 or the handle is a replacement. The sockets needed to be deep as alternating heat and cold tended to crack the wood. Ebony and rosewood handles have been seen on Sheffield plate coffee-pots. The small handle sockets on some early coffee-pots of plated copper were inefficient. The wood handles were shaped merely by bending and to prevent splitting were bound with heat-resistant wicker. In the majority of plain cylindrical coffee-pots a long metal socket was attached to the body. Into this was fixed a turned handle of stained hard wood. This projected from the side of the body at right angles with the spout and at about 30 degrees above the horizontal. Although these were common during the Sheffield plate period few appear to remain.

The vogue for neo-classic designs and decorations brought with it a demand for coffee-pots studiously following contemporaneous Greco-Roman patterns in silver. The fashionable coffee-pot lost its air of sturdy solidity, its body deteriorating into a fanciful urn or vase shape, supported on a spreading foot, usually circular, sometimes square with a short slender stem. At first the diameter of the foot was too small in proportion to the body and caused many accidents until made heavier, with a thicker stem. Bodies might remain plain, sometimes hexagonal or octagonal, but fashionably they were decorated in all-over repoussé with fantastic flowers, foliage and scrollwork: later spiral reedings decorated the lower part of the body. Matching lids were designed with elaborate finials. The shoulder of a later vase-shaped coffee-pot might be encircled with a band of solid silver decorated with bright-cut engraving.

A coffee-pot in the Victoria and Albert Museum, formerly in the collection of the Viscountess Wolseley and attributed to the 1770s, has a vase-shaped body, domed cover, trumpet-shaped foot and spool-shaped neck with a channel spout. The joint between body and neck is encircled with a wide band of silver enriched with scrollwork in relief. Foot and mouth rims and the silver band are edged in silver. Similar examples are known with a narrower band decorated with bright-cut engraving. Sometimes a vase-shaped coffee-pot has a detachable cover and a slender handle extending downward, following the body curve, to a socket rising from the body-stem junction. There is no thumb-piece on the top of such a handle.

Concurrently with the vase-shaped coffee-pot in the 1780s was a new version of the pyriform body in which its lower part was larger in circumference than before and usually embossed and the spout decoration less graceful. The low-domed cover returned with an attractive flower and leaf finial and the circular foot supported a short slender stem. Circuits of beading encircling the lid and foot might be duplicated down each side of the spout, ascending in diminishing sizes from the spout entrance. When newly burnished these beads responded to candle-light with a myriad twinkling gleams.

Coaching coffee-pots were made in Sheffield plate until about 1815. These were of pyriform shape but instead of being circular or elliptical on plan had flat sides. The spout was a curved open channel applied to the lip rim from which a piece was cut to allow the coffee to be poured. The handle was of strap plate and covered with wicker. These coffee-pots were fitted into small travelling cases with other coffee-making equipment.

Early coffee-pots in Sheffield plate were of one pint capacity. By the 1770s coffee, 'a ruddy Mocha, clear, luscious and dark', was served in breakfast cups and the pot was necessarily proportionately larger. Until 1815 coffee-pots, chocolate-pots and tea kettles were of wine-measure capacity, a pint containing 26 cubic inches: all other hollow-ware was made to Winchester measure. Thereafter imperial measure was used and this has been noted in several reproduction Georgian coffee-pots tested.

Until about 1815 coffee-pots were constructed by the methods described above. But a more plastic copper plate was then evolved enabling the body to be spun in the lathe. This involved much less cost than stamping with dies and soldering, except in the case of long runs. By then silver itself was returning to early Georgian form to be catalogued as 'Queen Anne' although encumbered with a wealth of florid ornament. Decorations on Sheffield plate followed by becoming more assertive.

The melon-shaped coffee-pot with six or eight wide lobes then became popular in Sheffield plate, although this pattern had been used by the silversmiths more than 20 years earlier. During the 1820s the melon shape was flat-based and from about 1830 catalogues show it raised on four decorative feet. The low-domed cover was surmounted by a carefully modelled fruit and leaf finial in silver. These were sold at £6.10.0 each.

Straight-sided coffee-pots were in demand during the 1830s and 1840s, circular, hexagonal, octagonal and sometimes with 10 flat sides, all tapering more conspicuously than formerly and with flat covers topped by modelled flower and foliage finials. These hinged directly from the lid to the rim of the pot. At the same time appeared the now rare coffee-pot in the shape of a Turkish ewer, the trade sign shown on many tokens issued by the seventeenth-century coffee-house keepers. The Sheffield plate version had a collet foot, flat handle, minimal hinge between cover and rim, plain knob finial and spout. These were catalogued at £4.15.0 each undecorated.

Connoisseurs of coffee had long been aware that boiling was altogether too fierce a treatment for this exquisite infusion, when the process of filtration was devised. By this method boiling water dripped through a bag or boggin containing finely ground coffee. To keep the coffee simmering whilst infusing, the pot was placed over the flame of a spirit lamp, on the warm hob of a grate, or on the stone flag before a down hearth. Jean-Michel Moreau le Jeune's painting of the 'Last Words of Jean-Jacques Rousseau' (d. 1778) shows a flat-based coffee-pot in front of a down hearth fire. Dean Swift, who customarily dined in great elegance at a table set with silver plate, always demanded that his after-dinner coffee should be prepared at the fire in the dining room.

Filtration coffee-pots were known to Georgians as coffee-biggins. Most authorities declare the device to have been invented in 1798 by the silversmith George Biggin: a coffee-biggin struck with his mark and the London date letter for 1799 has been recorded, but many by other silversmiths bear date letters 10 years earlier. The name biggin had long been used in England for a conical cap worn by small children, the Georgian night-cap in fact. The shape resembled that of the Hippocrates sleeve (see Chapter 12), a conical bag of cotton, linen or flannel strengthened at the rim and used for clarifying wines and straining fruit juices from Tudor times. The name biggin, then, had been in common use for a filter at least two centuries before it became associated with the filtering of coffee.

The coffee-biggin was a short, cylindrical, flat-based covered jug containing a conical filter or biggin. Such vessels might be in silver, Sheffield plate, copper or heavily tinned iron plate and were usually sold in matching pairs. Coffee poured from the biggin was found to be stronger and more fragrant than from the more conventional coffee pot.

The body of a coffee biggin in Sheffield plate might be slightly tapering and was usually severely plain. Height ranged between six and seven inches and they were in three sizes: large; the pint of wine-measure capacity containing 26 cubic inches; and small. The body was made from a single sheet of plate and silvered on one side only, the coating being thicker than standard. This was rolled into a cylinder and seamed with a roman joint, absolutely invisible when new, but detectable now after more than a century and a half of cleaning.

Some examples of the 1790s were made in the barrel shape then in vogue. The convex barrel-shaped body might be chased to resemble vertical staves and encircled with two or three applied hoops, usually plain but sometimes reeded or beaded. From about 1800 to about 1815 a pair of applied hoops might encircle an otherwise plain cylindrical body made from plate of lesser gauge than formerly, the ribs adding strength to the body. Thinner plate was used because of the war-time stringencies in silver and copper. The rim was further strengthened by encircling it with thicker, wider and altogether more substantial gadrooning than formerly.

Another pattern popular throughout the coffee-biggin period had a convex body, the lower half usually decorated with vertical reeding, the number of hand-raised lobes determining the cost. Careful inspection of the interior will reveal whether the reedings were stamped or hand-raised. The top and lower rims might be encircled with reeding or bold gadrooning. The double-domed cover was decorated with 24 hand-raised reedings, each one inch long and radiating from a reeded finial. Plain convex bodies are also found. The body of a fine-quality coffee-biggin was usually engraved with a coat of arms or crest.

A coffee-biggin of Sheffield plate needed to be heavily tinned inside and re-tinning was an essential part of its maintenance. Inside the body immediately below the rim was a ledge into which fitted a wire ring of spring steel, heavily tinned, from which to suspend the conical muslin or flannel biggin. This extended to the base and into it was spooned finely ground coffee fresh from the mill. Boiling water was poured into this. The bag was cleaned by washing in hot water and letting it stand in cold water when not in use. Replacement filters were sold by coffee dealers in three standard sizes. The coffee-biggin was fitted with a substantial handle of hard wood, usually boxwood, less commonly ivory or ebony. Such a handle was carved in three units including a thumb-rest set into its upper curve. The handle-sockets were plain: only on rare occasions were they decorated and then usually with a plain drop.

The spout was usually of the curved beak variety and was positioned at the rim opposite to the handle, not at right angles as was often the case with the conventional coffee pot. It was shaped from the plate and was soldered to the top of the body from which a v-shaped piece had been cut to allow the coffee to be poured. A beak spout might extend as much as half-way down the body or to immediately above the bulge in the case of the convex body. It curved slightly upward above the rim and its front edge might be sharply straight or cut with a graceful inward curve. The opening might be fitted with a small hinged flap to minimize loss of heat. A touch of ornament was applied to an otherwise plain body by introducing a shaped drop immediately below such a spout. Those who required a quick-pouring vessel preferred the wide, shallow, upward and out-ward curving spout encircling about one-quarter of the rim immediately above the strengthening gadrooning. Such a spout might be enriched with a mask or foliage mount.

The cover was low-domed and usually of the detachable lift-off pattern with a rim fitting tightly into the mouth of the body. When hinged the simple three-lug hinge was used, the flaps made to close flat against each other. When the body was reeded the cover might be decorated with a central circle of straight or spiralled reedings to match. The centre of the cover was raised in a plain circular platform supporting a finial in one of a variety of simple forms such as a plain ball or knop, acorn, baluster, orb, vase, mushroom or button. The finials of reeded coffee-biggins might be reeded to match, dating from about 1810. The finial was attached to a vertical hand-turned screw passing through the circular platform and attached beneath with a square nut. The scar was concealed by a disc of plate measuring about one inch in diameter: in the case of a reeded cover the washer's edge was serrated, the points fitting between reedings.

Usually the base of the coffee-biggin was perfectly flat to facilitate warming on a stand containing a hemispherical spirit lamp which might have two or three burners. The gadrooned ring of the stand fitted the base of the pot and was supported by three or four legs, usually scroll shape with the outer surface fluted or reeded and terminating in ring, paw, claw or foliage feet. From each leg extended a strut to a ring containing the spirit lamp below the coffee-biggin.

Other coffee-biggins were footed. The low circular foot enabled the vessel to be heated on the fireplace hob. The coffee-biggin infuser retained its supporters into the Victorian period, but by as early as 1818 an available alternative was the coffee percolator.

Chocolate-pots in Sheffield plate are now uncommon and rarely is an example found complete with its boxwood mill. Drinking chocolate was already a fashionable beverage when the *Publick Advertiser*, 16 June 1657, recorded that it could be bought 'in BISHOPGATE Street, in Queen's Head Allee, at a Frenchman's house and is an excellent West Indian Drink that is ready at all times and also unmade at reasonable rates'. Statute books first mention chocolate in 1660 when a duty of fourpence a gallon was levied upon every gallon made and sold, to be paid by the maker. At this time a pound cake of chocolate cost half a crown: if perfumed the price ranged between four shillings and half a guinea.

John Worlidge in 1675 described the method of preparing drinking chocolate. It was bought in rolls or cakes and 'sliced and scraped fine, then boiled in water with a little sugar. Whilst it is boiling keep stirring, and when it is off the fire, whir it with your hand mill. That is, it must be mixed in a deep pot of silver, tin, copper or stone, with a cover with a hole in the middle of it, for the handle of the mill to come out at, or without a cover. The mill is only a notched knop at the end of a slender handle or stick, this being whirled between your hands, whilst the pot is over the fire. The rough end in the liquor causes an equal mixture of the liquor with chocolate and raises a head or froth over it. Then pour it out for use in small dishes.' This procedure was continued throughout the Georgian period.

Chocolate-pots resembled contemporaneous coffee-pots with one important difference: there was a small hole in the centre of the domed lid through which projected the end of the wooden mill. After the chocolate had been beaten to a light froth the mill was removed and the aperture closed by a small hinged flap to the surface of which the finial was attached. Throughout the period the common form of chocolate-pot, whether in silver or copper or, from about 1760, in Sheffield plate, was a tapering cylindrical body with a collet foot to lift the base above the surface of the waiter upon which it stood. This assisted stability. It had been found that pressure of the whirling mill and vigorous cleaning tended to produce a downward bulge in the base.

In the Sheffield plate chocolate-pot the mill aperture might be closed with a small sliding disc, one side loosely riveted to the cover, the opposite end provided with a small hook which clipped beneath a tiny stud. In some late examples, reverting to an early eighteenth-century style, the apex of the cover was fitted with a short open cylinder through which the end of the mill extended. This was covered with a slip-on cap secured by a silver chain.

Some straight-sided examples might be incurved at the base, giving the impression that the pot was raised from the plate, when actually it was shaped from two pieces of single-sided plate, seamed vertically back and front, the seam concealed by a collet foot. Decorations resembled the hand chasing seen on contemporaneous coffee-pots. The pyriform body was also made, fluted around the base. An example has been noted raised from the plate as if it were silver.

The spout was always placed diametrically opposite the handle and in some instances was merely a hand-wrought slender tube with a single outward curve. Octagonal spouts are also found. Hinges and handles resembled those on coffee-pots. On silver examples after 1760 the hallmarks were struck with rectangular spacing beneath the base. When Sheffield plate began to be marked widely from 1784 many platers struck their registered marks in a line a little below the rim, visible to the casual observer and often resembling hallmarks.

# 15. Epergnes

When Lady Grisell Baillie in 1721 spent 10 days at Twickenham as the guest of Sir Robert Walpole she was entranced by the magnificence of the newly fashionable silver epergne displayed in the centre of the table at every formal meal. The epergne, introduced from France in about 1715, was a masterpiece of silver plate carrying a variety of pungent relishes, sauces, pickles and condiments, thus saving space on the lavishly laden table: its name derived from the French *epargner*, meaning to economize. The units composing an early Georgian epergne were listed in an inventory of plate taken in 1725 at the Jewel Office in Whitehall: 'An aparn containing one Table Basket and Cover, one Foote, four Salt Boxes, four small Salts, four Branches, six Casters, four Sauceboats.' Additionally there were, of course, an elaborate frame or stand and a top basket or dish. These superb centrepieces were used also for the display of sweetmeats on the dessert table.

Until the late 1740s a single epergne would enrich the centre of the table: then silversmiths launched lighter designs in matching pairs. It was these that the Sheffield platers produced in less elaborate forms from the early 1760s. Mrs Delany in 1752 sketched a dessert-table lay-out which included 'a pair of epergnes and 8 baskets for fruit'. Pennant in his *Bill of Fare*, 1761, advised '2 grande Epergnes filled with fine Pickles' for the dining table. By the 1770s a single epergne might serve for either purpose and for sweetmeats.

A fashionable Sheffield plate epergne of the 1760s and 1770s was composed of three basic units: a square, openwork frame supporting a stand holding a table basket or dish. The four scroll legs of the frame were linked at the top by an oval or circular ring strengthened by four aprons. To the knees of the legs were fitted sockets from which radiated upward-curving branches. These terminated in ring brackets for containing shallow round or oval saucers, their rims approximately on the same level as the base of the stand. Evenly spaced between these, four more branches rose above and beyond the lower set, based in sockets attached to the aprons. The branches might be fixed or swivel in their sockets.

Branches might terminate in hooks for baskets suspended by loop handles, fixed or hinged. At first the pendant basket's swing handle was a light openwork arch between a pair of heavier terminals. This was contemporaneous with the handle of flat Sheffield plate ornamentally pierced. Later handles were slender and might be of cable twist wire with scroll and leafwork mounts at the ends connecting with the hinges. Swinging baskets on Sheffield plate epergnes are uncommon and date earlier than about 1800.

In many instances an epergne was fitted with only four branches, these being continuations of the legs and supporting four dishes. By the 1770s the Sheffield plate epergne might combine four shallow saucers with four deep baskets. Both were fitted with flint-glass linings for relishes and pickles: for dessert the glasses were removed and the outer vessel filled with an array of colourful dry sweet-meats and comfits. Spare branches fitted with candlesockets might accompany an epergne so that it could have an alternative use as a candelabrum. Ornamental finials were supplied to fit into any branch sockets not in use.

Into the upper ring of the frame fitted the flaring lower rim of a stand resembling a giant narrow-waisted dish ring, its upper rim shaped to form a narrow shelf fitting the foot of a table basket. At first the outer surface of this rim was plain: later it was encircled with beading or ornamental wire matching similar enrichment on the rims of the accompanying baskets and dishes.

Sheffield plate epergnes were made in a greater range of designs than any other article – 269 patterns are known to have been issued by Watson & Bradbury between 1788 and 1815. Their height varied from 12 to 21 inches, with an overall spread measurement about one-third greater. The Sheffield platers often adapted designs from the light-weight patterns of the specialist silversmith Thomas Powell who operated workshops at Craig's Court, Charing Cross, from 1773 to 1789.

Oval and circular platforms with pierced galleries superseded square frames from about 1780. The platform was carried on four spreading scroll legs with claw feet and linked by laurel festoons or swags of drapery with central medallions. The legs were continued upward, each terminating in a branch fitted with circular dishes. From the centre of the platform rose a decorative urn. This supported two or four branches and also an openwork pillar terminating in a ring containing a two-handled canoe-shaped basket. At first the basket was in ogee outline, its lower solid part usually fluted and its deeper upper part pierced in a border pattern and sometimes also engraved. The ogee shaping from the 1770s became more pronounced, the rim strengthened with bead work and the body perforated all over in designs composed of conventional motifs such as sparsely spaced circles, ovals, crescents, scrolls, quatrefoils, diamonds and crosses. Less expensive ornament consisted of rows of vertical and horizontal perforated pales. A rare design for top basket and swinging basket consisted of six or as many as a dozen panels pierced with geometrical motifs, alternating with narrow strengthening panels embossed with scrollwork. Designs now became innumerable and so far have proved impossible to classify. The feet of dishes and baskets were short, plain cylinders which fitted tightly into terminal sockets on the branches.

By the 1780s the fashionable Sheffield plate epergne might be displayed with additional grandeur on a long oval or rectangular mirror plateau, framed with a low gallery perforated in a design matching the rims of top basket and dishes. This stood upon four low feet in scrolled or cabriole outline. From the late 1780s the frame and stand might be combined in a single open-frame unit of complicated design and by 1800 might be further embellished with festoons of chased flowers and foliage, lions' or rams' masks. A formal ornament such as a flame, urn, pineapple or berry was displayed on the central joint of the stretchers.

Less costly epergnes constructed almost entirely of plated wire (see Chapter 27) were made too for about half a century from the mid-1770s. The wire used for epergnes was not round but flat on the interior surface, the exterior reeded in various patterns. The arched top of each unit was hard-soldered in position as the soldering surface was very small. The ends were soft-soldered below and concealed behind a circular piece of plate. At first the oval base of the top basket was solid with wirework radiating from its edge. Ten years later the base might be lavishly pierced, a central reserve of solid plate being left for engraving a coat of arms. Branches might terminate in hemispherical cups of wirework containing linings of cut-glass with projecting rims bordered with deep scallops. In others each branch terminated in a horizontal ring of flat plate fitted with a shouldered flint-glass bowl elaborately diamond-cut. In some instances the bases of wirework baskets were so devised that candle-sockets could be inserted instead of glass vessels.

In the 1790s and early nineteenth century there was a vogue for top baskets perforated with ribbon effects such as a series of flat loops with overlapping ends forming a trellis. The exterior surface was chased to resemble woven wickerwork and from about 1800 the rims were enriched with silver mounts.

Pedestal epergnes date from the late 1780s and in many instances were so designed that the pedestal itself, a fluted pilaster or baluster, pivoted upon the centre of a square or tripod plinth or an oval stand on scroll feet. In others, the branches, four or five to the set, radiated from a loose ring sunk into the pedestal. Each branch terminated in a ring to fit a hemispherical bowl of cut glass and a matching master glass was set on the finial of the pedestal. In the nineteenth century a pair of revolving rings might rotate upon the pedestal at different levels; in some instances only the lower branches rotated.

A large openwork epergne rising from a plinth or galleried tray on a pedestal base combined the functions of cruet and epergne. The tray contained eight equally-spaced guard rings equipped with flint-glass condiment bottles fitted with appropriate mounts in Sheffield plate – sometimes in hall-marked silver. From this tray rose four brackets each supporting a canoe-shaped dish and centrally a large matching bowl for fruit and used later for flowers. Such an epergne is illustrated in a contemporaneous plater's catalogue in the Victoria and Albert Museum. This has a deeply cut master glass and three branches with canoe-shaped baskets with wavy rims. This is priced at eight guineas; with four branches, 10 guineas, and with six branches, 13 guineas.

Epergnes of the early nineteenth century might be double mercury-gilded, their vessels heavier and more lavishly cut. It was intended that a guest should find it difficult to distinguish these from the costly epergnes in gilded silver. A pattern much in demand consisted of a circular, triangular, square or octagonal plinth raised on three, four or five short legs with hoof or paw feet, which continued vertically as ornamental pillars. In a fashionable series these were in the form of female terms, each head supporting an elaborately designed ring containing a cut-glass bowl with a serrated or everted rim or a scallop-shell border. From the plinth, between each pillar or term, curved a branch fitted with a matching glass. In some instances the brackets on the branches were removable and could be replaced with candle sockets.

The elaborately stemmed epergne was a late Georgian and early Victorian development, its florid style suiting its ornate setting. A fashionable design was composed of acanthus leaves or vine leaves and trellis in naturalistic relief. Each high, out-curving branch would terminate in an expansive flower, the blossom itself being a cut-glass dish.

Early Victorians catalogued epergnes as centre-pieces and usually included a plateau. The bowls might be fitted with loose linings of ruby glass. The top basket was fashionably filled with wax flowers. At the Great Exhibition, 1851, some extraordinary varieties of epergne were shown. The catalogue refers to 'epergnes with pedestals formed of palms and tropical plants under which repose cattle, birds, camels and Arab horsemen'.

# 16. Dinner ware; breakfast and supper dishes

*Entrée dishes; venison dishes and covers;*
*dish wedges; vegetable dishes; breakfast dishes and*
*supper sets; cheese toasters*

Georgians of wealth and fashion dined in great elegance even when alone. In 1810 the Countess of Granville recorded that 'Dinner [for the earl and herself] consisted of soup, fish, fricassée of chicken, cutlets, veal, hare, vegetables of all kinds, tart, melon, pineapple, grapes, peaches, nectarines with wines in proportion. Six servants wait upon us, a gentleman in waiting and a fat old housekeeper hovers round the door. Four hours later the door opens and in is pushed a supper of the same proportion.'

Formal dinners were on an equally lavish scale. Dolby's *Cook's Dictionary*, 1833, directed that tables should scintillate with splendidly appointed silver and Sheffield plate. A first course menu for 12 persons consisted of '2 soups, 4 removes, 6 entrées . . . the entrées being fricandeau of veal with macedoin sauce, Neapolitan timball, scallops of pheasants with sauce supreme, glazed lamb cutlets and tomato sauce, oyster patties, attelets [small silver skewers] of sweetbreads with Italienne sauce.' These were served from two soup tureens, four dishes for carving the removes and five entrée dishes. Dolby and other Georgian cooks defined an entrée as 'any dish of butcher's meat [hash, stew and so on], fowl, game or fish, dressed for the first course of a dinner.'

Entrée dishes in Sheffield plate were uncommon until the mid-1780s. They were shallow rectangular, octagonal or oval dishes with low covers and without the warmers of the later period: they were used with dish crosses (see Chapter 17). A pair in silver struck with the hallmark for 1761 were described contemporaneously as 'two handled plain, with low domed covers, reeded borders and loop handles'. A pair made by Paul Storr in 1793 were similarly catalogued but with ebony finials. This long-lived pattern was copied in Sheffield plate. When the cover was without a finial it could also be used as a serving dish.

Entrée dishes were illustrated in trade catalogues and described variously as 'double dishes', 'steak stew dishes' and 'hash dishes'. The double dish included a lower vessel containing a warming unit. Such an entrée dish then consisted of four units: the base dish that contained the warming unit, the perforated plate placed on top of the unit, the food dish resting on this plate and its cover. Heat was supplied by an ingot of red-hot cast iron resting on a frame in the base dish. The top plate of thin plated metal tinned on the underside was sunk into the base dish, being shaped so that it rested upon the dish's edge. Base dish and top plate were counted as separate purchases. Entrée dishes might be sold singly, but more usually were in matching sets of four which could be used as 12 serving dishes if so needed. Dish, cover and warmer were shaped by stamping.

From early in the nineteenth century the fashionable entrée dish was enriched with decorative mounts around the rim and on the crown of the cover. By 1820 mounts had become elaborately patterned and as much as one inch wide, the shell and gadroon pattern being most popular. Pairs of mounts in thin silver were struck from a single die: caps and handles were similarly stamped.

Dish and cover might be encircled with narrow or wide fluting from 1815, the shape usually rectangular, sometimes in the attractive cushion shape. Covers were more highly domed than formerly. The Watson & Bradbury catalogue of 1815 illustrates two popular entrée dishes: a plain oblong with gadrooned rim and cover crown, made in three sizes: small, 105s; middle size, 115s 6d; large, 126s; and a fluted pattern with shell and gadroon mounts priced at 168s. All had silver handles, mountings and rubbed-in shields expansive enough for engraved coats of arms. Warmers were not included at these prices.

Hot water might replace the hot iron in the lower vessel of the entrée dish from about 1810 and had almost entirely superseded it in fashionable designs by 1815. This meant that the lower vessel was a complete unit, filled by an orifice with a screw plug on its upper surface and no longer required a perforated top plate. At the same time the dish tended to become deeper. The hot water base dish was fitted with four feet usually ornamented in harmony with the handles, their patterns including scroll with oak leaves, paw and foliage, shell and foliage, winged paws. At first the foot attachment extended no more than about one-quarter the depth of the warmer: later this decorative detail reached almost to the rim.

Handles on the ends of the warmer were necessarily substantial to support the considerable weight of the entrée dish complete with food and water. These were near horizontal, usually screwed to an inner boss and elaborately designed. A detachable vertical ring handle, often reeded or with foliate ornament, was screwed into a thick plaque soldered inside the centre of the cover so that it could be removed and the cover used as a dish. Crest handles were fashionable, the extra cost depending upon the intricacy of the device. Handles made by scrolling outward the end rims of the warmer have been noted.

A plain set of four oval entrée dishes and covers cost 20 guineas in the mid-1820s: two-handled warmers with top plates were 17 guineas extra. A set of four with dishes and domed covers fluted cost £40: the matching warmers £30 extra.

Entrée dishes in sterling silver might be accompanied by warmers and top plates in Sheffield plate.

Entrée dishes heated by specially made lamps were also used. Edward Thomason, Birmingham, had by 1820 devised a type for the service of curry in which the heater was not visible. He described the lamp as 'independent and fits upon the stand inside of and under the lining of the curry dish. When the body of the dish is lifted, the warmer is taken away from the stand, around the outer edge of which stand perpendicular figures and decorations.'

In 1822 George IV bought from Thomason a comprehensive dinner service which included 'six curry dishes' – there were no entrée dishes. Curry, a favourite dish of the king and made fashionable by him, was a preparation of meat, fish, fruit or vegetables, cooked with bruised spices and turmeric. This was also used to flavour hash or stew. After the death of George IV the platers made similar dishes with lamps named in the early catalogues as hash dishes. These, if plain, cost £7.10.0, 10s extra if gadrooned.

By the 1830s the platers were making entrée dishes heated by means of spirit lamps. The oval entrée dish was placed into the oval top ring of a stand supported by four short scroll legs joined by four curved cross stretchers. A methylated spirit burner was introduced where these met. A set of four such dishes, decorated simply with beaded mounts, cost £25; stands and lamps were £20 extra. In some patterns the heating lamp was set in the base of a warmer which was encircled with a wide band of ventilating perforations. Entrée dishes were known to early Victorians as corner or side table dishes and covers.

The Earls of Shrewsbury from 1393 to 1617 were Lords of the Manor of Hallamshire, a division of Yorkshire composed of the parishes of Sheffield, Ecclesfield, Bradfield and Hansworth in the ancient wapentake of Strafforth and Tickhill. Gilbert, the seventh earl, displayed unusual interest in the welfare of the people of Hallamshire and in 1614 he granted the Sheffield cutlers permission to hold an annual day of amusement and feasting for which he supplied numerous deer. These were turned loose in a meadow where they were eventually killed and cooked whole: he also made a substantial beer allowance to honour the occasion. From this function stemmed the Venison Feast held by the Master of the Company of Cutlers in Hallamshire on the first Thursday and Friday of September.

Until the 1750s the term venison was applied indiscriminately to the flesh of any game animal killed in the chase and used as food, such as deer, boar and hare. Since then the name venison has been restricted almost entirely to the meat of all breeds of deer. Although *The London Cook*, 1762, affirmed that 'the flavour of venison, especially if it is fat, is inimitable', it was little appreciated by the kitchen staff as several hours of close supervision were essential during roasting to prevent scorching. *The London Cook* emphasized that 'no sauce should be put in the dish, but that which comes out of the meat, but provide some good gravy in a sauce boat or basin and sweet sauce in another basin'.

Welsh venison, served in lesser families, was mutton dressed with allspice and claret. A recipe for 'roast MUTTON to eat like VENISON' was recorded by William Gellery who declared that 'the haunch of mutton should hang for about a fortnight; dress it as you would real venison; and be careful not to over-roast it. Less than two hours will do it.' Gellery was cook to Alderman Samuel Plumbe, a Sheffield gold refiner who held the monopoly of melting all bullion received by the Mint, and was elected Lord Mayor of London in 1772. Meat scarcity during the Napoleonic wars created a heavy demand for Scottish venison and the Welsh pseudo-venison.

A strong serving dish was necessary to support a haunch of venison. This prompted the Sheffield platers, familiar with the formal service of the meat, to design and manufacture special table equipment for ostentatious display at the Hallamshire Venison Feasts. The venison dish proper dates from the 1790s and was a four-piece dining table appointment allied with entrée dishes, consisting of a hot-water stand into which fitted a serving dish sunk with channels leading to a deep well. Upon this stood a plain vertical band of plate fitting into the bouge and supporting a highly domed dish cover large enough to enclose the cooked haunch completely. The majority are oval in shape and very heavy. They are to be found in sizes ranging from 18 to 28 inches long. By the 1830s venison dishes were made in the standard length of 24 inches. Without a cover such a dish cost 18 to 20 guineas according to the quality of the ornamental mounts.

The warmer, standing upon four ball or scroll feet, was an essential unit as the fat and gravy from the venison congealed quickly under the slightest draught. The water entrance was sealed with a screw plug. Two very strong near-horizontal lifting handles were fitted to the ends, usually decorated in a pattern matching the silver edges of the dish and its cover: a water-lily design appears on some high-quality late examples. Although similar sets were made by the silversmiths few examples have been recorded in silver throughout; many exist with the serving dish in silver and the remainder in Sheffield plate, the cover and warmer often having solid silver enrichments.

Upon the rim of the hot-water stand rested a tightly fitting shallow dish where the venison was placed for carving. This dish was sunk with a well at one end to receive the great quantity of fatty gravy directed by a central draining channel fed by three branches from each side: from about 1825 two branches were used. This well-dish, which might have a shaped outline, was bordered with silver mounts such as shell and foliage, gadrooning, reeding or beading or, from about 1820, by a wide, elaborate pattern. The well-dish was evolved by the Sheffield platers during the 1790s, at first hand-raised, but by the end of the decade usually stamped in heavier plate with tools made from the harder cast steel then available. It may be mentioned that until the four-piece unit was devised the venison dish and cover might rest on a dish-cross (Chapter 17). Rectangular dishes have been noted, without handles, and ovals with handles.

An improved well-dish was patented during the mid-1830s by John Gray of Edinburgh. The inventor's specification stated that his dish 'possessed the peculiar merit of separating the liquid fat of roast or boiled venison from the gravy, and of thus rendering the gravy as it flows from the meat as pure as if the fat had been lifted off whilst both were in a cold state'.

A plain oval band of plate stood loosely upon the dish, fitting closely against the bouge and the flat plate to prevent accidental splashing of the gravy-drenched meat during carving. Top and bottom rims of this band were edged with plain mounting, the lower being substantial and weighty. Venison dishes are seldom found complete with this unit.

Upon this band rested closely the everted edge of a dish cover, highly domed to enclose completely the haunch of venison and keep in the heat. Dish covers were usually plainly oval and encircled with silver mounts to match those of the dish. More expensively the upper half of the dome might be fluted or, from about 1815, the entire cover might be fluted with spreading sides. Some late examples were widely lobed to match the covers of melon-pattern serving dishes. Plain dish covers might be decorated with deep borders of chased flowers and foliage or fruiting vine. Early dish covers were hand-raised from the plate: because of their size and the labour involved they were costly. Those raised by stamping required as many as 50 carefully calculated blows with the drop hammer. Both types were raised from copper plated on one side only. They were tinned on the interior with pure grained tin burnished so that it was difficult for the casual observer to distinguish it from silver.

The apex was topped with a detachable loop or ring usually in a chased relief design matching the handles of the warmer. The majority were corded, beaded or gadrooned but other patterns were known such as shell and flowers, scroll, foliage, fruiting vine, oak branch, lion and coronet and the rare serpent of the early years of the nineteenth century. These handles might be of cast silver, but commonly they were of silver stamped in two halves, joined and filled with a lead-tin alloy. The handle screwed into a sturdy disc of similar metal welded directly to the dish cover. A plated cover might conceal a silver serving dish which itself was supported on a plated hot water stand. Dish covers were also made for meat dishes, usually in pairs and in sizes ranging from 10 to 24 inches, without oval supporting bands. A set of covers might consist of as many as a dozen graduated sizes. Edges were for the most part gadrooned, beaded or reeded; less commonly gadrooned with foliage and, rarely, with fluted ties at spaced intervals. Prices for a set of six ranged from £10 to £16.10.0 according to the amount of decoration. Oval, circular and rectangular dish covers were also sold singly.

The setting out of a formal dinner table might require a service of 25 dishes (see Chapter 18), each accompanied by its appropriate cover. These were all made in Sheffield plate edged with silver mounts. In addition there were heavily silvered circular dinner plates of 10 to 10½ inches diameter and nine-inch dessert plates.

Serving dishes, dish covers and plates are not in great demand by collectors. They are usually highly priced, however, as they are a source of genuine old plate and are bought by craftsmen for transformation into more desirable articles of Sheffield plate such as dish rings which sell at a considerable profit.

Dish-wedges were table accessories for giving the appropriate slope to well-dishes when these were not mounted on warmers. A pair was placed beneath one end of the dish lifting it so that the gravy flowed down the channels into the well. The earliest design was a wedge-shaped box with four or five ridges on the upper surface and a small loop handle attached to the vertical flat end. The alternative type was U-shaped with triangular sides and sharp corners, solid or perforated, and joined at the points by a sharp rod. The upper edge of each arm was cut with six notches permitting adjustment of the angle of slope required. These were sold in pairs at about 21s a dozen and used mainly with meat dishes.

Vegetables were handed by servants in circular dishes with short handles. These were shallow bowls with three divisions. The highly domed covers had detachable ring handles and reeded or foliate ornament. They were made with and without warmers. In many instances the dish was made deeper and fitted with a loose plate with three divisions and a central knob for lifting and handing. The partitions might each have a detachable liner. The shape of the dish itself might be three-lobed. Handles, when present, were usually near horizontal, of ebony, ivory or stained hard wood. They screwed into sockets attached to the dishes so that they were removable for storage purposes: the socket, too, formed the entrance to the hot-water compartment, but many lacked this refinement and were fitted with a loop handle at each end, often with petal rosette attachments. The cover finial was detachable and was usually of the ring variety ornamented to match the rim mounting or was a well-modelled flower. The cost of such a vegetable dish with a warmer was 10 guineas and 6½ guineas without a warmer.

Breakfast dishes, a late Georgian refinement of the newly emerging middle classes, fall into the group of table equipment that included entrée dishes. In the late eighteenth century a breakfast dish consisted of a 14-inch oval dish, plain rimmed and heated by a dish cross. By 1810 breakfast dishes consisted of pairs of shallow dishes. Each pair was contained in a long oval or rectangular hot-water warmer with a low domed cover and four ornamental feet. The most popular pattern from 1815 consisted of a pair of small square dishes each with a low domed cover set in an open rectangular stand with a gadrooned D-handle at each end. Four slightly bowed legs with cross-stretchers supported a spirit lamp beneath each dish.

Supper sets, usually elaborate self-service table appointments for four people, were designed to keep a late-night meal hot for an entire evening awaiting late-comers. The set consisted of four fan-shaped entrée dishes and covers and a matching soup tureen all placed into a large hot-water warmer on a revolving stand of mahogany with four salt cellars. In a design made by Nathaniel Smith & Co. and illustrated by Bradbury, the vessels all have vertical sides, fluted and with straight gadroon mounts. More elaborate supper sets date from about 1815. One well-known pattern contained four fan-shaped dishes with water heaters. Each dish had gadrooned borders and a chased shell at the apex. They rested on the arms of a cross-shaped plate, also of Sheffield plate, with a central ornamental finial. This was mounted on a mahogany tray and the whole unit protected with a domed cover.

Another pattern of supper set consisted of a hot water drum measuring about 28 inches in diameter and about four inches deep with a screw plug for sealing the filled aperture. The top was sunk to contain four dishes with a highly domed cover encircled with heavy gadrooning. Rising from the centre was a pillar handle of the cruet style. This was fitted with four hexagonal casters with highly domed covers pierced in the eighteenth-century style.

Toasted cheese has been a favourite savoury with English gastronomes for more than three centuries. In 1669 *The Closet of Sir Kenelm Digby Knight Opened* recorded that 'you may scorch it [the cheese] at the top with a hot Fire Shovel'. This was actually a salamander shaped at that time like a garden spade and doing double duty as a shovel for the wood ashes in a down fire grate. Phillip's *Dictionary*, 1700, defined 'toasted Cheese and Bread, and Toast and Cheese' as a ramekin. More correctly it was Welsh rabbit, as described by Hannah Glasse who gave her recipe for Welsh rabbit in 1760: 'toast the bread on both sides, then toast the cheese on one side, lay it on the toast and with a hot iron [sala-mander] brown the other side. You may rub it over with mustard.' In a second recipe she repeats Sir Kenelm Digby's advice to 'brown it with a hot shovel'.

Mrs Glasse recommended the use of a pan of tinned iron for browning the cheese surface of English rabbit: 'Toast the bread on both sides, then lay it on a plate before the fire, pour a glass of red wine over it and let it soak the wine up. Then cut some cheese very thin and lay it very thick over the bread and put it in a tin oven before the fire. When toasted and browned it should be served hot immediately.'

Some of the finest cheeses for toasting were made in Lancashire farmhouses, those from the Leigh district being highly praised in contemporaneous cookery books under the name of 'Leigh Toasters'. The art of serving toasted cheese was to get it from the fire to the plate and into the mouth without delay: in fact it was always eaten sitting around the fire. The rubbery pulp so often associated with twentieth-century toasted cheese was unknown to the Georgians.

A special contrivance for the toasting of cheese at the fireside was devised early in the reign of George III by London silversmiths and copied by the Sheffield platers from the 1770s. The cheese toaster became very popular in English middle-class homes but was virtually unknown on the continent. Louis Simond in his *Journal of a Tour of Great Britain*, 1815, reported his astonishment at the 'extraordinary cheese-toasters' in silver and Sheffield plate in the Birmingham show rooms of Edward Thomason and described them as 'a wonderful invention'.

Cheese-toaster design was based on the hot-water dish consisting of a shallow sealed rectangular compartment containing boiling water. Its rim was encircled with a mount either plain, reeded or gadrooned: by 1810 mounts had become wider and might be enriched with elaborate foliage or shell corners. Into its sunken top were fitted six loose rectangular pans and over these hinged a domed cover raised from the plate. The cover interior was burnished to a mirror-like brilliance so that when partially open and facing the fire heat was reflected from it on to the cheese, toasting its surface to a uniform brown. The early cover was fitted with a waisted finial plainly turned in silver, ivory, ebony or hardwood. In the nineteenth century the finial, usually in silver, might be a melon or vase-shape, a ring or vine leaf and, eventually, a skilfully worked rosette, also in silver.

Hinges on early light-weight cheese toasters were of the five-lug variety and measured about $3\frac{1}{2}$ inches in length, the end lugs being shorter than the one in the centre. Seven-lug hinges might be used in the nineteenth century when cheese toasters were made heavier and stronger than formerly. Early examples measure nine to 10 inches in width and by the early-1820s 12 inches was common. The cover was usually held partly open by a silver chain fixed to a small metal eye screwed into the handle and ending in an open hook made to encircle the waist of the cover finial, thus holding the cover at the angle that would best direct the fire's heat on to the cheese.

The hot-water compartment was filled by one of three methods. It might be necessary to unscrew the ivory, ebony or hardwood handle set horizontally behind the hinged cover and pour the boiling water down the hollow metal socket connecting with the sealed container. Alternatively there might be a flat plug screwing into the hollow socket which could be opened, or a small beak-shaped lip with a hinged cover set into one side (sometimes one each side) of the hot water container. This heat was ample to keep the toast hot whilst the cheese was bubbling or browning.

Toasted bread was placed into each of six detachable pans fitting exactly into the sunken dish. These were raised from the plate, and in the nineteenth century the design might include a short flat lip soldered horizontally to a long side, thus simplifying removal from the dish. The toasted morsels had to be served quickly from the pans on to heated plates and when a cheese toaster was in regular commission the individual pans inevitably showed signs of wear and knife scratches made in removing toasted cheese that tended to adhere firmly to the metal. Replacement pans of Sheffield plate could be bought, but usually the damage was masked by tinning. The warmer might be in Sheffield plate and the loose pans in sterling silver, each fully hallmarked. The presence of hallmarks on the pans served to guests was counted as a status symbol.

During the Regency period of 1810–20 there was a demand for elaborately designed cheese toasters with fluted sides and covers standing on four feet – claw, paw, ball or scroll. Oval toasters were also made from about 1815 with gadrooned sides and cover and a substantial D-handle at each end. Four of the six pans were suitably rounded. Attached to each end of the warmer, between the struts of the handles, was a beak-shaped spout with a hinged cover. Hot water was introduced through this. The Watson & Bradbury catalogue of 1822 illustrated a Sheffield plate example with a pair of elaborate D-handles based on acanthus foliage. The handles were stamped silver shells filled with a tin-lead alloy. This was priced at 105s and annotated: 'Whether made with handles at the ends or a handle at the back, but is never made with both.' Many of these later cheese toasters are engraved with coats of arms or crests. The demand for cheese toasters declined during the 1820s and very few were made after 1830 in silver or Sheffield plate.

# 17. Dish rings; dish crosses and stands

Dish rings were dining-table accessories throughout the seventeenth and eighteenth centuries, at first in silver, pewter and brass and from the late 1760s in Sheffield plate. In 1649 Randle Holme defined a 'stand for a dish' as a common article of household equipment 'to be sett on a table and upon which to sett another dish upon; which kind of stands being so sett, make the feast looke full and noble. These stands are made round or six or eight squared; the top and bottom straight so that either end may be set high most.' The shape of a dish ring suggests that it evolved from the spool-shaped salt with scroll arms rising from the rim. According to the Victoria and Albert Museum publication *Charles II Domestic Silver*, 1949, these arms were intended for supporting a dish. The first reference so far noted to dish stands named as rings appeared in the *London Gazette*, 1697, in an advertisement: 'stolen 2 Rings for a Table'.

A contemporaneous table ring remains, hallmarked 1704. Made by Andrew Raven of London, this is a plain spool of solid high-standard silver, embossed with a scroll-framed cartouche for engraving a coat of arms or crest and otherwise entirely plain. Not until early in George II's reign did silversmiths realize that the practical dish ring could become a showy table ornament. At first it was chased with designs composed of flowers, foliage and scrollwork and from about 1750 with low repoussé work characterized by ornate open-cut designs of figures, birds and, on occasion, scenic views.

It is well to keep strictly to the contemporaneous name for these rings. Invariably when assayed in Dublin they were entered in the books of the Goldsmiths' Company as dish rings; the London assay office termed them 'dish stands' and charged an assay fee of twopence each. *Falkiner's Dublin Journal*, 1762, described them as dish stands and in 1780 as 'rings for the centre of the table'. Illustrations in the Sheffield plate catalogues of about 1800 in the Victoria and Albert Museum caption them as 'dish rims'.

It has long been assumed that their purpose in Ireland was to support a bog oak bowl from which potatoes were commonly served: hence their popular name of Irish potato rings. This term indicates, however, that the purpose of the ring was to stand on a dish in the centre of the table and thus transform it into a bowl with perforated sides. Those to whom potatoes are served as a moist mash overlook the fact that an Irish potato baked in its jacket, with white 'flour' frothing through cracks in the crisp skin, is an epicure's delight. Such potatoes have their own recognized manner of serving even today. They are as easily spoiled by a closed container as a slice of toast: instead they must be piled on a snowy napkin and merely held loosely in position by a perforated ring. Indeed it was found that no more than a skeleton shape of plated wire was required to support the folded napkin. After serving the potatoes the napkin was removed and a bowl of bread substituted.

Dish rings of sterling silver for the most part are struck with the hallmark of the Dublin Assay Office – Hibernia seated with her right hand outstretched – and the maker's mark of an Irish silversmith. The majority of dish rings in Sheffield plate were exported to Ireland where they were in great demand for everyday use. In Dublin certain plate workers bought sheets of unworked plate from Sheffield and converted it into table ware, including dish rings.

Dish rings are no more than flat strips of fused plate measuring about 21 inches long and five inches wide. The plate was silvered on both sides and therefore dish rings in Sheffield plate can date no earlier than the late 1760s when this practice was introduced. The strip was rolled into a cylinder and hammered upon a wooden block into a giant concave spool shape. In early examples the silhouette was deeply concave. The ends were then seamed vertically by means of a roman joint, so skilfully made that it is always difficult to detect its position. The ring's diameter measured between seven and eight inches at the top, about two inches less at the waist and an inch or more wider at the base. An example with a top diameter of $7\frac{3}{4}$ inches would have an inner diameter of six inches at the waist and about $8\frac{1}{2}$ inches at the base. The edges were turned over to form a slender round tube, thus concealing the raw edge of the copper. From about 1780 the edges were covered by reeded ribbons of flat plate. When dish rings became slightly taller from about 1780 the inward curve was less pronounced until eventually there was a tapered outline due to the base retaining its outward flare whilst the top became less spreading. The waisted design enabled the ring to be reversed and so function for serving bowls of two sizes: it might also be used for the display of fruit during dessert.

The Sheffield platers incorporated as many characteristics as possible copied from fashionable dish rings made by the silversmiths. It was, of course, impossible to interpret into Sheffield plate the silversmith's ornate repoussé work.

Such decoration on a deeply concave surface was severely limited when applied to plated copper. The great majority, then, display only perforated designs enriched with engraving and slight chasing and thus lack the naïve figures and other similar motifs in relief that add so much interest to a long series of high quality dish rings made after 1780. It was customary for a cartouche to be included in the design upon which the owner's coat of arms, crest or cypher could be engraved. Patterns on dish rings were so positioned that they may be viewed correctly with the smaller diameter uppermost.

From 1780 embossed and chased effects were produced by mounting ornament of thin silver on blank spaces left in a complex openwork field of piercing such as could be cut in the metal with a repeating press tool. This enabled the plater to reduce the metal to a delicate trellis work and simultaneously conceal copper edges. Naturalistic motifs such as flying birds and squirrels with classic swags of drapery were obtained in thin silver from factory silversmiths and filled with a lead-tin alloy. After hand finishing of the surface detail they were applied to a perforated ground of vertical pales with cusped ends or other geometrical designs incorporating crosses, crescents, circles, stars and squares. In a very popular pattern the waist remained solid and was encircled with a band of bright-cut engraving, with rows of vertical pales above and below, interspersed at intervals with floral roundels.

From the early-1790s silvered plate of lighter weight was used. This was often thinly plated. In this work, top and bottom rims were bent sharply over to form plain strengthening bands. The raw edge was concealed beneath a silver thread. Occasionally the upper rim was expanded outward horizontally and finished with a reeded edge of flat wire.

Magnificent dinner table equipage was described and illustrated by Elizabeth Raffald in *The English Housekeeper*, 1763. For example, a table laid with 25 serving dishes included: '4 large oval dishes for the roast; 2 small oval dishes; 6 scalloped round dishes; 4 plain round dishes; 1 large round dish; 4 rectangular with incurved sides; 4 very small round dishes for savouries'. But the cheerful clatter and pungent odours of the kitchen regions had to be kept discreetly remote from the formal elegance of the dining room and this involved problems for the hostess who wished the array of dishes to be proffered temptingly hot to her guests. Dish covers (Chapter 16) protected them from draughts as they were hurried along the corridors but even so it proved desirable to apply gentle heat upon their arrival on the sideboard-table. This was the function of the dish cross, long indispensable yet now barely recognized. Dish rings were already in use to protect side table marquetry veneers from hot dishes: the dish cross was a more practical version since it could receive any size and shape of serving dish and soon acquired the additional advantage of a warming unit.

The dish cross was thus a purely functional innovation introduced early in George II's reign, displaying ingenuity rather than aesthetic taste. Hallmarks on silver specimens indicate their continuing use into the reign of William IV: two or three of the several units were hallmarked. The *Directory of Sheffield*, 1774, includes dish crosses among the Sheffield plate then in production.

The dish cross consisted of four horizontal pivoting arms radiating x-like from a central spirit lamp, each arm fitted with a sliding socket supporting a shaped bracket for the dish above and linked to a small foot below. The arms and the sockets were adjustable so that the stand could hold any flat-based table dish within the current range of standard shapes and sizes. With the arms and sockets fully extended a dish cross would support a large serving dish; by drawing the arms closer together and sliding the four sockets towards the centre it could be used to hold, for instance, a small oblong muffin dish. Each pair of arms radiated from a flat central ring so constructed that they could revolve one above the other around the neck of the spirit font. This served as an axis from which they could be swung horizontally.

It was only during the 1750s that the dish cross acquired its heating unit. In February 1957 Christie's catalogued one of the preceding design, a rare example struck with the 1740 hallmark and described as 'George II, on four shell feet with scroll brackets above, the arms revolving around flat circular discs'. This pattern is found in Sheffield plate of a much later date.

During the early 1750s a circular spirit lamp was introduced as the central point in the x-design. The top of the font was covered with a tightly-fitting screw-on concave wick holder. Its overhanging rim, strengthened with an applied mount, beaded, gadrooned, corded, fluted or otherwise serrated, permitted easy removal for replenishing the spirit. The plaited flax wick was passed through a burner rising in the centre and usually encircled with narrow relief ornament. The single burner trained its heat only at the centre of the dish base, tending to scorch the contents at that point. This was overcome by centring the flame in a concave disc cut with geometrical perforations or a circle of radiating pales and sunk a short distance into the font, a device that distributed the heat more evenly upon the base of the vessel above. It is sometimes found as a replacement in a spirit lamp of an earlier period. For instance, a dish cross made in the 1770s incorporates this improvement but the device in question was made by Kirkby, Waterhouse & Co., a firm established in 1793. The font was usually plainly spun, whether in bowl-shape, ogee outline, vase-shape or spirally fluted. It might be engraved with a crest or monogram.

The dish cross arms themselves were hollow and square in section, each shaped from a single piece of plate invisibly seamed along the inner side. This ensured that the socket-foot units moved freely along them yet provided rigid support when adjusted to receive the vessel. Each socket measured about one-third of the arm's length and its two visible sides might be ornamentally perforated, but remained plain on an undecorated dish cross. A small rosette or fluted stud screwed into the end of the arm prevented the socket from sliding too far and falling off but permitted removal for cleaning. To the upper surface of each socket was soldered a bracket for supporting the dish; to the lower surface a short leg and foot of such a height that the base of the lamp font was lifted clear of the table.

The four brackets for supporting the dish rose an inch or more above the dish cross arms, usually shaped as small scrolls matching the legs below and just high enough to keep the dish clear of the spirit flame or dispersed heat. For pushing them close around the dish the brackets were fitted with small thumb-piece finials soldered to the backward-curving bracket ends and matching the outlines of the feet below. Design varied considerably: bracket and finial might together form the slanting support for a shallow dish, sometimes with a serrated surface for a better grip. Legs usually repeated on a larger scale the attractive scrolls above just as the feet repeated the decorative patterns of the finials. Shell and petal, sometimes pierced, and ram's mask and hoof foot were among the most fashionable designs. Circular reeded feet have been noticed on some early examples and others had small round feet with beaded edges.

An alternative dish cross design dates from the 1790s. Four fixed arms extended at right angles to each other from the central axis and were fitted with sliding brackets. These were made either for circular or for oblong dishes. The arms extended from an axis consisting of a central ring containing a concave pierced disc. Immediately below this was placed the spirit lamp, a separate unit, its plainly spun font supported by three paw or claw feet or, later, scroll and shell feet.

Contemporaneous with the dish cross was the open-frame dish stand. This contrivance for warming food or drink on table or sideboard was constructed from a pair of flat wire rings which might be plain, reeded or chased with leaves and scrollwork. The rings were connected by curved or double scroll supports of round wire. Dish stands were reversible, one ring for oval dishes, the other for circular. In the centre, supported by wires extending from the rings, was a circular heat disperser, its concave surface perforated with radiating pales and circles. Beneath this was placed a spirit lamp with double or triple burners. An uncommon type was so designed that the dish rings revolved on a pair of movable bands sunk into the axis. Others were made for use with octagonal and oblong vessels.

Dish crosses and dish stands were invariably well finished despite the subordinate role they played in the dining room. Early in the nineteenth century dish crosses began to be replaced by dish warmers containing red-hot irons or boiling water.

Folding dish stands were made by Watson & Bradbury and other platers from about 1810. Four oval loops of flat wire, each strengthened with a cylindrical vertical centre strut, were hinged together vertically. The four units could be adjusted to support an oval or circular dish.

# 18. Sauce and gravy vessels, boats; tureens; argyles; saucepans

Pungent sauces, relishes and pickles were invaluable to cooks of earlier generations. Unappetizing dried and salted meats and fish constituted much of the everyday fare, masked by strong scents and flavourings. In a great household these were prepared in a department known as the saucery, superintended by the yeoman of the sauces, a livery-wearing servant who attended table 'redye with vynegar and colde water' to minister to any diner who found his sauces too fiery. At first such sauces were tabled in deep flat dishes measuring about six inches across and with up-turned rims. These were known as saucers, a term defined in *Bailey's Dictionary*, 1728, as a 'little dish to hold sauce'. Canoe-shaped or 'shipp saucers', pointed at both ends, were also recorded as early as 1620.

George I introduced to the English dinner table the fashion for smoothly flowing semi-liquid sauce, dominated by a single flavour. This type of sauce was tabled cold in a deep boat-shaped vessel which had a pointed beak-shaped spout upcurving at each end, a wavy rim, a scroll handle attached vertically to the centre of each side and a low oval foot. In the 1720s the centres of the sides were incurving and rose higher than the spout ends. This pattern was made by a few of the early Sheffield platers after the introduction of double plating in the late 1760s, and was again revived in the early 1820s with florid silver mounts. The body in this design was stamped in two halves. A third series appeared in the late 1840s, with a hand-raised body usually on an oval stemmed foot and with a pair of upward and inward curving scroll handles rising from the rim.

The sauce-boat with a single, wide up-curving spout was devised in the 1720s. This was the most common form made by the Sheffield platers who at first copied it as closely as possible from 1765 and repeated it again during the 1830s–40s, catalogued as 'Queen Anne' pattern. Sauce-boats were necessarily severely smooth, as embossment or other ornament in relief interfered with pouring. Four elaborately designed legs topped by lion masks were fashionable on the silver sauce-boat from the early 1730s, but this pattern is seldom seen in Sheffield plate. Three short legs with hoof, shell or claw and ball feet were preferred, one beneath the spout and two at the back, one either side of the handle.

The Sheffield platers found it convenient to make the body incurved towards the everted rim: helmet-shaped examples were catalogued. The same shape with and without applied festoons of flowers dates from about 1800. An example illustrated in a catalogue of this period shows a high, uprising spout, curved downward at the tip, and a high upcurving handle with an expansive leaf attachment at each end. It has a short, spreading oval-stemmed foot. It is of half-pint capacity and a pair cost 32s plain. The shape of the three-legged sauce-boat in Sheffield plate was fairly constant, although few identical examples are seen.

The shell-shaped sauce-boat of the early Georgian silversmiths was revived in Sheffield plate early in the nineteenth century. These appear to have been intended to contain sauce to accompany a fish course for handles might be shaped in an appropriate form such as a lamprey or a dolphin. Elaborate loop handles are also found, sometimes terminating in the head of a sea monster. Diarists at this period have noted that each person was served with 'an almost entire fish' – confirmed by contemporaneous caricatures. The oval foot was decorated with shell and scroll mounts: examples have been noted with eight scallops around the foot. In other instances smaller versions of the foot ornament were repeated around the rim, usually encircled with narrow scroll mounts. Shell-shaped sauce-boats were fashionably accompanied by matching ladles.

By 1820 the single-spout low-bellied sauce-boat had become fashionable. This had three legs with hoof feet, each attached to the body with a spreading shell motif. The scroll handle had an acanthus leaf thumb-rest. Although sauce-boats were usually plain, heavy gadrooned rims date from this period. Examples have been noted with upstanding free-scroll handles, double-scrolled – virtually copies of a pattern made by the silversmith Walter Brind, Foster Lane, London, in the 1750s and made again in Birmingham in the 1840s.

The Victorian single-lipped sauce-boat often was plain of body with bulging sides and a gadrooned rim which might be scalloped. It had a double scroll handle and three hoof feet. Such vessels were made in three sizes: large, £3 a pair; middle, £2 a pair; and small, holding half a pint, £1.11.6 a pair. The helmet shape with a chased pedestal foot, its edge shaped into four feet, cost £4 a pair. Pattern books show that footed sauce-boats were at least 30 per cent more costly than those with three short legs – sometimes 50 per cent more. They were always sold in pairs, but double and triple pairs might be bought and occasional sets of a dozen have been recorded.

Although Sheffield plate sauce-boats were shaped for pouring sauce or melted butter, it was fashionable to spoon out the sauce with a ladle, one ladle to each sauce-boat, the handle shaped to the curve of the spout against which it rested.

In a sauce-tureen a rectangular space was cut from the edges of the cover near to one side and from the early 1780s to the 1820s might have a feather edge or a border of engraving. Then came, in this sequence, thread and shell, king's pattern, queen's pattern and husk.

A change in culinary fashion during the 1760s required some sauces to be less spicy but served piping hot, bringing into use the covered sauce-tureen – catalogued by Sheffield platers as 'tureen sauce boats'. This was usually accompanied by a matching stand with a raised centre, the better to protect the table surface from damage by heat and as a rest for the ladle when no provision had been made for a handle by cutting a slot in the cover.

The earliest sauce-tureens were canoe-shaped with a handle at each end rising from the rim in a high semi-circle, and recurving downward, gradually tapering to beneath the base of the body. From about 1790 handles might be made from heavy cast sterling silver. Examples have been noted in which the outer surface of the handle is in silver, the under-surface in fused plate. From about 1800 a strengthening piece of plate, usually in silver, extended from the foot to about halfway up the handle, terminating in a simple ornament. The upper curves of the handles and the top of the cover finial were of equal height: formerly the finial rose above the handles. The body-foot join from early in the nineteenth century was strengthened by introducing an expansive decorative washer between it and the end of the handle, made necessary by the use of thinner plate. Ring finials were corded and the accompanying handles similarly decorated. Squared-off reeded handles were usually associated with an octagonal loop finial, also reeded sometimes with the upper corners incurved, in which case the outer corners of the handle were incurved to match.

The stand or dish was also canoe-shaped, shallow, each up-curved end terminating in a substantial scroll. The centre was hand-raised to form a low flat platform with a shallow rim to receive the pedestal stem of the tureen. The rise, though shallow, was made slightly higher than the rim to prevent the hazard of accidentally catching the foot against the latter when lifting the tureen. The rim of the stand was encircled with strengthening reeding or gadrooning matching similar ornament on the vessel.

The body rim, the edge of the short-stemmed foot – oval or in some more ornamental shape – and the rim of the stand were strengthened by simple mounts in a matching design. The lid was centrally domed and an urn or berry finial might rise from a spreading rosette of palm leaves. The majority were smooth-surfaced: others might be gadrooned on bowl and cover, chased, or ornamented with applied swag medallions.

A sauce-tureen and its stand from about 1800 might be circular, canoe-shaped or oblong. The oblong had rounded ends, D-handles and a square plinth supporting a short-stemmed oval foot, usually with a reeded edge. Sometimes the plinth rested on four feet, often dolphin heads, animal paws or scrolls. Introduction of the square foot to sauce-tureens brought about the abandonment of loose trays until the 1830s when once again the fashionable sauce tureen stood upon a dish, deeper than formerly and with long loop handles. At this period sauce-tureens might be gilded.

The majority of Sheffield plate sauce-tureens were assembled from factory-made units. The body was seamless, usually smooth inside; the foot also was in one piece, shaped by means of a die. An alternative was a partly reeded body, flat based, with lion's mask and ring handles. This might be ornamented with a band of decorative chasing below the rim. In some examples the top of the rim, the cover, the lower part of the body and the rise of the stand were all encircled with reeding. The upward points of the canoe-shaped body were not so tall as formerly but it was more capacious.

From the opening of the nineteenth century a series of covered sauce-tureens appeared in a design which had a rounded-oblong body with bulging sides supported on four wide scroll feet. By 1810 this was elaborated with filled handles and feet of silver, a style fashionable on silver half a century earlier. With the exception of a few early examples these were factory built and continued in production until early Victorian times, when they might have gadrooned feet and rims, with ring handles to the covers. It was a fashionable conceit at this time for vertical crest handles to be fitted to the covers. Throughout the period of manufacture in Sheffield plate the sauce-tureen might be engraved with a coat of arms in the centre of one side of the body and a crest on the cover. Very few sauce-tureens were made after the 1850s. None was shown at the Great Exhibition of 1851, nor are any entered in a plater's catalogue issued in 1852. Their omission followed the reappearance of the sauce-boat at this time.

An interesting series of sauce-tureens fashionable from about 1815 was evolved on the principle of the argyle. A heavily tinned interior lining made a compartment which, when filled with hot water, kept the sauce steaming hot. The water was introduced through apertures with hinged covers cut into the tops of the hollow handles which connected with the water compartment.

Carving at the dining table by the hostess was a novelty introduced to London by the Hanoverian Court in about 1720. Etiquette had formerly required that game and joints of meat should be carved by a servant at the side table. After the wedding of the Princess Royal to the Prince of Orange in 1733 the Countess of Hertford carved at the high table. By the 1740s the responsibility had been passed on to the host, but this still meant that the meal was served slowly. When the gathering was large and he wrestled with the carving, the hot gravy gradually cooled and congealed. Epicures of the period insisted upon being served with 'drawn gravy' prepared from blood freshly drawn from the animal. Gravy was considered an important detail of the menu, replacing the old pungent sauces, but the customary design for a sauce vessel was still an open boat.

Tepid gravy was heartily resented by John, Fourth Duke of Argyle (d. 1770), who expressed his dislike by designing gravy servers for his own table. These were internally heated by boiling water. The enterprising silversmith who made a pair for the duke in the early 1760s marketed similar articles under the duke's name.

Argyles obviously became standard productions for they are entered in the London Assay Office price list of 1777, the cost of assay being threepence. Whether its association with the Duke of Argyle has any substance or not it appears from the hallmarks on silver examples that the original type was made with a hot water jacket. The argyle resembles a small teapot with an excessively long, slender swan-neck spout. It continued, with variations, to be fashionable for about a century. The typical argyle is of two gills capacity and measures about seven inches in height, including the lid finial.

Almost at once argyles were made by the Sheffield platers. Collectors recognize four methods of keeping the gravy hot within its container: a simple hot-water jacket; a central hot-water container; a central box iron; a hot-water compartment in the base. Hallmarks on silver examples reproduced in Sheffield plate show that the earliest heater was the hot water jacket. The central hot-water chamber was in production contemporaneously with the jacket from the early 1770s. The box-iron heater may be dated exactly to 1774 when the idea was patented by John Wadham of St George-in-the-East, London (see Chapter 13). No example with a hot-water compartment in the base has been noted dating earlier than 1774.

The argyle with a hot-water jacket had a cylindrical body with a detachable cover. This was fitted with a double lining or outer jacket to contain boiling water poured through a small socket entrance at the rim near to the handle and sealed with a screwed stopper, superseded from about 1790 by a self-closing hinged cover. Either opposite or at right angles to the ebony or hard-wood handle, which might be bound with cane, rose a swan-neck tubular spout, long and thin. This was set low on the body and passed through the hot-water jacket into the bottom of the gravy container where the gravy would be richest. The inner vessel might be plated with silver, but many were tinned. The long, curved and extremely slender spout served the double purpose of preventing over-large servings of the rich liquid and of minimizing the escape of heat through the outlet. Although particularly difficult to clean such spouts continued in use throughout the period.

Body shapes followed chronologically those of teapots, the low-domed lift-off cover being succeeded by the hinged lid. The body usually remained plain so that heat from the water was not expended uselessly upon extraneous ornament. From about 1785, however, the body might be fluted. A coat of arms or crest might be engraved on the side to the right of the handle. The rims of lid and base were strengthened with reeded, gadrooned or beaded mounts.

Early argyles were flat-based and, when heated by the gravy or hot water, might disfigure a polished table even if protected by a baize undercloth as was usual. The immediate solution was a separate stand with three ball or scroll feet. The stand was discarded in about 1800: rarely are the pair found complete. Subsequent development was the flaring foot rim attached to the argyle.

The central hot-water chamber was fitted at first into an argyle with a cylindrical body and swan-neck spout. During the 1780s and 1790s, however, the body was fashionably oval or hexagonal with a detachable domed cover and a straight tapering spout rising exactly to the height of the body rim. The cylindrical hot-water container rose centrally from the base and was sealed with a screw stopper. The gravy was poured around this.

The argyle containing a box-iron heater inside was usually designed with a vase-shaped body rising from a low stem in the form of a slender spool expanding downward towards a circular foot, often on a square plinth from about 1800. Within, rising vertically from the base, was a lidded socket of fused plate or, more usually, of tinned copper, designed to contain a cylinder of red-hot iron – usually cast. The argyle lid was shaped with a high dome to accommodate the longest box-iron possible for such a small vessel.

The argyle with a baluster-shaped body expanding into a spreading base was water heated by dividing the interior horizontally so that only the swelling upper portion contained gravy, an entrance to the spout being cut into the dividing partition. The lower section was filled with boiling water through a projecting socket covered with a hinged lid. A deep convex foot ring lifted the hot-water container above the table. Handle and spout were at right angles to each other. The Sheffield platers had acquired the bulk of the argyle trade by the mid-1790s. Cylindrical and barrel-shaped bodies, circular or oval on plan, appeared early in the nineteenth century. In these, the expansive beak-shaped spout had a hinged lid fitted to the rim, which simplified the addition and removal of water.

These versions continued uninterruptedly until the 1840s when the Victorian argyle made its appearance. This was of the hot-water jacket type with a cylindrical body usually engraved. The spout might be chased and its opening sealed with a self-acting cover. The handle had ivory insulators and leaf-flange sockets; the cover was double domed with an ornamental finial. A contemporaneous catalogue named them 'argyles or gravy-warmers', the factory price being £3.15.0 plain and £4.3.0 engraved.

Hazards associated with the use of brass and copper saucepans left in the charge of careless servants prompted Georgian medical men to advise the use of silver by those who could afford the luxury. These vessels were not intended solely for warming brandy as assumed by many collectors. Jonathan Swift, for instance, in his *Directions to Servants*, 1729, recommended a silver saucepan for such culinary duties as melting butter, declaring that brass and copper, even when tinned, 'gave it a taste'. Particularly important were silver saucepans in the preparation of piquant sauces which for centuries disguised the salty flavour of preserved foods. The acids contained in many of these sauces were liable to act upon the surface of base metal, affecting flavour and endangering health. Families using silver were served directly from the covered saucepans which were carried into the dining parlour on stands fitted with spirit lamps.

Silver saucepans were a rich man's privilege until Victorian times: in Sheffield plate they were used by the middle classes from the early 1750s in five standard capacities of $\frac{1}{4}$, $\frac{1}{2}$, $\frac{3}{4}$, 1 and 1$\frac{1}{2}$ pints. Joseph Hancock is known to have been making them by 1750. These were impressed on the socket with his name IOS$^H$ HANCOCK SHEFFIELD: there are marked examples in Sheffield City Museum and the Victoria and Albert Museum. The ogee-shaped pan was flat-based and hand-raised from copper plate with silver fused to one side only, the coating being substantially thicker than for other domestic ware. The interior of the pan was thus silvered and the copper exterior was highly burnished. This was the typical saucepan until the introduction of double plating in the late 1760s. The brim was turned outward to make a quarter-inch flat rim of silver, the plainly smooth curved surface being free of crevices that might harbour food when carelessly cleaned. Few single-plated saucepans date later than about 1780. Thomas Mitchell, a relation of Bolsover, who entered the plating trade in 1751, made similar saucepans.

Small-capacity saucepans could be spun from copper alloyed to a suitable degree of softness, but the majority were hand-raised until about 1780. At first the pouring lip was made by expanding the rim slightly outward into a v-shape at a point at right angles and to the left of the handle. This was soon superseded by the beak spout, much more expansive than could be made by raising the copper. A v-shaped section was cut from the rim extending almost halfway down the body and a triangular beak lip was soldered into position. Occasionally a hinged flap covered the opening of the spout on a pan equipped with a hinged cover. The usual cover was a low dome with a plain, simple curve topped by a turned finial of material matching the handle. The centre of the dome was flattened in nineteenth-century design.

The pan's most important feature, however, was the handle which determined how long it would give useful service. The socket was of Sheffield plate and at first was but slightly tapering, the taper becoming more pronounced by the late eighteenth century. The pan attachment was in the shape of a shield or heart, the socket being inserted and hammered over a slight depression encircling the hole. This was hard-soldered and could not be pulled away. The completed handle was then attached to the pan at a high angle, flat-headed rivets being used.

The handle that fitted into the socket was turned with a collar to fit flush against the plain rim of the socket which was strengthened with encircling swaged ribbon. For additional security a silver rivet was driven through socket and handle. The handle was a decorative feature of ebony, ivory or hard wood. Green-stained ivory was fashionable, made easy to grip for pouring by being cut in hexagonal section. In the nineteenth century the turned handle was more robust with a greater diameter and the socket was made shorter.

The much less costly cylindrical saucepan made of sheet plate ran concurrently with the shapely hand-raised pattern. The body with a slight outward taper was seamed vertically and fitted with an inserted base strengthened with an encircling ring of swaged ribbon. The spoutless rim might be slightly everted and the nearly flat cover had a central knop of material matching the handle. The typical size of such a pan was $3\frac{1}{2}$ inches diameter and $2\frac{1}{2}$ inches deep, the depth increasing in the early nineteenth century when large numbers were made.

The Sheffield plate saucepan stand was a simple contrivance. A plain, deep ring to fit the rounded base of the pan was supported by three legs, at first square and terminating in paw feet of the style of contemporaneous chair legs. From the early 1790s the supports might be composed of swaged or drawn ribbon, usually reeded and shaped with a high inward curve. The legs were connected by a ring immediately above the feet and a smaller, slighter ring was placed between them immediately below the pan-ring to support the plain cylindrical spirit lamp.

This lamp was shaped from a rectangular sheet of single-side fused plate, a disc base and a loose-fitting concave cap without a hinged dome to the wick aperture. After about 1800 the cylindrical lamp might contain a large mortar light instead of spirits. These mortars, usually of fine beeswax with wicks of flax, were specially manufactured for the purpose. Cotton wicks could not withstand long-continued heat and were not so uniform in their capillary action.

# 19. Cruets and soy frames

Silver vessels for oil and vinegar stood separately on the English dining table from early in the fifteenth century. By 1690, however, an openwork silver frame might be provided for a pair of flint-glass cruet bottles with silver caps. The frame, of thick moulded ribbon, had a lateral handle and a flat solid base. Two small handles projecting horizontally from the sides held the silver caps whilst the bottles were in use. From about 1710 the cruet stand of this pattern might be enlarged by the addition of three small circular platforms each with a guard ring. A vertical column terminating in an oval loop handle rose from the centre of the platform and the design included four short feet.

This pattern continued fashionable until the 1750s when it was superseded by a more ambitious design made in silver and in Sheffield plate. This was a cruet frame with a flat platform bordered by a deep gallery usually ornamentally perforated but occasionally embossed or chased with such designs as anthemion or birds among scrolling foliage. A beaded or corded rim matched the guard rings. The loop of the central standing handle might be plain, scrolled, spirally fluted or of twisted wire. The platform was cut from heavy plate and might be circular, quatrefoil or cinquefoil, supported on feet shaped as ball-and-claw or spreading escallop shell. The result somewhat resembled a decanter coaster with a central standing handle. Few of these remain in Sheffield plate. Such cruets were fitted with flint-glass bottles and casters, pyriform in shape, each with a silver or Sheffield plate cover or mount to suit its duty on the table. By the 1770s the platers were using stoppers of cut glass with oil and vinegar bottles, a feature quickly copied by the silversmiths.

Cruet frames and their silver bottle mounts from 1790 to 1825 might be decorated or severely plain. Frederick Bradbury has recorded that the catalogues of the family firm illustrated more than 500 cruet frame patterns between 1788 and 1815, covering a wide range of styles and usually light in weight and con-sisting mainly of mechanically made units. The engravings show that the galleried platform might be oval, circular, square, rectangular or canoe-shaped, usually with a central handle of the looped pillar design. Silver mounted mustard pots were included as standard cruet fitments from early in this period. The shapes of all vessels now harmonized.

The less expensive rimless oval platform was common, too, from the 1780s. This was bordered with gadrooning or other silver edging with matching supports rising from the plate to the guard rings. It had D-shaped handles and an apron of curved gadrooning. The deep guard rings, usually reeded, were supported by four fluted pillars on paw feet, leaving the bottles fully exposed. Oval frames with high galleries enriched with openwork piercing or engraving date from the early 1790s, ornament often including ovolos or bands of flowering foliage. These might have mask and shell supports to the guard rings: shell and dolphin ring handles were popular. Such frames were made in Sheffield plate and silver by J. & T. Settle, Norfolk Street, Sheffield.

The oblong frame became fashionable at about the turn of the century and might have a shaped outline or a corkscrew scroll at each end, with paw, bracket, ball or fluted feet. From 1810 the gadrooned or reeded border might be replaced by gadrooning with shell and foliage motifs at the corners and the centre of each side. The guard rings might be chased with anthemion ornament. The fashion for circular cruet frames was revived in about 1810 in substantial Sheffield plate. Square frames with four bottles date from about 1815.

Another cruet pattern evolved by the factory silversmiths shortly before 1820 but made largely in Sheffield plate was the box design. This was an oval frame, rising at each end, with a high gallery, elaborately pierced or mechanically embossed, and four short scroll feet. This was covered with a plate recessed to receive five cruets, two casters and a mustard pot. The plate was secured by the central looped column which passed through to the base where it was fastened by a small fly-nut. These were catalogued as 'Elizabethan cruet frames with pierced boxes', to meet a current vogue for period names to articles lacking any resemblance to anything made by the favoured reigns.

Contemporaneous with the Georgian cruet frame was the soy frame. Early in George II's reign the East India Company began to import a new, highly flavoured relish known as soy, described in 1776 as 'a sauce as thick as treacle and of a clear black colour'. Soy was prepared from beans of the *Soja hispidi*, salted and mixed with finely ground barley or wheat. To this might be added *yu* oil from Japan, but olive oil was more commonly used.

The vogue for soy, first served from shallow saucers of silver or porcelain, created a demand for specially designed silver-mounted bottles of flint-glass. By the 1750s soy bottles were tabled in special frames with two or three other sauces. At first these were differentiated by gilding or engraving a label upon each bottle: from the 1770s the bottles could carry silver or Sheffield plate tickets suspended by chains around their necks – miniature versions of contemporaneous wine labels (Chapter 12).

In the nineteenth century a soy frame might accommodate as many as six, eight or ten matching bottles each containing a different sauce such as soy, kyan, chili, anchovy, catsup, quin, lemon juice, tarragon, harvey and innumerable others including the Indian sauces mogul, nepaul and carrache. Quin was a sauce evolved by the actor James Quin, its ingredients including walnut pickle, garlic, mushroom catsup, horseradish, anchovies and cayenne. The basic flavour of kyan was derived from the smooth red seedheads of the South American cayenne pepper known contemporaneously as garden coral and today as capsicum.

The earliest soy bottles, dating to the 1740s, were tabled on a graceful frame of silver. A flat circular or quatrefoil platform supported three or four cast scroll brackets attached by soldering and topped by circular guard rings shaped from drawn silver wire to contain the bottles. The brackets also extended downward from the platform as short legs terminating in spreading feet to provide stability. From the centre a standing loop handle rose above the bottles. These were of flint-glass, their long slender necks fitted with silver covers and handles. The fashionable design was ewer shaped with spout and graceful handle curving upward and downward from a silver mount. Richard Boult's trade card of the late 1740s illustrates such a soy frame.

Thomas Heming, goldsmith to George III, at the King's Arms, Bond Street, illustrated on his trade card the fashionable soy frame of the late 1760s. A row of three soy bottles with shallow diamond-cut necks and bodies are shown set in pierced galleries standing in a rococo canoe-shaped dish. This design with and without uprising ends continued fashionable until the Victorian period, usually with a row of four bottles and less frequently with six or eight. These were generally facet cut, but the pattern included a narrow plain reserve to be engraved with the name of the sauce. The pantry usually contained several spare bottles inscribed with the names of fashionable sauces. Sometimes eight bottles were offered, six engraved with the sauce names and two carrying silver bottle tickets which could be selected from a set of six bearing the names of unusual sauces.

Late Georgian silversmiths and Sheffield platers produced many costly conceptions of canoe-shaped soy frames, ornately enriched with cast and chased decoration and containing superbly cut bottles of the finest flint-glass made specially in the glass-man's piling pots.

By the early 1770s Tudor & Leader, Sycamore Hill, Sheffield, were manufacturing light-weight soy frames, the platform usually of heavy wood such as Spanish mahogany to ensure stability. The upper surface and edges were concealed beneath thinly rolled silver plate or Sheffield plate silvered on one side only. The gallery of an example made by this firm in 1776 was pierced with vertical pales, ovals and lozenges and accommodated six cut-glass soy bottles with loosely fitting lift-off silver caps. Claw and ball feet continued fashionable, but foliage and bracket feet were more common. Soy bottles were now short-necked, deep diamond-cut and might be footed, round or square. They were fitted with glass stoppers, usually with ball finials and cut ornament.

By the end of the 1780s cruets and soy bottles might be brought together to form a single unit placed conveniently in the centre of the formal or semi-formal dining table. At first the bottles were placed in guard rings fitted to a revolving stand of mahogany, its surface covered with a sheet of silver or Sheffield plate. Such pieces were catalogued by the Sheffield platers as 'cruet and soy frames'. Soon this device was enlarged into an unwieldy epergne with branches spreading from a decorative pierced ring supported on stays extending from the guard rings encircling the edges of the revolving stand. Each branch terminated in a silver or cut-glass saucer with another set high in the centre. Several elaborate variants were made: in some examples the epergne was hung with gilded baskets for pickles.

A catalogue of about 1850 illustrates 27 examples of combined cruet and soy frames, the number of bottles ranging from five to eight and each with four cruet bottles. These are shown set in circular frames with very deep galleries elaborately pierced with festoons; in so-called Gothic patterns; with vertical pales below shaped and festooned rims; and in ovals with substantially moulded uprights at the ends and sides supporting plain guard rings. Examples of the so-called crescent may be noted too, containing three vessels, the central one projecting in front of the others, with an elaborate near-horizontal scroll handle at the back rising appreciably above the guard rings. At this time, too, there was a fashion for a soy frame consisting of four conjoined cylinders elaborately pierced and set around a central standing handle and each containing a cut-glass bottle.

Although the majority of soy bottles were blown from clear flint-glass of varying qualities, there was a fashion for opaque white glass enriched with decorations and labels in coloured enamels, from about 1770 to the early 1790s, and again in the mid-nineteenth century when the inscription was usually black. Typically these bottles were pear-shaped. Bristol blue glass was a satisfying alternative, lettered in gold. Green soy bottles achieved some popularity in the mid-nineteenth century.

Collectors expect cruet and soy frames to contain their original – or at least contemporaneous – bottles of flint-glass. These display a chronological development from which there was little deviation although shapes and decoration naturally followed fashionable styles. The quality of the glass itself is of some assistance in recognition. The demand for glass accessories by manufacturing silversmiths and platers caused glass-houses to be established within easy reach of Sheffield and Birmingham. The cost around 1820 of plain uncut flint-glass cruet and soy bottles was 1s 10d a pound; as much as 2s 6d for fine quality.

At the time that the Sheffield platers entered the cruet trade flint-glass contained less lead than formerly and in consequence was more whitely transparent. Progressive improvements in clarity and flawlessness continued throughout the Sheffield plate period. Prismatic fire was lacking, however, until the last decade of the eighteenth century when new methods of annealing or toughening resulted in a glass strong enough for deep cutting with fine prismatic diamonds.

The glass cruet bottle copied the footed pyriform outline with a tapered neck such as was used by the fashionable silversmiths. The body was cut with shallow diamonds and narrow vertical flutings above the shoulder. A flat circular foot, alternately cut and under-cut, was joined to the body with narrow moulding. Cruet bottles of this form enriched with cutting in accordance with contemporaneous fashion were popular for about a century.

At first the body might be square-cut with hollow diamond cutting above, or cut all over with simple shallow facets. During the 1770s and 1780s the fluted body might be intersected horizontally by two or three shallow prisms. From about 1780 there was a vogue for long flutes extending from neck to foot, the sharp edges being softened with small intermittent oval facets. This style of cutting continued very popular during the nineteenth century.

From 1770 until the end of the century the thick foot might have a scalloped edge or be solidly square and cut beneath with a simple or ornate star. From the early 1790s the foot might be cut with a six-pointed star, common after 1820, and occasionally with a 16-pointed Brunswick star. Hallmarks on the silver bottle mounts show such cutting to have been usual from 1775, its purpose being to conceal the depression made by grinding away the punty scar.

From about 1790 until 1805 flat convex diamond-cutting combined with fluting was fashionable. The cross-cut diamond in all its variations, but in a less carefully worked form, is found on cruet and soy bottles with silver mounts dating from the early 1780s. From about 1790 a prismatic ring might encircle the neck, this being a common feature until the 1830s.

Cruet bottles became less elaborately decorated, the majority being cut with six or eight flat sides, flat-cut necks and widely everted mouth rims. Galleried frames might display bottles cut with large diamond facets, with tall stopper finials to match, of heavy-cut diamonds. Many reflected the nineteenth-century Gothic influence.

Towards the close of 1790 light-weight cruet bottles of soda glass, blown very thinly and but slightly cut, were used by the Sheffield platers in an endeavour to cut costs.

Throughout the Georgian period cruet and soy frames stood upon the table, often in pairs; matching sets of six, eight or a dozen are recorded in Sheffield plate. The influence of the celebrated chef Alexis Soyer brought about a change. In 1849 he wrote: 'the cloth being laid with the proper side uppermost over baize, I order a napkin, two knives, two prongs, two tablespoons and two wine-glasses to be placed to each person, a salt cellar between every other, that being a condiment which everyone uses: the cruet frames are kept on the sideboard'.

# 20. Mustard pots and salt-cellars

Mustard-making 500 years ago was already an established and prosperous craft, qualified tradesmen becoming members of the Grocers' Company. Caxton in 1483 wrote of 'Nicholas the Mustard Maker', and a century later Thomas More recorded 'a musterde maker in Cambridge'. The mustard-makers grew, harvested and dried their seed and ground it in hand-operated querns. The pungent powder was then mixed with pea flour, dampened and rolled into small balls which were dried hard for marketing. For table use the ball was crushed in a mortar and mixed into a paste with strong wine vinegar: unfermented grape juice, cider and claret were alternatives. This was stored in a pot made air-tight with parchment.

Although mustard pots for the table were in use much earlier, the first reference so far discovered dates to 1380 when John Wycliffe, writing from Oxford, suggested that his 'lettis on parchment mai do good for to covere mustard pottis'. These pots were small earthenware containers glazed with smithum inside, but coarse glass was also used.

Mustard as a relish rather than a sauce tabled in deep, rimless circular dishes, dates from the Elizabethan period when it was served in small silver pots, usually inventoried in pairs. But mustard sauce, served from double-lipped sauce boats and accompanied by lumps of ice on a glass plate, continued fashionable until about 1720.

Mustard seed kernel separated from its husk as in wheat flour and sold as a dry unadulterated powder of great pungency dates to the early years of the Hanoverian regime when a Mrs Clements of Durham travelled the country twice yearly booking orders for 'Durham Mustard'. This might be either in brown or white or a blend of the two: its full strength was brought out by mixing with water immediately before serving. This was used sparingly as a condiment.

This mustard was usually tabled in small tin-glazed earthenware pots, but silver mustard pots were obviously in considerable production by 1739 for the London Assay Office in that year issued a price list including 'mustard cans'. The term can for centuries had been applied to cylindrical drinking vessels with handles. The term mustard can remained unaltered in the revised price list of 1777, although they had for many years been invoiced as 'mustard tankards'. This description continued until the introduction of other forms in the 1820s made it convenient for catalogue compilers to revert to the Stuart name of mustard pot.

Mustard cans in Sheffield plate resembled small lidded tankards measuring about three inches in height and two inches in diameter. The flat hinged lid was fitted with thumbpiece and spoon aperture. The cylindrical body was rolled from the plate and seamed vertically. Edging applied on the outer surface strengthened the brim and deeper edging lifted the flat base, which might be made uneven by careless cleaning, slightly above the table top. The body contained a flint-glass liner to facilitate daily cleaning.

The closely fitting lid might be flat, domed or, less commonly, double domed, and with a spoon aperture cut into its rim opposite to the thumbpiece. The lid was opened by slight pressure upon the thumbpiece, known to Georgian crafts-men as the purchase or lever. The thumbpiece rose vertically from a three-lug hinge, one leaf soldered to the top of the lid, the other extending to the upper surface of the S or D handle. This might be of filled silver or a flat strip of fused plate curving from below the rim, its tail ending immediately above table level. The thumbpiece itself, cast in silver and chased, appeared in several standard patterns, the most common being in openwork, the escallop shell running it close in popularity.

Mustard tankards with perforated bodies enclosing Bristol-blue glass liners were a fashionable innovation of the mid-1760s, displaying the silver pattern to perfection. Trellis, large honeycomb, fishnet and other widely spaced geometri-cal designs have been noted. Early piercing was hand-cut into plate of a gauge strong enough to accept the stresses caused by lifting, pressing the thumbpiece and cleaning. These hand-pierced mustard tankards were commonly fitted with flat lids, their rims encircled with plain or ornamental mountings: others were boldly domed with a flat edge fitting closely upon the brim. Designs were also made by extending flat double-plated ribbon between brim and base, arranging it in all-over repeat patterns such as pointed ovals.

Less costly stereotyped piercing by the hand-press quickly followed. These perforations on mustard tankards were mainly composed of repeat motifs. The body might display narrow bands of circles or other geometrical motifs top and bottom with a wider circuit of upright pales between, interspersed with minia-ture urns. The range of designs possible with only a few press tools reached many hundreds. Later work was more elaborate and might comprise top and bottom bands of pierced and engraved flat shells, with three expansive motifs pressed between – one in front and two at the sides.

Commonly the Sheffield plate lid was highly domed in the centre with a broad flat flange. These were more speedily shaped by spinning than by hand-raising. Unpierced surfaces of the body and lid might be enriched with engraving, a feature fashionable, too, on unpierced mustard tankards, most of which were flat-based.

A mustard tankard from about 1780 might be made *en suite* with four cylindrical salts pierced to match. The latter stood upon four short-legged feet, but the mustard tankard remained flat-based. During the 1790s, however, it might be raised on three feet such as claw and ball, scroll or pillar.

Mustard tankards and mustard pots were differentiated from the 1770s following the introduction of the neo-classic vase mustard pot by master silversmiths for the fashionable trade: the platers had them in production by about 1780. These were for the most part shaped by spinning and might be solid or perforated, the solid type being embossed with classic motifs: examples have been noted with the lower third of the body encircled with reeding. Piercing consisted of a wide rim band of geometrical design with three equally spaced motifs below.

The vase-shaped body was supported by a pedestal foot, again usually spun in the lathe, encircled with bead or other simple edging to match the rim and might stand upon a square plinth. The domed or bell-shaped cover, also spun, was topped by a cast and chased finial of silver, the pineapple and urn being common. A thumbpiece might be fitted, but more usually the hinge extended upward from the body rim and curved over the rise of the handle.

Oval mustard pots were designed in silver from about 1780 and appeared in Sheffield plate a few years later. These were shorter than the cylindrical or vase-shaped type, but of the same capacity: the body length was about equal to the overall height. The majority were made with uprising ends and the lid, curved to fit closely upon the body rim, might lack any other shaping or be raised into a high dome, topped by a silver finial. The body might be encircled with two bands of press-piercing. When the thumbpiece was omitted, a five-lug hinge was used. A flat ribbon handle was attached, usually on the long side, with a spoon aperture opposite. Rectangular, hexagonal and octagonal mustard pots were made until the 1820s: these were rarely pierced.

The mustard tankard continued concurrently with these until by the early nineteenth century the cylinder tended to have a slight upward taper and in many instances the flat or slightly convex lid possessed no spoon aperture in a fashionable desire to exclude air from freshly prepared mustard. Vertical reedings decorated the body during the 1820s, rim and base encircled with wide mountings bearing relief designs. The lid was urn-shaped and the handle a bold D.

A change in the proportions of the cylinder occurred in the 1830s, diameter measuring only half as much as the height, with top mountings more elaborate than formerly. The lid, usually flat, was now sunk into a square-cut recess shaped in the rim, the two surfaces forming a single plane when the lid was closed. Harp- and s-shaped handles were fashionable.

Gothic decoration became popular during the 1830s, the lid extending upward as a tall, Gothic spire. A smooth-faced hexagonal or octagonal mustard pot might be engraved with two designs repeated on alternating panels and stood upon four heavy scroll feet. A scarce octagonal type had a collet foot, the body sloping inward and terminating in an irregular rim edged with an elaborated mount. Embossed bodies were produced mechanically: six vertical panels displaying differing flower and foliage arrangements between double corrugations being popular.

Early Victorian mustard tankards normally measured about three inches in height, encircled with perforations or embossments. The lid overhung the body to the same diameter as the expansive mount encircling the base. Handles of all former shapes were made: the flat top of the harp-shaped handle was in line with the flat lid.

The richly worked standing salts of past centuries are symbols of a vanished social system in which ceremonial and colour reigned supreme. This impressive piece of ancient table silver has received full measure of attention from collectors, but more immediately interesting, perhaps, is the trencher salt in silver and in pewter, the direct forerunner of the salt in Sheffield plate. Until the seventeenth century trencher salts were short cylindrical containers measuring about one inch in height and three or four inches in diameter, with applied strengthening moulding at rim and base. They were filled with salt 'sutille, whyte, fayre and drye', and its surface smoothed with a salt-planer of ivory, three inches long by two inches broad. By the time of Charles I they might be circular, square, triangular or octagonal, with sides vertical, sloping or concave. Slight changes were made in their shape and size in about 1720 when the fashionable trencher salt became rectangular with clipped or rounded corners and contained an oval well. Concave sides extended outward to the foot. This pattern continued until the early 1730s, and there was a revival in Sheffield plate early in the nineteenth century.

Ornamental salt-cellars, superseding trencher salts, appeared on fashionable tables from the early 1720s, the deep well or bowl no longer enclosed in a silver carcase. The bowl, almost hemispherical and about $2\frac{1}{2}$ inches in diameter, was raised from the plate, its outer surface either smooth or decorated with an applied calyx of palm leaves, usually 12. The bowl rested on a low collet foot of lesser diameter, built from a series of low mouldings. This pattern continued until the mid-century, but was revived in Sheffield plate during the second quarter of the nineteenth century and catalogued as the Queen Anne pattern.

The Sheffield platers entered the salt-cellar trade after openwork pattern had been made fashionable by silversmiths from about 1760 with liners of Bristol blue glass. This rich smalt blue was found to be a superb ground for displaying patterns perforated in the plate. These salt-cellars were oval, the body about one inch deep raised upon four short legs terminating in claw and ball feet. Wavy rims in Sheffield plate date from the mid-1770s. These vessels were sold in pairs and catalogued in three qualities, the first two supplied with blue-glass liners: (a) tinned inside; (b) plated inside with silver edges; (c) gilt inside with silver edges. Until about 1820 they were fitted with three or four feet.

Ready-pierced galleries for both oval and round salt-cellars were sold by specialists in this work such as Tudor & Leader, Sheffield, and Matthew Boulton, Birmingham, who issued the same designs in rolled silver plate and in fused plate. The factory men used fly presses and in the large number of flat-surfaced formal designs on various articles the same skilfully arranged patterns of geometrical piercings may be detected over and over again. An early favourite was composed of vertical Gothic arches such as were more skilfully reproduced in the 1830s. Later came the standard vertical pales, light trellis work, cross patterns, circles, crescents, diamonds and conventional scrollwork.

A band of engraving encircled the body of many a pierced salt from about 1780, either above a narrow circuit of piercing or between a pair of narrow circuits of geometric perforations. Four taper or scroll feet might be substituted for the claw and ball pattern. The gallery of an oval salt-cellar was sometimes taller at the narrow ends than at the centre.

This was a reflection from the canoe-shaped salt-cellar dating from the 1770s, supported by a slender stem rising from a spreading trumpet foot. In some instances the instep was pierced to match the body. The bowls of the majority of canoe-shaped salt-cellars were decorated with engraving; some have an ogee outline. The ends of the body were usually plainly pointed or, less commonly, shaped with scroll terminals. These were abandoned in the 1780s in favour of loop handles rising above the rim, then curving or bending squarely over and extending downward beneath the body towards the stem. The plinth foot was diamond-shaped with a short capstan stem. The canoe-shaped body might be given eight batswing flutes, the rim scalloped in harmony with their outline. The factory sales price was 20s a pair tinned inside and 24s a pair plated inside with silver edges. Each flute was decorated with chased ornament and in some instances the edge of the foot was shaped in scallops matching those of the bowl rim.

Salt-cellars with hemispherical bowls and short slender stems rising from spreading feet accompanied the canoe-shape. The bowl might be solid and gilt inside or the rim press-pierced with a rim border, a similar band of piercing encircling the body and the space between engraved with urns and pendant swags. These were contemporaneous with and followed by stemmed salt-cellars in which the top of a plain hemispherical bowl was encircled by a pierced rim and the edge might be scalloped. Two-piece salt-cellars, now very rare with both parts intact, were made early in the nineteenth century, a small flat rectangular dish supporting an oval salt container and also serving to carry a silver salt spoon. In early examples the dish measured about three inches long with a central depression for a shallow salt bowl with a collet foot. Both units might be enriched with chasing or engraving.

Melon-shaped salt-cellars, eight lobes alternately wide and narrow and mechanically raised, appeared during the 1830s. The expansive masks or shell motifs of the four legs were attached to the narrow lobes. Rococo shell patterns became popular during the 1830s and continued long into the electro-plate era. Examples, gilded within, will be found representing the spotted tridacna shell, catalogued at 25*s*; the spinous cassidaria shell, 35*s*; the echinus shell with a coral foot, 22*s*. All of these were later reproduced in pearl-glazed Belleek porcelain. The rare shell and triton was catalogued at three guineas. Shell-shaped salt-cellars are to be found with feet modelled in the form of turtles – often mistaken for tortoises. The most popular salt-cellars of the late Sheffield plate period, from William IV, were circular, pierced with arabesque scrollwork and with widely everted rims of wavy outline. These contained flint-glass liners, clear or coloured.

The majority of salt-cellars from about 1815 fall into one of three main groups, continued from silversmiths' designs of the eighteenth century: hemispherical body with mask legs; rectangular body with collet foot usually raised on four ball feet; pierced, with a flat base. These were either gilded within or fitted with glass liners. The flint-glass works at this time catalogued 'salt linings' at 1*s* 10*d* a pound, a penny a pound extra for colour. The hexagonal Gothic salt-cellar mechanically shaped with six Gothic arches and with a blue glass lining forming windows, was popular from the early 1830s. These were catalogued at 16*s* each. Catalogues until about 1820 refer to salt-cellars as 'salts'; thereafter the term salt-cellar was general.

A Sheffield plate salt-cellar was always accompanied by a silver salt spoon. This was usually a deep-bowled oval ladle, the stem following the fashion of contemporaneous table spoons. The majority, however, possess the old English pattern handle chased with a shell. The early Georgian salt spoon had returned by the 1830s, catalogued as in the Queen Anne style. This was a miniature shovel with a flat-faced scoop and rat-tail stem terminal, the scoop itself being gilded. The scoop might be heart-shaped with a D-handle. Shell-bowled spoons also belong to the period.

218 Inkstand, 1785

219 Combined inkstand and candlestick, 1770s

220 Globe inkstand, c. 1805

221　Inkstand, *c.* 1800

222　Inkstand, 1830s

223   Snuff-boxes, 1750s

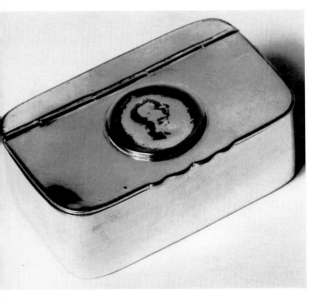

224   Snuff-boxes, *c.* 1800

225   Snuff-boxes, 1750s

226  Loving cup, 1760s

227  (*right*) Tankard, *c.* 1780

228  Pair of late eighteenth-cent tankards

229  Pair of presentation goblets, George IV period

230  Loving cup, 1758–70

231 and 232    Cake baskets

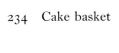

33    Interior view of plate 232

234    Cake basket

235 Hot-water warming pans: (*left*) 1790s; (*right*) 1770s

236 Pipe lighting bowls, 1780s

237 Portable pipe lighter fitting into vase for table use

238 (*top left and right*) Pair of pipe lighters, 1790s. (*centre*) Pipe lighter with handle. (*bottom*) Snuffer trays, 1790s. (*centre*) Mustard pot, 1780s

240    Honey pot and plate, *c.* 1800

239    Cucumber slicer, 1820

241    Monteith used as wineglass cooler, 1780; double decanter coaster, *c.* 1810; egg-boiler suite with spirit lamp and timer

242    Pipe-lighter, 1785

243    Urn, *c.* 1790

Egg-coddler, *c.* 1800

245   Egg-boiler, late eighteenth century

Pipe-lighter, *c.* 1785

247   Table snuff-boxes, *c.* 1800

Kettle, 1820s–30s

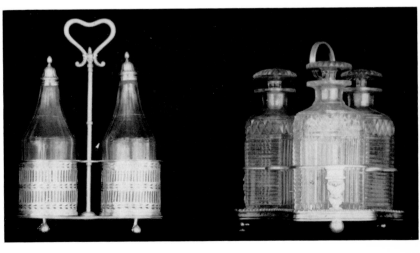

249   Soy frame, late eighteenth century; spirit frame, *c.* 1820

250   Centrepiece for dining table,
      c. 1840

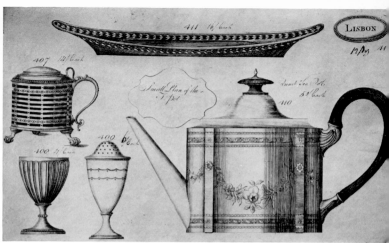

251   Snuffer tray, teapot, mustard pot, egg-cup and pepper
      caster, from pattern book of early 1790s

252   Soup tureen, c. 1820

253   Cruet stand, from early nineteenth-
      century pattern book

254   Miniature tea equipage
      for dolls' house, early nine-
      teenth century

255 (*top left*) 1820s

256 (*top right*) 1760s

CAKE BASKETS

257 (*left*) *c.* 1810

258 (*below*) 1790s

259   Wirework cake basket

260   Cake basket of interlaced wire, *c.* 1800

261   Wirework cake basket

262   Wirework sugar basket, *c.* 1790

Sweetmeat stand with three removable shell dishes, early nineteenth century

264 (*top left*) Taper holder. (*top right*) Inkstand, late eighteenth century. (*below*) Pair of tapersticks, 1750s, flanking a candelabrum base

265 Late Georgian Sheffield plate, including (*behind*) a pair of muffineers and a sauce boat and (*front*) a pair of decanter coasters and a pair of salt-cellars

266 Trug tray, early nineteenth century

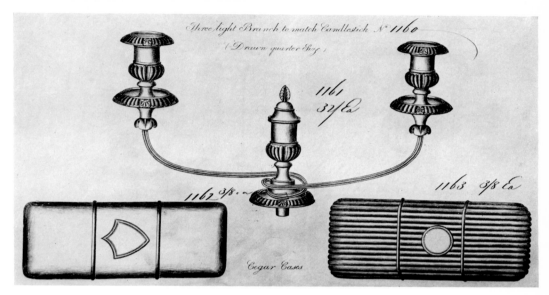

267 Three-light branch and two cigar cases, from late eighteenth-century pattern book

268 Group of Sheffield plate table ware showing flamboyant ornament fashionable from the end of the Georgian period

269 Sheffield plate in use at a banquet, 1814

# 21. Egg-cup stands, egg-boilers and toast racks

For centuries boiled eggs have garnished the English breakfast table. The early custom was to cook them over a charcoal brazier on a side table. Then for a century, from the 1770s, it was fashionable to have them carried boiling hot to the breakfast-room sideboard in an egg-cup stand protected from draughts by a highly domed dish cover.

Egg-cup stands date from about 1770 but few were made earlier than about 1780. An early example fitted with six egg-cups consisted of an oval wirework basket with claw and ball feet. From the centre rose a pillar terminating in a loop handle. Such a design might be made from round or oval wire.

A stand with a platform supporting four circular guard-rings for the egg cups was introduced in the 1780s. Between each ring was a loop for an egg-spoon, held vertical with the bowl upward. There was a central pillar for lifting. At first the platform was solid and square, but the sexfoil outline soon became fashionable, followed by a shaped oval. This held six egg-cups with a central pillar handle supporting a salt-cellar which might be of cut-glass or Bristol blue glass, fitted into a canoe-shaped wire frame. Another contemporaneous pattern consisted of an oval wire-based stand from which rose eight vertical supports, with four guard-rings around a pillar handle. Canoe-shaped egg-cup stands were made too, some with the ends extended and scrolled. Others were bordered with pierced ornament but the majority were constructed from round wires sometimes with a vertical heart-shaped handle.

Egg-cups were made from two units either hand-raised or, more commonly, spun from the plate. The plain-surfaced cup and the hollow pedestal foot were joined by soldering and burnishing. A rib with a flat or rounded surface encircled the egg-cup a little below the rim to permit suspension in the guard-ring. In some early examples the rib was omitted but the interior surface of the guard-ring was shaped to follow the curve of the egg-cup. The interiors of egg-cups and spoon bowls might be mercury-gilded to avoid the unpleasant effect of egg upon silver.

Early nineteenth-century egg-cup stands had horizontal members of wide beading or gadrooned mounts. These were joined vertically by slender pillars with paw feet. By 1810 gadroon-and-shell ornament was preferred. The upper member was fitted with egg-cup rings and slots for spoons and supported a stemmed salt-cellar in the centre. The rims of egg-cups and salt-cellars were encircled with matching mounts. The handle consisted of crossed arches with a finial at the join.

Egg-cup stands between 1790 and 1825 were made in patterns too varied to be tabulated, the majority in Sheffield plate: one firm alone issued 64 designs during the period 1788 to 1815. The Sheffield platers concentrated on light plain styles, and in some instances the stands were in Sheffield plate and the egg-cups in factory-made sterling silver. Makers' marks struck conspicuously on the egg-cup rims gave the guest the impression that the entire set was in sterling silver.

Customarily for breakfast a man might eat two boiled eggs and a woman one. Special stands were evolved, such as those containing three egg-cups and two spoons, suggesting use by husband and wife. Examples have been noted containing two egg-cups with a loop for a single spoon. A collector may even find an egg-cup stand with two spare egg-spoons attached to pillars and guard-rings that can be extended to receive two additional egg-cups. The rims of these egg-cups were widely everted with slender stems to the pedestal feet, matching a salt-cellar on a central raised platform. The stand was supported on four ball or scroll feet.

Among special patterns may be mentioned the triangular egg-cup stand with baskets of wirework to contain the egg-cups and a substantial central pillar handle rising from a solid platform. Similar stands were made in hexagonal outline. The upper part of the egg-cup might be encircled with an ornamental mount and the spoons, in shell and hour-glass pattern, were usually of silver.

Heavier moulding, usually semi-circular or reeded, was used for the stand from about 1820. The feet were elaborately designed paws and the supporting columns florid. The egg-cups at this period might be turned from cast silver, but were usually spun. The central salt-cellar was fashionably urn-shaped with a bail handle and a ladle. One pattern of this period included an oblong tray with a pair of D-shaped handles and scroll feet. This carried six openwork egg-cups fitting into openwork containers, supported by columns, and had a central pillar handle. Foliage supports were a new feature. The lozenge-shaped basket egg-cup stand dates to the same period, with four egg-cups and spoons.

Early Victorian egg-cup stands were over-decorated and difficult to clean, thus creating a preference for finely decorated bone china to the virtual exclusion of Sheffield plate. They were now catalogued as egg frames: earlier makers had entered them as egg-cup stands. The guard-rings were, curiously, catalogued as 'holes'. In many instances a flat platform with a pierced gallery or a very deep rim was supported on four claw and ball feet. The central pillar handle remained. The borders of the egg-cups were pierced or encircled with heavy mounts. The spoons were placed with their bowls or their finials projecting beyond the rim.

Other styles of Victorian egg-cup frames included a shallow dish on four ornamental feet with a central handle topped by a horizontal loop finial. The canoe-shape pattern was again fashionable, with four or six egg-cups, the rims of stand and egg-cups shaped to a repeating cyma outline. The galleries of most egg-frames of the mid-nineteenth century were chased with ornament such as intricate bird and flower designs, closely engraved scrollwork or pierced trellis work. The egg-cups were similarly decorated.

Egg-cup frames were often ingeniously combined with other objects associated with the Georgian breakfast table, such as toast rack, salt-cellar, pepper caster, or egg-boiler complete with spirit lamp and sand-glass egg-timer. Sheffield platers produced a century-long range of egg-boilers in which the vessel was filled with boiling water, carried to the breakfast table and there set on a stand containing a spirit lamp which kept it boiling. Each person could cook eggs to his individual liking. In most instances the contrivance consisted of a two-handled cylindrical or vase-shaped vessel with a flat or domed lid divided centrally and opening on two hinges. Fitted within the water pan was a frame of plated wire with rings to hold four or six eggs individually while they boiled. They were lifted from the water by a central uprising loop handle of flat metal.

Such was the egg-boiling unit as at first conceived and made until the mid-1790s. The stand was then encircled by four, six or eight guard-rings for the egg-cups: these alternated with loops for suspending eight spoons. The handle was now made of plated wire shaped at the top into a simple cage to display a three-minute sand-glass mounted on a horizontal swivel. By 1800 the stand for the boiling vessel might be fluted and raised on four reeded legs with hoof or paw feet, flat struts extending inward from the ends to support a ring containing a spirit lamp. Such a boiler was fitted with a pair of fixed horizontal loop handles or with the period's lion-mask and pendant ring handles. Almost a dozen patterns have been collated in Sheffield plate.

Toast racks – known contemporaneously as toast trays and sold in pairs – were made following the invention of solid plated copper wire from about 1780. They are not entered in the assay office price list of 1774, nor in a Sheffield plater's catalogue issued in the same year. The majority were skeletons constructed entirely of plated wire, at first in round section and from about 1800 oval and in flat ribbons with variously curved upper surfaces. The seven-barred pattern for containing six slices of toast was the most popular but a nine-barred pattern for eight slices and five-barred designs were made too. The bars rose from a rectangular or oval frame usually made from a strip of flat plate: the ends were sometimes slightly upturned. The central bar usually rose higher than the remainder, its apex fitted with a plain vertical ring handle. A ball foot at each corner was usual, but paw, scroll and bracket feet are to be found. Watson & Bradbury's series of pattern books illustrated 78 different designs between 1788 and 1815, in addition to many combined toast racks and egg frames.

Samuel Roberts of Roberts, Cadman & Co., in 1807 patented a folding toast rack requiring much less storage space than the usual pattern. The frame folded lengthwise on the lazy tongs principle, the wires that formed the bars rising from hinged junctions. These are stamped R C & CO PATENT. Almost immediately A. Goodman & Co., also of Sheffield, devised a folding toast rack that closed sideways, across the width of the frame. The apex of each bar was so hinged that unscrewing slightly a knob at each end of the base permitted the bars to shut together. The handle swivelled downward from the central bar.

From about 1820 more elaborate seven-barred toast racks became fashionable, their bases very shallow trays stamped from the solid plate and bordered with wide, elaborately designed mounts, such as the gadroon and shell pattern. These stood upon four shell and foliage feet with handles in a matching design. In some instances an oval plate with a low, raised border might be perforated with a band of leaf or shell motifs encircling several large medallions. Each bar consisted of three tall loops rising from decorative plaques in the plate.

At this time appeared the five-barred toast rack fitted lengthwise into an oval tray bordered with a deep, elaborately perforated gallery, on claw and ball feet. In some of these the bars were removable to facilitate cleaning, each being attached to the tray by means of a fly-nut concealed beneath. An invoice dated 1821 from Kirkby Waterhouse & Co., illustrated by Bradbury, shows that ' 1 Toast Tray with silver mountings and shield, silver handles and feet – strong' was sold for £1.4.0. This would retail at about £1.12.6.

From 1842 original toast rack designs could be registered at the Patent Office, thus securing three years' protection against piracy. Among the recorded examples was a toast rack registered in 1851 by Roberts & Halls. This had a wheat-stem column handle rising from an engraved oval tray with oblique bars rising from each side.

Toast racks combined with egg-cup frames were made in numerous designs. Early examples were complicated arrangements of round wire bars with a guard ring for an egg-cup at each corner. The majority were of the seven-bar pattern from about 1800 with a rectangular stand of solid plate. A five-bar type intended for a man's use had a guard ring for an egg-cup at each end.

# 22. Fish slices; asparagus servers; mazarines

The Duchess of Northumberland, in her *Diary* of the home-life of George III, recorded in April 1762 that 'Their Majesty's constant [dinner] Table at this Time was as follows: a soup removed with a large joynt of Meat and two other dishes such as a Pye or a boyl'd fowl. On the side table was a large joynt, for example, a large Sirloin of Beef cold and also a Boar's Head and a Sallad: 2nd Course always one Roast, one of Pastry and Spinage and Sweetbreads, Macaron, Scollopt Oysters, Whitebait or the like.' Under such royal approval whitebait became a fashionable dainty. Farington in his *Diary* many years later commented that 'the King sat at the head of the table and served the whitebait'. A special table accessory had already been devised by 1760 for its service, being listed at the London Assay Office as a fish trowel, the cost of assay being three-halfpence. Within a few years such fish trowels were being reproduced by the Sheffield platers. Quite apart from the whims of fashion, fish were important in the Georgian's diet and every country house possessed a 'fishing warren' of two or three well-stocked ponds to supply fresh fish for the table in a day when highly seasoned salted foods constituted a large proportion of winter provisions. When the host took on the duty of carving at table the tools for serving fish became important.

The trowel blade at first resembled a builder's mortar trowel, flatly triangular, its length about one-eighth less than its breadth, six being cut from a circular piece of fused plate. Each blade was handsomely perforated in a delicate all-over openwork pattern of foliated scrollwork and other fashionable motifs enclosed in a narrow border with square-cut edges. The perforations were made by the fly press, which removed the background of the design, leaving the pattern in solid, flat-surfaced silver. In some instances this was further ornamented by flat chasing. The disc was then cut into six sections, the points rounded off and the edges squared. The short edge of the blade was given a wavy outline, its curve being an arc of the original plate.

The slender handle was attached to this edge with a shell- or fan-shaped bracket.

The fish trowel was superseded in fashionable use during the 1770s by the less expensive fish slice, eight blades being cut from a circular plate. Such a scoop, finished with the left-hand edge bevelled, was used for serving prepared portions of fish, the perforations allowing surplus liquor to be strained off: for dividing large fish at table two matching slices were provided. Fish tabled at this time were usually boiled in heavily tinned copper fish kettles, covered and containing straining plates. The standard size was 21 inches long and eight inches deep.

Piercing in the fish slice was less elaborate than formerly, usually with repeats of such conventional motifs as lunettes, shells, semi-circles and vertical and horizontal pales. The bolster joining the blade and handle usually had a short up-curving shank ending in a tang for insertion into the handle. A silver ferrule fitted over the handle to prevent splitting whilst in use or being cleaned. Ivory hafts were fashionable, at first plainly turned, stained green and polished. Later the ivory was preferred in its natural colour and might be cylindrical or octagonal in section and tapering towards the blade. A smooth cap fitted over the end of the handle to conceal the riveted end of the tang: this was usually in silver. Handles of mother-of-pearl date from the early 1790s.

Fish server hafts in Sheffield plate resemble knife hafts and were stamped in two halves and invisibly soldered together: even with a magnifying glass it is difficult to detect the join. The central cavity was filled with shellac strengthened by the addition of powdered pumice. This was poured in whilst semi-liquid and the tang of the bolster inserted: when the cement had hardened the handle was securely fixed. Sheffield plate hafts occasionally copied the handles of contemporaneous spoons, attached by soldering.

The fish slice with a fish-shaped blade had become fashionable by 1780, and for the remainder of the century and until the 1820s this was the most common shape. Conventional piercing was usual, but there was often a central full-length design resembling the backbone and ribs of a fish. The blade might be chased with a fish, sometimes a pair crossed, and foliated scrollwork, with the surrounding plate cut away to form a pierced design. In Sheffield plate, however, the blade of the fish slice was more or less standardized to a fish-shaped blade with a border of pales following its outline and an oval central rosette. In a more costly design the pales themselves were bordered by a series of repeating curved piercings such as leaves and medallions.

Diamond-shaped blades were devised in the early 1780s. One popular pattern consisted of three rows of pales alternating with circles bordering the four edges while the centre was decorated with a single classic motif in flat-chasing.

Rectangular blades with rounded ends date from the mid-1790s to the early 1820s. Decoration was confined to outlining the blade with one or two u-shaped bands of simple geometric piercing, sometimes with the addition of some flat chasing. These blades were usually fitted with Sheffield plate hafts: some early examples had hafts of plain ivory.

Fish slice blades were symmetrical until about 1800 when designers introduced the shape later perpetuated in individual fish knives. This shape had been used for knife blades from Anglo-Saxon times. There was a cutting edge with a smoothly curved outline bordered by a flat-chased double line. The blunt edge was incurved with an undulating outline meeting the cutting edge at a blunt point. The centre of the blade was pierced with a simple motif and the field chased with flower and foliage designs. This shape, with slight variations of outline, continued fashionable until the end of the Sheffield plate period, in stout gauge plate after about 1820.

The collector of fish slices will notice the existence of examples with asymmetrical blades designed for use with the left hand so that the host could use both hands when dividing and serving large fish. But the most elaborate development, dating from about 1810, was the single fish server intended to lift small fish from the serving dish to the plate. This one-handed tool was constructed from a fish slice with a long bolster shank and a smaller handle and blade directly above it. The two were linked by a fixed lever hinging from front to rear in a slot cut in the bolster-shank and a spring attachment. By pushing the upper handle forward with thumb-pressure upon its scrolled terminal, the upper blade was lowered on to the larger blade to secure the fish whilst lifting it from dish to plate. This would be especially useful to the servant moving from plate to plate with the serving dish on his left arm.

By about 1820 the fish slice might be accompanied by a matching fork with four broad flat prongs and a curved base pierced with a motif matching that on the blade of the fish slice. Pairs were catalogued as fish carvers and might be associated with sets of fish table knives introduced to the table service in about 1815. By the late-1880s the fashionable fish slice blade was again symmetrical: these are in electro-plate and liable to be confused with earlier issues.

Some authorities believe that fish servers with springs were used also for the service of asparagus. But catalogues from 1790 illustrate and name the asparagus server as a large pair of bow-spring tongs with a pair of wide rectangular blades measuring about two-thirds the length of the bow. The blades were pierced all over in geometrical patterns and flat chasing when present was carried over to the outer surface of the bow.

Fish slices were used in association with the oval mazarine or fish drainer. This lavishly pierced plate is edged by a rim that rises sharply then extends horizontally so that it rests upon the bouge and rim of a deeper serving dish underneath.

The fish was brought from the kitchen in a fish kettle of boiling water to ensure that it was hot – hence the need to drain it at table. The mazarine plate for the service of fish was strong enough to stand up to the strain of carving and cleaning.

The heavy serving dish would measure between 12 and 24 inches in length and was about three times the weight of an accompanying mazarine; some were circular. The shaped rim was usually edged with reeding which in its turn might be encircled with knurled ornament, usually gadrooning. The dish without the mazarine could be used for serving game or meat.

Mazarine piercings are found in a wide variety of patterns. Motifs included scroll cartouches pierced with scrolls, arches and trellis work; shell and diaper work; diaper patterns of stars, diamonds, quatrefoils. Early nineteenth-century piercings included geometrical patterns of crosses, stars, lozenges and circles; scrolling foliage and rosettes. Until early in the nineteenth century they were catalogued as 'fish plates'. In Sheffield plate mazarines were invariably illustrated and listed in pattern books as fish plates and date from the 1780s.

At first each motif was pressed individually: by about 1800 motifs were hand pressed in small groups. After 1820 power operated machines did this work more speedily. The collector will find it easy to distinguish between these methods. By using plate fused with an exceptionally thick coating of silver on one side it was possible to add further enrichment by surface engraving. Such pierced motifs were arranged in geometrical patterns.

# 23. Waiters and trays

Waiters were described in 1661 as 'new-fashioned pieces of wrought silver plates, broad and flat, used in giving Beer, or other liquid things to save the carpet [table covering] or cloathes from drops'. Square or round, they were proffered by servants when performing small personal duties such as the handing of letters. They were not set down upon the table and may thus be differentiated from trays. The term salver may best be restricted to the style with a hollow pedestal stem. A silver tray was indispensable to every fashionable Georgian hostess for displaying her magnificent tea equipage of kettle and spirit lamp, teapot, pair of tea canisters, milk jug and sugar bowl. Known contemporaneously as a 'solid silver tea table', it might be circular, oval or rectangular.

For 'second best' and in households unable to afford solid silver, tables were graced with accessories in Sheffield plate. The earliest authenticated waiter, measuring 14 inches in diameter, with an expansive double cypher in the centre, bears an inscription on the reverse as described in Chapter 2. This is dated 'Feby 14th 1760'.

The Sheffield platers manufactured waiters and trays in profusion, the shapes following those designed by the fashionable silversmiths. The basic plate was rolled from copper alloyed with one-fifth its weight in brass to ensure rigidity. Throughout the period when Sheffield plate was customarily covered with silver on one side only the early waiter or tray was sometimes constructed from two sheets laid back to back and soldered together. The primary intention of this was to ensure that only silver was in view when the waiter carried by a standing servant was glimpsed from beneath by a person seated. Double sheets of plated copper were rarely used on articles other than such flat ware because of the increased cost.

More commonly, however, a single piece of copper plated on one side was used, the underside coated with tin, polished and burnished until to the casual eye it closely resembled the hue of Sheffield plate. This feature continued until about 1830. From the later 1760s the copper plate might be silvered on both sides of plain and lightly chased examples and fine quality work might be gilded. The layer of silver on the upper surface of a tray or waiter required to be thicker than normal to withstand constant wear.

In eighteenth-century work the raising and shaping of the border was accomplished with a hand operated swage block invented in 1762 (see Chapter 4). The border had to be passed through the swage block many times to complete the shaping raised in this way. From early in the nineteenth century, however, it became more usual to shape the waiter or tray, including the raised border, by means of drop hammers. This was the work of specialist factories who supplied the shaped blanks to platers in a small way of business. Bradbury's inventory of a stamping shop in 1775 refers to a '6-inch waiter mettle die' costing £1.10.0. The base of the plate was flat-hammered to ensure rigidity and a perfectly smooth surface capable of displaying a mirror-like brilliance when burnished. The flat hammer, with a pair of $2\frac{1}{2}$-inch convex faces, weighed about four pounds.

Waiters were shaped in styles resembling the sunken tops of the contemporaneous mahogany tripod tables known to collectors as piecrust or Chippendale. The Chippendale term is misleading, for silver waiters of this type exist struck with George I hallmarks, whereas the Chippendale designs were not published until 1754. The Sheffield platers elaborated the piecrust border with a series of cyma curves based on a circle or octagon, linked by six or eight relief motifs such as volutes, shells and fans. Such motifs applied to the borders of waiters and trays, shaped by stamping, consisted of two pieces of plate soldered back to back. The line of demarkation was imperceptible as the raw edges of the copper were concealed by the carefully burnished silver solder.

Decoration on the flat plate of the waiter was restricted at first to a crest or cypher – more rarely a coat of arms. This was engraved which meant that the manufacturer had to prepare for this contingency lest the engraving revealed underlying copper (see Chapter 5). When surface ornament was introduced it took the form of chasing. From the 1780s the early narrow borders were expanded gradually until by about 1815 the entire plate might be covered with chased pattern around a central reserve for the cypher or crest. Patterns consisted mainly of flowers, foliage and scrollwork: much less commonly birds were included. If chasing in high relief was introduced the fused silver coating needed to be thicker than usual to stretch without cracking under the hammer blows.

The earliest waiters in Sheffield plate were fitted with three or four spherical feet without surface ornament, a type that continued throughout the period. These feet were succeeded until the close of the century by naturalistic types such as the hoof, claw-and-ball, bracket, and volute in several patterns. As new styles of waiters developed the feet were merely adaptations of previous patterns so that specimens of the early nineteenth century may show any of a wide variety of spreading feet.

A pattern book now in the Victoria and Albert Museum, issued in 1792 by John Green, described as a plate worker of York Street, Sheffield, records that round and oval waiters were made in sizes of six to 10 inches rising by inches, and 12 to 30 inches rising by two inches. Design included, optionally, a shield of silver in the centre set in an engraved oval and silver edges. Prices for the 12-inch sizes with gadrooned edges were: round, 48s plus 10s extra for silver edges and 7s for silver shield; oval, 36s plus 7s and 5s. There was a trade discount of 55 per cent.

Trays in Sheffield plate until the 1790s were in the fashionable oval shape with narrow thread or beaded edges of silver and might be accompanied by pairs of matching waiters. Plates were usually plain, but collectors look for examples decorated with bright cut engraving, fashionable during the 1780s and 1790s. This decoration was possible only on thickly plated copper as the edges and points of the gouges used produced a delicate faceted effect, outlining flowers and foliage, ribbons and other motifs by cutting narrow channels with variously slanting sides. On such plate no separate silver shield was required for the engraved coat of arms. Unlike flat chasing, bright cut engraving is not discernible on the underside of the tray. A pair of beaded or reeded loop handles of slender section were fitted to the narrow ends from the late-1780s.

During the 1780s and early 1790s there was a vogue for rectangular trays in which the ends of the rim were extended to form a pair of hand-holds, shaped as scrolls, usually enriched with expansive honeysuckle or acanthus motifs in relief. These trays were hand-raised from the plate. Less expensively they were made with applied vertical pierced galleries edged with gadrooning which continued to the scrolls of the hand-holds.

Rims were made deeper from about 1800, thread and gadrooned edges being usual. At the same time the oval began to lose its regularity of outline, piecrust edges becoming fashionable, with the cyma motifs separated by fruiting vine, shells, acanthus leaves and other relief work applied to the deeply concave rim. Loop handles were elaborated to match.

Large rectangular trays with rounded corners date to the early nineteenth century with wider rims, often coarsely gadrooned and incorporating rococo embellishments. The handles, D-shaped and weighty, were enriched with scroll work and other relief ornament. Such handles were die struck from very thin silver plate in two hollow sections which were filled with a lead-tin alloy, joined with solder and the seam burnished. Tea tray borders soon acquired a florid ornament applied to deeply concave raised rims. Mounts with mask motifs were especially popular – large masks at the handle openings and several smaller versions on the long sides. The entire plate might be flat-chased in complicated scroll designs laden with flowers and foliage. The variety of patterns was huge. The Watson & Bradbury pattern books dating from 1788 to 1815 illustrate 96 waiters and 74 tea trays.

# 24. Inkstands

There is a sense of pleasant seclusion in closing the door of a room and then, with pen and paper, sitting at a comfortable desk and writing to an intimate friend. Many celebrated Georgians chose this attitude when having their portraits painted. Gainsborough in 1783 posed the 23-year-old William Pitt, then Chancellor of the Exchequer, standing at a writing table set out with a fashionable silver inkstand. This and other contemporaneous portraits show that three silver-mounted glass bottles were arranged symmetrically on the inkstand tray, the central inkpot flanked to the left by a pounce dredger and to the right by a quill-pen cleaner.

Only the rich could afford the luxury of writing table equipment in sterling silver. In more modest homes metals such as pewter and copper were used until the 1760s when Sheffield plate inkstands appeared on the market, the first of a long series of more than 1,000 patterns. The term inkstand was used by Matthew Boulton in about 1770 to distinguish them in his catalogues from the earlier standish with its glass containers placed loosely upon a flat dish.

Inkstands in Sheffield plate date from about 1760. The design consisted of a shallow, rectangular tray with plain rim, four low scroll feet and dished channels for quill pens and penknife extending the full width, back and front forming a raised platform between them for three flint-glass vessels containing ink, pounce and shot.

The glasses were a matching set, their purposes indicated by the shapes of their Sheffield plate tops. At first they were plainly cylindrical: then they were cut with wide, flat, vertical flutes and facet-cut on the shoulders. By 1770 the lower portion remained cylindrical, the shoulders showing a circuit of diamond cutting which became deeper by 1780. From this time vessels inserted in the perforated guard sockets might be in Bristol blue glass, usually with facet-cut shoulders. Square glass bottles with near-flat shoulders such as had been used on standishes by silversmiths for more than a century had become fashionable with Sheffield plate by 1790, their faces decorated with shallow diamond-cutting. The vessels were taller than formerly, vertically fluted to the shoulder which was cut with deep diamonds.

Inkstand glasses from about 1810 were heavier than formerly, despite an excise tax of 1s 6d a pound, and they were usually cut with a field of diamonds in deep relief. Shapes from about 1820 included urn, vase, melon, shell and sphere with short stems and circular feet. Boldly cut panels date from about 1830, with shallow base rings to fit guard sockets of the same height.

The Sheffield plate covers of the three glasses were made to match, usually plain and slightly concave. A smooth-faced collet was cemented to the vertical rim of the mouth of the glass vessel and the collar of the appropriate cover slipped over this. The edges of these pull-off covers were strengthened with applied mounting, plain and reed being the most popular. The inkpot cover was pierced with a hole large enough for easy dipping of the quill pen. At first this hole was provided with a small loose cover removed by a knob when one vessel was in use. The hinged cover dates from about 1815 and was usually domed with a finial: from 1820 double and triple domes were fashionable.

Ink until the mid-eighteenth century was a thick liquid made by the user from a fine powder containing gum arabic and often mixed with beer. Sediment and gum from this ink that accumulated on the nib of the quill required frequent removal. This was done by the use of small lead shot contained in a glass quill-cleaner, its cover pierced with three, four or five holes placed near to the rim and large enough to receive a quill or quills when not in use. In some instances quill-cleaner and ink-pot were combined as a single receptacle in which the ink was contained in a glass liner surrounded by lead shot. In such instances the central ink aperture in the cover was surrounded by three perforations for quills.

The pounce dredger contained pulverized gum sandarac, a resin derived from the North African arar tree. Dr Johnson defined this powder as 'pounce because it is thrown upon paper through a perforated box'. Contrary to common assumption pounce was not used for drying wet ink after writing. Its purpose was to prevent the ink from spreading into the absorbent writing paper and the script thus becoming blurred. The cover of the pounce dredger was pierced with small circular holes as in a caster, occasionally, from the 1790s, with pressed crosses in a balanced all-over design. Surplus sandarac, known colloquially as 'sand', was returned to the dredger by funnelling the paper over the concave lid. Following improvements in the surface of writing paper early in the nineteenth century by glazing it with a rolling machine, the pounce became superfluous. In 1820 Charles Lamb was able to record that 'the pounce boxes of our days have gone retrograde'.

The written words now required drying and, although blotting paper had been used in the days of parchment, 'writing sand' was sprinkled over the wet ink from the pounce pot. Fine sand for this purpose was obtained from the Isles of Scilly.

As blotting paper came into use the pounce pot was replaced on the inkstand by a wafer box containing thin adhesive discs about the size of a shilling. These were made from flour mixed with gum or gelatine and dyed, usually Chinese red. The box stood between the inkpot and the quill-cleaner. At first the cover might support a taper socket for use with sealing wax; by about 1820 a miniature chamber candlestick had become fashionable for this purpose. Specially made smokeless wax tapers were burned to melt the sealing wax without discolouring it with soot.

The Sheffield plate inkstand from about 1770 was a rectangular tray bordered with a pierced gallery and supporting three applied sockets or guard-rings, pierced to match and containing glass bottles. In some instances the galleries were very low and the guard-rings might then measure as much as four times their height. Narrow swaged wire encircled the outside of the base of the guard-rings assisting the solder in anchoring them firmly to the platform of the tray. The conventional rectangle was continued throughout the period accompanied by the oval shape from about 1770.

Canoe-shaped inkstands were high fashion between 1780 and the end of the century, but continued into Victorian days. At first they were designed with highly up-turned ends, the gallery pierced with vertical or horizontal pales, stars and circles. The guard-rings were high and sparingly pierced and some examples enriched with bright-cut engraving. The tray ends might be turned over and carried beneath to form loop handles. Joints in the plate were so perfectly worked that handles and stand appear to have been cut from a single piece of double-plated copper, although actually consisting of three pieces. Occasionally swing handles were fitted.

From about 1790 the canoe-shaped inkstand might be almost flat with tri-angular ends and low unpierced guard-rings decorated with bright-cut engraving. In another design a simple wire frame incorporated the guard-rings. An elaboration of the canoe-shape was designed with a double gallery: that is, a gallery in reverse encircled the base of the tray which supported a secondary deck with a pierced gallery and three pierced guard-rings. The canoe-shape continued into the nineteenth century, and from about 1815 might have two low guard-rings and a pair of inkpots with hinged covers in the shape of truncated cones. An early Victorian type held only a single large glass inkpot, cut all over with deep diamonds, and a pair of rests for steel pens.

Design variants ran into many hundreds: one firm alone was responsible for at least 70 patterns between 1788 and 1815. There was a long series of inexpensive inkstands built almost entirely from plated wires of various sections.

Octagonal inkstands with reeded borders date from the 1790s, but these are uncommon.

A fashionable novelty in Sheffield plate was the globe inkstand. This was often gilded to resemble those in sterling silver devised by John Robins who occupied workshops at St John's Court, Clerkenwell Green, London, from 1774 to 1808. The design was introduced in 1787 and within a few years Sheffield platers and factory silversmiths were competing with less costly versions, the majority measuring six to nine inches in height with the occasional foot-high giant.

The globe inkstand is constructed with a hollow body composed of two separate hemispheres. The lower section is fitted with a recessed plate cut with slots and circles to hold writing equipment. This is contained in a framework which may be supported on four outspreading scroll legs of sturdy plated wire, oblong or round in section and terminating in simple scroll feet. More commonly, however, the framework rests on a circular foot measuring about two-thirds the diameter of the globe, being shaped by spinning in the lathe and bordered with reeding. The four junctions of the frame with the horizon circle may be decorated with female or lion masks or, from about 1800, open flowers, shells, acanthus, honeysuckle and other motifs stamped in low relief from silver and filled with a lead-tin alloy, these being linked by pendant swags of drapery.

The globe was opened by touching a tiny ball rising from a pine cone, pineapple or acorn knop covering a hollow cylinder fitted to the upper curve of the astrolabe. This contained a patent lock incorporating a barrel spring and pulley, allowing the upper hemisphere to slide downward within the lower hemisphere. This revealed the writing equipment, usually consisting of two or three glass bottles, often in Bristol blue glass cut square with chamfered shoulders and fitted with plated covers, together with penknife, pencil and ivory tablets.

Anyone unfamiliar with the mechanism might find difficulty in opening or closing the globe as has occurred with some inherited examples. The flat horizon circle was made thick enough to conceal the joint around the centre of the globe when the inkstand was closed and was supported by four flat quadrants with reeded lower surfaces. These rose from a plain compressed ball knop. A short pillar rising from the apex of the knop supported the astrolabe circle.

A Sheffield plate pattern book of the mid-1790s illustrated an exceptionally massive example, 12 inches in height with a globe measuring $5\frac{3}{4}$ inches in diameter. The gadrooned frame was decorated with four lion masks around the horizon ring linked by swags of drapery. These were stamped from silver and filled with lead-tin alloy. It was supported on a spool stem, itself standing upon a six-inch square plinth containing a drawer and based on four ball feet. The sphere contained four matching bottles in blue glass cut with flat surfaces and mounted with lift-off covers of Sheffield plate, and also several items of writing equipment. The price was quoted as 105s. An example from the collection of the

Viscountess Wolseley is in the Victoria and Albert Museum. The majority of globe inkstands were much smaller and closely resembled the original version in silver.

Globe inkstands have been wrongly styled Pitt's globe inkstands. This name can only date from December 1806 when the cabinet-maker George Remington designed and patented globe writing desks and sewing tables following the design of the globe inkstand which by then had lost its popularity. The makers, Morgan & Sanders, Catherine Street, Strand, acquired the patent and named their globe writing desk after William Pitt, the prime minister who had died a few months earlier.

Small inkstands in a variety of patterns were made from about 1800 such as an oval tray containing inkpot and sand sprinkler, each in its pierced guard-ring. In some instances these were accompanied by a wafer box of Sheffield plate. The tray was supported on scroll or ball feet with a horizontal lyre-shaped handle projecting at the front. Cube-shaped inkstands achieved some popularity, having formerly been made in pewter of crowned-rose quality. The top plane of the cube lifted to disclose a covered inkpot: beneath were four small drawers.

Early in the nineteenth century were made the now rare Sheffield plate inkpots without stands and containing glass liners. They were catalogued at the time as ink stands and cost 4s 6d each at the factory, either plain or reeded. These were a pointed-dome shape with a flat base and a quill aperture at the apex. To ensure stability the base diameter was about equal to the height.

Inkstands from about 1810 were enriched with wider mounts, more elaborately designed as the years progressed. The ends of the rectangular tray might be cyma-shaped, sometimes with a pair of handles attached. The guard-rings might consist of gadrooned wirework shaped into three conjoined rings supported at the ends and centre by matching wire. By 1820 the front and back edges of the tray might display plain aprons, shell motifs at each end, and expansive corner feet. The platform was higher than formerly with a deep bouge all round. Paw and paw-and-foliage feet came into use at this time.

Ink caskets, sometimes gilt, date from the early 1820s. The design consisted of a circular flat box with a lift-off lid and the interior divided to hold a pair of circular inkpots in the centre and a pair of quill holders all in a glass liner, the intervening space filled with small lead shot. The lid was engraved with a crest or monogram: crests might be bogus. Another design, with a lift-off lid, contained only a pair of inkpots, for red and black ink: this might have four ball feet.

# 25. Snuff-boxes; patch-boxes and bonbonnieres; nutmeg graters

For more than a century and a half the snuff-box occupied the position in national life held by the cigarette case today. It was made in materials ranging from spectacularly lovely jewelled rock crystal and precious metals glittering with costly gems to the plebeian pewter. The rich man paid as much as a guinea an ounce for his favourite snuffs and the working man as little as threepence. The newly-rising middle-class Georgians turned to the silversmiths for snuff-box designs based on traditional good craftsmanship. These might be embossed, chased or engraved and enriched by treble-gilding with burnished high-lights: some were set with colourful gem-stones or sparkling pastes. Sizes ranged from the miniature for suspending from the fob or the chatelaine, through the pocket boxes to large boxes for table and mantelshelf.

Less expensive alternatives were the snuff-boxes in Sheffield plate. It has long been assumed that snuff-boxes were among the first articles made by Bolsover when he started his factory at Baker Hill, Sheffield. These, however, were large circular boxes with vertical sides and pull-off covers – most unsuitable for the pocket and it is most improbable that they were so used. The first essential of a snuff-box is that box and lid are entirely snuff-proof and air-tight to preserve aroma. The fashionable snuff-taker carried his snuff-box in his left-hand pocket. When it was withdrawn he gave the cover three smart taps near the hinge. He then lifted the lid and placed a pinch of snuff on the back of the left hand or on the thumb-nail and inhaled. More usually the snuff was carried directly to the nose. The snuff-box was tapped to attract the powder away from the box rim so that opening produced no cloud of dust: three taps were considered lucky. Women snuff-takers usually took their snuff from a tiny spoon or nose shovel, usually included among the fitments of the Georgian etui. This device kept the finger nails free from discolouring dust and excluded other people's fingers from one's powder. The snuff-spoon was of silver, about two inches long, with a shallow oval bowl: some were shaped as ladles or shovels.

Sheffield plate snuff-boxes were usually rectangular, but other forms such as oval were made. Those intended for everyday use required to be made from strong metal to prevent warping whilst being carried in the pocket. From 1780 the cover-mount might contain a skilfully decorated Staffordshire enamel. After about 1790 the sides tended to be concave or rounded in bombé form, depth varying from $\frac{3}{4}$ to $1\frac{1}{4}$ inches. The pointed oval or shuttle-shape had a late eighteenth-century and early nineteenth-century vogue, but these have proved less enduring than the plain, straight-hinged rectangle. Snuff-boxes normally contained no more than a two-day supply of snuff as body heat drove off the moisture, resulting in a dry, unpleasant flavour.

Fashionable snuff-boxes in sterling silver from about 1800 were given heavy cast lids, elaborately decorated with pictorial subjects in high relief. This feature made it possible to distinguish silver from Sheffield plate at a passing glance. The Sheffield platers then competed by using dies sunk from the recently improved tool steel which was capable of embossing clear-cut impressions such as pictorial scenes, with minor motifs on the back such as baskets of fruit in conventional scrollwork. These were much lighter in weight than the silver-smith's originals. Silver snuff-boxes could receive intricate engine-turned surface ornament, impossible on Sheffield plate without revealing the under-lying copper – hence the insatiable demand for engine-turned snuff-boxes until about 1850.

Until the introduction of double plating in the late 1760s interiors of Sheffield plate snuff-boxes were gilded, tinned or lined with a thin veneer of highly polished tortoiseshell, usually blonde, to prevent oxides forming on the copper and discolouring the snuff and also adversely affecting added perfuming in-gredients such as mustard, ginger, jasmine, ambergris and orange flowers. Treble gilding remained brilliantly radiant.

Tortoiseshell was used variously as lining, base and cover of Sheffield plate snuff-boxes, fashion demanding light-coloured shell until about 1800. The shell of the hawksbill turtle (*Testudo imbricata*) was used for finer work. The shell grows upon the surface of the turtle's external skeleton from which it was separated by heating the entire shell. The epidermal plates then lifted from the bone and were levered off with a long knife. A turtle provided 13 large hornlike scales known as blades and 25 smaller scales termed feet, all brilliant, finely marked and semi-transparent. They are mainly composed of a substance resembling gelatine in its chemical character, with a small quantity of inorganic matter. This consists of cells which are naturally compressed, but, under the influence of heat and potash, become spherical. The shell then becomes plastic and may be shaped, pressed or moulded, as desired, these forms being retained when cold. It can be welded under pressure of hot irons. The shell was approved for its texture and translucent hues, and the fact that it seldom cracks or warps. As snuff does not cling to its smooth surface it proved ideal for snuff-boxes.

Tortoiseshell formed a good background for silver and lids of snuff-boxes and bonbonnieres might be decorated in this way. This was known contemporaneously as inlaid tortoiseshell: more recently it has been included in the general term piqué more exactly restricted to patterns of metal dots. The silver was used in a pure state without the addition of any alloy. The metal was thus soft enough to be rolled or beaten to paper thinness. Cut to shape it was pressed upon the surface of tortoiseshell heated by court quality charcoal. The foil was hand-worked into position. The contraction of the tortoiseshell in cooling held it firmly in place without cement which would mar the clarity of the blonde shell. The surface was made perfectly smooth by scraping away superfluous tortoiseshell, then polishing and burnishing the whole. The silver was so soft that it could be shaped over embossed tortoiseshell, but in this case a clear varnish adhesive was used. This is rare on Sheffield plate.

The underside of a snuff-box was often press-ornamented with flowers, foliage and scrollwork. A very rare series of snuff-boxes in Sheffield plate, adapted from silver originals, had tortoiseshell covers set with figures in landscapes. Another series illustrated Aesop's Fables adapted from designs on Chelsea porcelain. The sides of such boxes were in Sheffield plate. In pre-1770 examples strips of thin silver, shaped by passing through a steel swage, were hard-soldered to ribbons of plate, the silvered side forming the box interior.

By far the greater proportion of remaining snuff-boxes in Sheffield plate are rectangular and severely plain, design including a five-lug hinge running the entire width. Edges and corners are usually pocket-worn, revealing the copper. A popular decoration on otherwise plain snuff-boxes was a cartwheel copper penny dated 1796, soldered to the cover and close-plated to match the box. The pennies were minted by Matthew Boulton at his Soho works and it has been assumed that these boxes were made by his firm. Another design has a silver plate rubbed into the lid and engraved with the name of the original owner.

Bonbonnieres or comfit boxes were devised as gifts for ladies, but were also carried by many men. These contained small breath-sweetening comfits. Linings other than silver or tortoiseshell might give the comfits an unpleasant taste. These small bonbonnieres closely resemble patch-boxes. From the mid-eighteenth century similar boxes might be used to contain tiny sponges soaked in aromatic vinegar. Sir Ambrose Heal's collection of trade cards, now in the British Museum, illustrate several such 'spunge boxes'.

Patch-boxes, often mistakenly catalogued as snuff-boxes, date from the earliest period of Sheffield plate. They were made still earlier in precious metals and usually jewelled. They were often hingeless with pull-off covers: air-tight fitting was not essential as there was no powder to escape. Some authorities are inclined to classify circular boxes measuring about 2½ inches in diameter as patch-boxes. This use was unlikely as even a very small box would contain an adequate supply of patches for any occasion. The lid might be fitted with a steel mirror.

Splendid colourful effects could be displayed on snuff-box or bonbonniere covers by setting them with English hard stones such as veined agate, variegated marble, blue john and so on. These formed backgrounds to perforated designs, flat and in relief, worked from paper-thin silver and harnessed to the stone. The silver was cut into intricate patterns incorporating figures, birds, animals, flowers and foliage enclosed in scrollwork cartouches or forming all-over scenic subjects. These contrast splendidly with the colourful stone. In most instances the cover was inset with a single stone, sometimes with a mosaic pattern of several stones. The box and mount were in Sheffield plate.

Excellently finished double boxes, common enough in silver and pewter, are occasionally found in Sheffield plate. These were meant to contain two qualities of snuff when fitted with a pair of inner lids hinging from the ends of the box. Sometimes both base and top were fitted with hinged covers, a horizontal partition separating the box into two containers, one for snuff, the other for comfits. These were often shuttle shaped. In a rectangular pattern the box was divided centrally with two lids hinging from the top edge of the vertical partition.

Essential to well-to-do Georgians was a pair of large table snuff-boxes, sometimes gilded. One was handed with the wine, the other stood on the parlour table or mantelshelf. A tiny scoop was included for guests to replenish their own personal supply. The majority of table snuff-boxes in Sheffield plate were circular with lift-off covers and measuring from four to six inches in diameter. A popular design consisted of a hemisphere supported on a trumpet-shaped foot and with a domed and finialled lift-off cover.

Pocket nutmeg graters came into popular use during the last quarter of the seventeenth century when freshly ground spice gave zest to many foods and drinks. Mulled ales and wines, hot negus, punch and toddy were rarely taken without a sprinkle of nutmeg. Like highly flavoured comfits the spice was welcome, too, as a breath-sweetener.

Nutmeg graters were made in silver, ivory, bone, hard-wood and, from the 1760s, in Sheffield plate. Their heyday was during the hot toddy period, about 1780 to the 1840s: few existing Sheffield plate examples date earlier than this. So emphatically was the nutmeg associated with toddy that a popular Regency series of graters were made in the shape of rum and whisky kegs.

Nutmeg graters in Sheffield plate for the most part were made by garret masters employing only members of their own families. These graters were so designed that they could be constructed from flat plate, requiring little more labour than cutting and bending and the soldering of joints that were made invisible from the outside by vigorous burnishing. Spun units could be bought from the factory platers.

Among the earliest of nutmeg graters in Sheffield plate were those with heart-shaped boxes, a form fashionable in silver from the late seventeenth century. The steel grater fitted into a heart-shaped frame hinging immediately beneath the cover on the same seven-lug hinge. The outer lid was slightly convex and swaged with a reeded rim. The body was shaped into a heart from a single strip of single-sided plate, soldered vertically and tinned within. Another series of heart-shaped graters were made with top and bottom lids, each swinging on a projecting three-lug hinge. One lid opened to reveal a permanently fixed steel grater: the other gave access to the nutmeg. In many of these the perforations were drilled in concentric heart-shaped designs. Circular, oval, rectangular and square boxes were made to this double-lidded design. Those double-plated date from the 1780s and the presence of a blued grater suggests a date later than 1800.

Small egg-shaped nutmeg graters were common during the fourth quarter of the century: thereafter they tended to become larger. This pattern unscrewed into two sections, the lower usually about twice the depth of the upper. A circular grater was fitted into the lower rim by pressure. Surfaces were usually smooth with the exception of swaged ribs encircling the screw joint. Early examples were hand-raised from the plate by garret masters and the rims thickened deeply enough to take the threads for screwing the parts together. Others were factory-spun and bought by garret masters for finishing. In spun examples vertical marks caused by the pressure of the wooden tool and circular marks caused by revolving in the lathe remained visible on the interior surfaces. Associated with the egg-shaped nutmeg graters were acorn designs with slip-on covers.

Another popular small design was the oval or cylindrical box with slip-on interchangeable lids, top and bottom. The upper lid might be slightly domed to house the nutmeg as well as giving access to a fixed grater, the lower one could be opened to release the powdered spice. In a series of somewhat larger square or rectangular nutmeg graters the lids, top and bottom, were hinged but the grater itself was rigid. The lower lid, which required opening carefully, was extended a little beyond the box at the end away from the hinge for easy handling. When the box was closed the hinges were virtually invisible, the lower lid being designed to open at right angles and no further. Typically the body of such a box was strengthened by the addition of a band of plate encircling the interior of the upper lid, the hinges being concealed inside the box in a narrow box-like projection extending the length of the lid.

Most of these nutmeg graters were plain, but some were decorated with bright-cut engraving, giving an all-over scintillating effect. In another series, outwardly similar, and dating from the 1790s, the lid opened to reveal a steel grater fitted into a plated frame hinging to the right and slightly beyond the vertical. This design is found too with an oval or shuttle-shaped box.

A different design was the long grater consisting of a round or flattened cylinder. In this style the grater was set in one side of the cylindrical tube and the lid closed lengthways. This was hinged at the bottom, while at the top a second hinged section fitted over the top of the cylinder. In some instances a third hinge permitted the base to be opened also, so that the nutmeg could be more easily grated, with base, cover and top lying flat.

The urn-shaped version dated from about 1780. This was oval on plan and split down the sides from the rim to the square or round foot where the sides were hinged. The oval lid was domed, with a narrow strengthening rim and a ball finial. Lid and foot had three-lug hinges. The sides were shaped from double-plated copper; the foot and stem cast and close-plated; the cover shaped by pressing. When opened vertically a steel grater was revealed, shaped to follow the outline of the urn.

The table nutmeg grater, either canoe-shaped or half-cylindrical, fitting into a frame with a semi-circular handle at one end, enabled the nutmeg to be powdered more speedily. Accompaniment of the home or tavern toddy bowl, this resembled a kitchen grater, four to ten inches in length, with each end covered, the lower cover being hinged to permit removal of the ground spice. The blue steel grater perforations formed a pattern of concentric circles and might be protected by a sliding cover of double-sided Sheffield plate.

The frame was usually rimmed with gadrooned or reeded mountings: in small examples the frames were decorated across their entire width. There might be an ornamental motif in the centre of the bow. In others a cylindrical steel grater was set in plated rims, the side pieces continuing over the top to form a semi-circular handle. A very rare early-nineteenth-century type resembles a rectangular cricket bat set in a wire frame extended at one side and shaped to form a handle.

One collection of more than 100 nutmeg graters examined was found to contain no duplicates and none, either in silver or Sheffield plate, engraved with a crest. Many were monogrammed or initialled, however, suggesting that those who drank the more costly wines did not require the nutmeg's aromatic flavour.

The rasping unit of the grater consisted of a series of small protruberances roughly broken into the steel plate by punched holes. In early Sheffield plate nutmeg graters the rasp was usually framed in plated copper in such a way that it would lie snugly within the body of the box, resting upon a narrow ribbon of plate soldered to, and encircling, the interior rim. Hammered iron sheet was used until the 1770s. Then rolled steel came into use. These rasps were thinly coated with tin to prevent rust, but friction of the nutmeg eventually removed this. French plating was even less permanent.

The rolled steel used for graters from the early 1790s was annealed in a bed of hot charcoal about two feet deep, the lower part being in a state of incandescence while the heat gradually lessened towards the upper layer. This produced conditions suitable for the development of oxide colours. After removal from the fiery charcoal the steel was hardened by being plunged into raw whale oil and then vigorously rubbed with an oil-soaked pad of beaver felt. This process surfaced the steel with a hard blue film capable of resisting the friction of the nutmeg. Signs of scaling are by now often visible, but numerous rasps in silver boxes bearing hallmarks of the late 1790s are still in excellent condition. Perforations were made in this steel by raising small hemispheres with a fly-press in such a way as to leave a perfectly flat ground: each hemisphere was then broken by a hand tool, giving a jagged edge.

This was specialist work for the platers appear to have bought steel graters by the sheet, cutting and shaping the metal as required. Many an old rasp shows severed perforations around the edge, usually concealed by the plated metal frame.

# 26. Buttons

English costume buttons until the time of Elizabeth I were purely ornamental: garments were fastened by aiglets or hooks and eyes, or by pins or girdles. Tudor portraits display dresses with buttons sewn in rows and so close together as almost to touch. From the 1570s the wealthy fastened their outer clothes with buttons of jewelled gold. By the end of the century buttons of less precious metals had become fashionable and a few years later more than 40 master button-makers were established in the City of London making buttons of silver, pewter, tin and brass. Hallmarks were struck conspicuously on the face of silver buttons until about 1720 when they were concealed at the back. This, naturally, had made them unfashionable and few silver buttons of an earlier date are known. Early in the eighteenth century legislation made it illegal for buttons to be worn unless they were made of precious metal or covered with textile twists. Metal buttons were, of course, outmoded until this restriction was removed in the late 1740s. Jonas Hanway in 1753 recorded 'the new fashion of metal buttons'. In the following year the importation of buttons was prohibited.

By this time Thomas Bolsover had discovered fused plate: with the removal of the restrictions concerning metal buttons he at once began the manufacture of Sheffield plate buttons. This branch of the trade quickly flourished, particularly in Birmingham where button-makers had been concentrated for more than a century.

*Sketchley's Birmingham Directory*, 1767, described the local button-making trade as very extensive, 'and is distinguished under the following Heads viz. Plated, Gilt, Silvered, Lacquered and Pinchbeck'. By 1770 more than 80 master button-makers were established, a number increased during 1783 by at least a dozen specialists in Sheffield plate stamped buttons following the expiry of Richard Ford's patent for shaping buttons by a die stamp without the hazard of splitting the metal. This gave form to the cap of the button, a separate hand-press giving relief to the ornament. The idea had been anticipated by

Matthew Boulton who in 1782 had established the Matthew Boulton Button Company.

An Act of 1796 regulated and defined the various qualities of buttons, specifically laying down that 'plated buttons shall be made out of copper to which plate silver has been previously affixed by fusing and rolling the sheet'. This prevented silvered or close plated buttons, of poor endurance, being passed off as Sheffield plate. The Act laid down, too, that on double gilt buttons the 'gold shall be equally spread upon their upper surface exclusively of their edges, in the proportion of ten grains to the surface of a circle twelve inches in diameter and in that of treble gold shall amount to fifteen grains in the same proportion'. Treble gilt buttons were sold under a guarantee of permanency for seven years. *The Book of English Trades*, 1815, records that the wearing of buttons covered with cloth was prohibited, penalties being very severe, and that the laws prohibiting the importation of foreign buttons had not yet been repealed.

Sheffield plate buttons were made in huge quantities during the scarcity of precious metals due to the Napoleonic wars. Officers' uniform buttons, formerly of 18-carat gold or gilded silver, now might be of treble-gilded Sheffield plate. The colour tone of this heavy mercury gilding could be distinguished from gilded silver buttons only by an expert. Gilded silver buttons, hollow or raised, had been exempt from hallmarking since 1739. In a later Act of 1790 they were described as 'buttons to be affixed to or set on any wearing apparel and solid sleeve buttons'.

Collectors will find little difficulty in attributing approximate dates to Sheffield plate buttons by close inspection of the manufacturing processes. Buttons are also grouped according to the ornament displayed, and these may be more numerous than a cabinet of coins.

Hunting buttons might display a fox mask or other trophy in relief with the name of the hunt engraved around the edge. A set of hunting buttons consisted of 12 medium-size, six large and six small. These were usually flat-faced and engraved with named portraits of individual hounds, one button showing a huntsman. Sets of racing buttons are known, mostly of the Regency period: excellent shooting and cockfighting buttons date from about 1790. Plain flat-faced buttons were sold upon which local engravers could add designs and inscriptions to commission. A thicker layer of silver than normal was applied to flat-faced buttons.

Charles Dickens devoted one of his early magazine articles to the subject of sporting buttons. He wrote: 'There is a series of buttons, gilt or silvered, which one may see as one would so many pictures – that sort of badge called "sporting buttons". Members of a hunt or fancy sporting association distinguish themselves by wearing these miniature pictures: here is a covey of partridges with almost every feather indicated in the highest finish; there a hound clearing a hedge; now a group of huntsmen and pack; and again, a fishing net meshes its prey; or the listening stag or bounding fawn.'

Livery buttons were usually decorated with crests in high relief, but others were engraved with a coat of arms or crest. Even the three rows of tiny globes that decorated the page's jacket might each be engraved with a crest or cypher. Private coachmen and footmen wore convex buttons: other servants flat-topped buttons. In identifying armorial buttons *Fairbairn's Book of Crests*, 1905, proves invaluable. It is emphasized in the introduction that details of the illustrations may not always agree with the actual blazoning. Army and navy uniform buttons with badges in relief are found in Sheffield plate: these were worn by officers: buttons for the men were in brass. Designs in relief were innumerable and included the heads of royalty, naval and military heroes, political figures and other celebrities.

The leading button dealers in London were Firmin & Co., established in the reign of Charles II and still in business. One of their old bills prices 58 plated buttons for coats bearing the crest of the 13th Regiment at 1s 8d a dozen. Princess Charlotte's livery buttons made by this firm in 1816, engraved with her arms, were as large as five-shilling pieces.

The shaping of early plated buttons was carried out by hand processes. Suitable discs were cut from thin metal, plated on one side only, by means of punches on a wooden block covered with a thick plate of lead. Each blank was hammered into the shape of a button cap with a progressively deeper series of steel punches and dies. The rough cap was annealed from time to time to make it more ductile. Finally the decorative impression was struck with a fly press.

Wood or bone moulds were inserted into early buttons to provide solidity. Their manufacture was a special branch of the button trade. A log of hard wood was cut across the grain into suitable slices. The moulds were cut from this by a bow saw operated by a woman piercer. Very small moulds were turned from a wooden rod on a small lathe. The mould was drilled with four vertical holes through which cat-gut was threaded to form crossed loops which served as a shank. The space between the cap and the mould was filled with a hard composition preventing accidental flattening of the relievo and making the button firm and solid. The cap was then placed downward in a shallow dish of sand over a chafing dish of burning charcoal. When the cement melted in the cap, the mould was slipped into position. After cooling the edge of the cap was lapped over the mould. The face of the button was then burnished.

This tedious process continued until 1783 when Ford's patent die stamp for button-making was thrown open to all. This gave form to the cap of the button by a single fall of the hammer, the die being so formed that by being cut deeper than the thickness of the metal it was turned up all round the rim. This enabled it to be lapped over the body of the Sheffield plate underplate containing the shank.

*The Book of English Trades* illustrates such a stamp with the description: 'The machine by which buttons are stamped is well illustrated in the plate. The man stands in a place sunk into the floor, by which he is nearer on a level with the place on which his dies stand. By means of a single pulley he raises a weight, to the lower part of which is fixed another die; he lets the weight fall down on the metal which effects his object' – that is, shaping the button cap. Devices in relief were then raised with a hand-operated fly-press. After the invention of a harder tool steel in 1793 the relief work was more meticulously finished than formerly. The fused plate used for caps pressed with designs required the silver on the copper to be rather thicker than for plain buttons.

From about 1770 moulds began to be replaced by metal underplates on Sheffield plate buttons. These were shallow blanks made in the same manner as the cap, but much flatter and undecorated. A wire shank was soldered to the underplate. Cap and underplate were then jointed with solder and cleaned on the lathe.

Buttons made by locking together the edges of cap and underplate were the invention of William Saunders of Birmingham who patented the process in 1823. The hollow space between the two units was filled with cardboard or cloth. Buttons were made in this way almost entirely after the expiry of the patent in 1838.

The shanking of buttons was an important process as the length of their life depended upon it. Eventually specialist workshops run by master-men were established. A wire loop was soldered to the underplate of the early hand-punched button, each individually attached by blow-pipe and flux. The two ends of the loop were merely brought together. Since the point of contact was small there was always danger of a breakaway in use.

Such buttons were made for about 10 years until 1780 when an improved method of shanking was evolved. The ends of the wire were continued into two short flat extensions, thus providing a large attachment area with its consequent greater safety. These early wire loops were made from hand-drawn wire, recognized by not being perfectly round: it was also of finer gauge than that used on nineteenth-century buttons. Shanks tended to be oval rather than circular as in later buttons.

A more speedy method of shanking dates from about 1800. Each shank was temporarily attached to its button by a tiny wire clamp resembling a pair of spring sugar tongs, and a small quantity of resin and solder placed on the attachment area. A gross of these were laid on an iron plate and heated until the solder ran, fixing the shank to the button. The heat from this process oxidized slightly the surface of the button which was cleaned by dipping quickly into dilute nitric acid.

Mechanization was speeding up production during the late 1820s. Sir Edward

Thomason in his *Diary* for 1830 recorded that the silver and Sheffield plate button room in his Birmingham factory contained machinery for forming and burnishing buttons, a machine for engraving buttons and one for making button shanks. Not until the late 1830s were shanks made automatically by machinery and levelled at the joint. Thomason possessed more than 1,000 different pairs of dies for stamping arms, crests, service badges and servants' livery buttons.

# 27. Wire-work

Among the most ingenious products of the Sheffield plate manufacturers was work in interlaced wires such as cake baskets, fruit dishes and sugar basins lined with dark blue flint-glass, a background that contrasted handsomely with the lustre of the metal. These wires were made round, half-round, square or triangular in section and sometimes ribbed. They may be grouped into four identifiable chronological periods.

The earliest plated wire, dating from about 1760, was made from thin copper strip fused with a film of silver and then hand-wrought into a tube seamed along its length. The surface of the wire was undulating and close inspection will reveal the joint in the metal. Its finish was poor and cleaning proved the impermanence of the silver coating.

This unsatisfactory wire was eventually discarded in favour of a rigid, seamless wire with fewer surface undulations. This was made under George Whateley's patent of November 1768. The specification required a rod of copper, slightly alloyed with brass, measuring about four feet in length by one inch in diameter and pointed at one end. This was wrapped around with a strip of rolled silver. Copper and silver were fused together by fluxing with borax and making them red-hot over a clear charcoal fire. The plated rod was gradually cooled and boiled in a solution of alum. To extend it into wire it was passed through a series of heavy steel blocks pierced with holes of diminishing sizes from one inch to the desired diameter of the wire. These blocks were fitted into a draw-bench operated by a large windlass powered by eight youths. The pointed end of the rod was inserted into the largest hole and gripped by a pair of wrought-iron pincers with serrated jaws, tightened by pressure from a looped rope extending horizontally from the vertical windlass which had four levers. The great pressure forced the rod through the hole, which was occasionally dressed with beeswax, gradually reducing its diameter and increasing its length. This process was repeated through successive holes, alternating with annealing, until the rod extended into wire. Finally, it was cleaned with dilute acid and burnished.

Whateley's patent was improved in the early 1780s by Wilks & Moteram, former employees of Matthew Boulton, Birmingham, but the basic fault, a slight irregularity, was only overcome when the drawing process was improved in about 1800. This was achieved by introducing a draw-bench powered by one man operating a winch. A regulating fly wheel ensured that the plated rod moved smoothly through the draw-plates instead of in fits and starts.

Plated wire drawing became a specialized trade during the 1790s. In Sheffield, Dixon, Hallam & Hudson established wire-drawing workshops in about 1793 and Eadon, Kibble & Weaver at 72 Holles Street in the same year, moving to a larger factory in 1805. Patten & Co., Norfolk Street, established short-lived wire-drawing workshops in 1805. Birmingham supported two plated wire-drawers: Partridge & Jones, later W. Partridge, Price Street, 1793 to 1825, and the Swingler family, also of Price Street, 1805 to 1839.

Table ware was constructed from these wires by cutting them into appropriate lengths, curving them as required and inserting them between the rim and base. Holes were drilled in rim and base to receive them and soldering made them secure. By 1790 each wire was given a single sharp curve making a hair-pin shaped unit: early in the nineteenth century they began to resemble elongated figure 8s. The sides of a cake dish, for example, would be composed of perhaps 50 such curves ranged side by side. By 1815 fashion preferred designs in which a single length of wire was shaped in a continuous curve to form a single pattern. Such a unit was soldered at intervals to the lower surface of the rim and the upper surface of the base ring, but without the costly drilling.

Collectors should beware of plated wire-work cake, dessert and sweetmeat baskets in period styles made by twentieth-century copyists. Round wires only are found in this series and the soldering lacks the experienced care of the old Sheffield platers.

Fruit and cake baskets with wire-work sides and foot rings were fashionable from about 1790. Designs were adapted from those made by silversmiths during the previous 20 years. Oval and measuring about 14 inches long, the basket had a solid base supported on an oval foot ring, usually in wire-work, but sometimes in deep plate, solid or pierced with one or two rows of vertical pales. The rim might be wide and everted or near vertical, pierced and chased and encircled with a wire strengthening edge. The swing handles, semi-circular, widened to the centre. In some less costly examples the rim consisted only of strong wire with a pair of hinges attached to it for the swing handle and with a simple ornament soldered to each end. Early swing handles were solid, but by 1795 openwork designs were fashionable, such as a pair of flat wires spaced with balls or other ornament.

A long series of baskets were constructed of flat wire, some with pairs of wires in various sections twisted together. The flat interior of a basket was often engraved with a coat of arms or cypher. Those intended for fruit and liable to become acid-stained were usually gilded over the silver to minimize the cleaning that would wear away the silver.

By 1805 rectangular table baskets were fashionable. These measured about 12 inches in length with solid dished bases raised from the plate. The hair-pin units were closely spaced and reduced to a narrow band. At about this time solid handles were revived: as an alternative there might be a pair of vertical units joined by a flat horizontal strut usually decorated and with a central reserve for engraving a crest or cypher. Wide shell and gadroon mounts date from about 1815.

A Sheffield plater's catalogue issued in about 1812 illustrated a cake basket with a deep solid base supporting sides composed of hair-pin wires all curved outward; the ribbed foot rim was raised on four ball feet. With silver mounts this retailed at about 72s 6d.

By then the blue glass lining might extend above the rim of the wire-work vessel: from about 1820 the glass rim might be cut with deep scallops.

The boat or shuttle shaped wire basket with pointed ends and a high wire-work foot dates from the early 1790s. Later came the canoe-shape with uprising ends and the rim pierced with a border of vertical pales. In some designs wire units were grouped in threes to suggest leaf forms incorporating round and flat wires: the straight centre 'vein' was flat and broader at the base than the pair that flanked it.

Round baskets without handles, intended for fruit, date from about 1800. Here single strands of wire rose vertically from a flat solid base, being encircled mid-way by a strengthening wire. Such a vessel was usually supported by a deep, solid foot ring. A canoe-shaped example illustrated in a catalogue of 1793 was priced at two guineas. By 1800 fashionable circular fruit baskets, about nine inches in diameter, were made with everted rims edged with beading. From about 1810 a popular design in flat wire ribbed on the outer surface consisted of a hemispherical vessel supported by a high trumpet-shaped foot. Fruit dishes were made, too, oval and circular with boldly everted bouges, the wires arranged trellis fashion between plain or ornamented rims.

Sugar baskets were made of wire-work with vase-shaped bodies and deep rims of solid plate which might be left plain or encircled with chased or pierced ornament. Supported on a slender stem rising from a circular foot such a vessel would be fitted with a blue glass liner and dated from about 1790. It was rivalled a few years later by the design with a boat-shaped body. By 1800 the body rim might be octagonal and the foot shaped to match. Covered sugar vases with spool stems set on square plinths date from about 1810 with rims deeper than formerly. Similar but larger vessels with urn-shaped bodies were used for the service of sweetmeats.

Epergnes constructed almost entirely from plated wire are described in Chapter 15.

# 28. Miscellaneous

*Charcoal braziers* for the table were in great demand by smokers before the days of friction matches. Design consisted of a low-footed bowl with a wide pierced rim, held slightly above table level by a tripod with three short legs: claw and ball or double scroll were usual but small buns of ebony or hard wood were often used. In most instances the brazier was fitted with an almost horizontal handle of wood. This stood upon a tray which held a pair of small ember tongs used to lift a piece of glowing charcoal to the tobacco in the smoker's clay pipe. Court charcoal was prepared from flexible woods stripped of their bark which might crackle and fly whilst burning. Such charcoal required little draught, yet emitted an intense smokeless heat until entirely consumed. A small blowpipe was used to revive the fire if necessary.

*Cucumber slicers* of Sheffield plate were very possibly the notion of George Stephenson (1780–1848). The celebrated locomotive engineer lived, after his second marriage in 1819, at Tapton House, a few miles south of Sheffield in the neighbourhood of his principal coalmines. Stephenson was an ardent gardener and counted among his horticultural interests the propagation of straight cucumbers. This he achieved by maturing each cucumber in a glass tube measuring about a foot in length and with a diameter of about two inches. These somewhat resembled test tubes, with a slight curvature on one side and with one end sealed with a knob. In clear moulded glass they cost 1s 9d a pound at the glasshouse and 2s 4d in flint-glass. Cucumber glasses could have been made at any one of the several glasshouses near Sheffield.

Stephenson amused himself and puzzled visiting celebrities by serving them with thinly sliced raw cucumbers of uniform size and thickness instead of the fashionable cucumber stew containing 'slices as thick as a crown piece' and of unpredictable size and shape from the distorted cucumbers then grown.

The Sheffield plate cucumber slicer consisted of a horizontal tube supported on a sturdy stand with a baluster stem and a round foot weighted with loom. The silver plating served to protect the salad from the unpalatable flavour of acidic cucumber juice upon base metal. Fitted to one end of the tube was the steel blade razor thin which could be revolved on a spindle operated by a hand crank. The blade could be removed quickly for cleaning by detaching a small thumbscrew. Cucumber slicers in silver and ivory have been recorded.

*Hot-water plates* were made throughout the Sheffield plate period. Early examples were hand-worked throughout. From about 1815 the upper and lower parts were stamped, the lower section fitted with a screw-cap filler. From this period, too, dates the now rare example in Sheffield plate fitted with a dish of the good quality white earthenware known as pearl-ware, decorated with blue transfer printing under the glaze. The mark of Josiah Spode II has been noted impressed in some fractured examples. Thomas Griffiths, a plater of Bradford Street, Birmingham, in the 1840s and later made 'stamped hot-water plates, some with earthen plates'.

*Punch and toddy ladles* in Sheffield plate exist in very large numbers. Punch drinking so captured the imagination and palate of the Georgians that puncheries were established in well-to-do homes, forerunner of the modern cocktail cabinet. Here modish punches were prepared, always cold until the introduction of hot toddy during the early 1760s. These were served from punch bowls with long-handled punch-ladles. Handles on fashionable examples were in turned ivory, usually in double baluster form, head to head with a carved finial and usually engraved with a crest. The majority, however, were in hard wood which tended to float on the surface of the potent liquor.

The efficient method of manipulating the ladle to ensure stability in the hand is well-illustrated in contemporaneous engravings and in George Knapton's portrait of Sir Bouchier Wray, painted in about 1760. The handle is shown grasped in the middle by three fingers and the thumb of the server's right hand, then passing beneath the palm so that its knopped finial rests against the wrist. The forefinger is shown pressing on the upper surface of the handle-socket joint.

Trade cards show that shallow-bowled ladles in the shape and size of a goose's egg were fashionable during the early Sheffield plater's period – the 1760s and 1780s. The pointed end of the ovoid bowl provided an excellent pouring lip. The handle was attached at right angles to its greatest length.

Sheffield plate ladles were usually intended for the service of hot toddy, an English drink that became fashionable with the accession of George III. This drink was defined in the *Sporting Magazine* of that time as 'hot grog with the addition of sugar'. The grog, a mixture of rum and hot water, was enriched with lemon juice and flavoured with grated nutmeg – hot rum punch in fact. In the

*Butlers' Compendium*, 1823, a toddy-ladle is defined as 'a small deep ladle used for conveying whiskey toddy from a rummer or punch-bowl to a wine-glass'.

The hard wood handles of the punch ladles that were taken into use for serving hot punch or toddy were adversely affected by the heat. Constant expansion and contraction of the silver and wood at different rates eventually caused the handle to become loose in its socket and liquor seeped into the joint. This was overcome first by shortening the socket and inserting between it and the ladle an extension of plated rod, rectangular in section and long enough to ensure that the joint between the wood handle and the socket rim was raised above the surface of the hot toddy.

This extension became unnecessary, although not entirely dispensed with, when whalebone handles were introduced in the 1780s: it should be remembered that these might replace the wood handles of earlier ladles. Whalebone handles were square or round in section near to the socket, with a length of twisting above to provide a safer grip on the smooth surface to prevent the hazard of slipping through the fingers whilst transferring the toddy to its glass. Such a handle usually terminated in a plated finial, often with a flat end engraved with crest or cypher.

Whalebone handles were usually attached to hemispherical ladles with sides incurving towards an everted rim, spoutless, but with a slight outward curve to facilitate pouring. This was shaped from rolled plate by spinning in the lathe. Vertical fluting and wide lobes were common in the early nineteenth century. Other ladle bowls were enriched with embossed and chased work consisting of an all-over design of grapes and vine-leaves or flowers and foliage. Although these bowls were light in weight, the whalebone handle was sufficiently heavy to sink the ladle to the bottom of the bowl of toddy. These continued to be made until the early Victorian period.

The early nineteenth-century ladle was more commonly hemispherical with a wide pouring lip extending upward above the rim at right angles to the handle in such a way that a full ladle could be carried across to the drinking glass without mishap. Double-lipped bowls were also made. From about 1820 very thin plate might be used: these bowls were encircled with a strengthening rib to prevent distortion in use. The handle socket was continued in a long slender taper of flat metal shaped to the curve of the bowl to which it was soldered. Occasionally punch and toddy ladles in Sheffield plate were gilded by the mercury process.

Toddy ladles became outmoded in the north of England and Scotland following the introduction of the glass toddy lifter in the early 1820s.

*Scallop shells* dominated the minor decorative arts through much of the eighteenth century, their pleasing curves introduced alike in house-porch and state bed-head and in gold snuff-boxes and silver table dishes. The great scallop, a hermaphrodite shell-fish of the genus *Pecten*, has a flat right-hand valve slightly overlapped by the convex left valve. This convex shell has 15 ribs, the central large one flanked by the remainder in progressively diminishing length and width.

For more than a century silver and Sheffield plate dishes in the form of scallop shells measuring about five inches long were used for serving oysters baked with bread crumbs, cream and butter. For some 30 years from about 1770 the same shells had an alternative purpose as stands to the handless cups then fashionable for hot chocolate. Silversmiths and platers invariably catalogued them under the heraldic term of escallop shells. The rare early plated shells were hand-raised from two sheets of single plated copper, closely fitting, copper to copper and soldered together. They were then fitted with a pair of cockle shell feet struck from dies. So skilful was the craftsmanship that it is difficult to differentiate them from the double plated type. The rim of the shell was turned outward to conceal the bare copper. Vigorous burnishing made the edge of the welt invisible.

From the mid-1770s escallop shells were stamped from double-plated copper. The rims usually remained plain, but might be decorated with narrow silver edging, gadrooned or beaded. The average escallop shell measured $5\frac{1}{2}$ by 5 inches and after improvements were made in cast tool steel in the 1790s it might have 19 clear-cut ribs. The handle or ear was an extension of the hinge line or beak, usually in the form of a flat T-shaped plate with a boldly shaped outline, usually scalloped. Shell-shaped handles have been noted. The feet on escallop shells are usually described as snail shells but presumably were intended as winkles.

Contemporaneous catalogues illustrate escallop shells with three scroll feet at 18s each, footless at 12s 6d each. A larger size with wider flutings and a sizeable flat handle and three scroll feet was 19s. Although priced singly they were sold in sets of four or six. Although some collectors refer to escallop shells in Sheffield plate and silver as butter dishes there is no contemporaneous evidence that they were intended exclusively for that purpose, if at all. Escallop shells are simple to copy and many reproductions exist.

*Chafing balls* were made in Sheffield plate for use as hand warmers in pocket or muff. The design consisted of a hollow sphere, three to four inches across the diameter. It separated into two halves either by twisting a pair of bayonet fasteners or by unfastening a flat hook and opening it on a substantial book hinge. Inside was a hemispherical heater or spirit lamp about $1\frac{1}{8}$ inches in diameter and it was the device for holding this for safe burning that made the ball a practical proposition. This device, known as a gimbal, was used for keeping articles in a horizontal position on a ship. It consisted of three concentric rings of flat springy metal pivoting inside the ball. The heater, fitted with a round wick and burning methylated spirits, swung in the centre of the gimbal. The ball was decoratively pierced in openwork designs of scrollwork, flowers and foliage, usually with an eight-pointed star at each pole. The background was enriched with simple chasing. One pole was slightly depressed inward so that the ball could stand safely without rolling. Sometimes loops and a fine silver chain were attached for hanging the ball around the neck. In Desagulia's *Natural Philosophy*, 1774, such a heater is illustrated and called a rolling lamp.

*Spherical soap boxes* containing sweet scented ball soap found a place on every fashionable dressing table throughout the Georgian period, at first in silver, pewter or brass and from about 1770 in Sheffield plate. The sphere, split across its diameter, stood on a narrow spool stem rising from a spreading foot, the upper hemisphere hinging from thick swaging encircling the rim of the one below. Both were hand-raised. The surface of a soap box was at first smoothly plain. Eventually it was realized that ornamental perforations in the cover would permit a pleasant perfume from the soap to pervade the room. Sheffield plate soap boxes are always of this type except those intended for shaving sets. The hemispherical shape of the perforated cover compensated for the removal of the metal, patterns being so planned that the strain was spread evenly. It was engraved around the perforations with scrollwork topped by a plain finial and fitted with a lifting knob on the lower front edge. The lower hemisphere was not pierced.

Typical dimensions for the box were a height of about 5 inches and diameter of about $3\frac{1}{2}$ inches, the cover being deeper than the lower section so as to allow a larger area for ornamental perforations, although in some nineteenth-century examples the perforations were merely circular holes arranged in geometrical patterns. The mounts encircling the rim and foot might be chased with relief motifs such as roses, acorns and oak leaves, thistles or a combination of all, such as was fashionable on silver soap boxes. Shape and dimensions remained unchanged until the spherical soap box went out of fashion in the 1820s.

*Toasting forks* were made with the metal parts in Sheffield plate. A long shaft of polished hard wood or japanned beech gave the tool an overall length of between 30 and 40 inches, long enough for the cook to sit or stand well away from the scorching fire. Attached to the end was a short cap finial fitted with a loose ring for hanging when not in use. A series was made with a handle of twisted plated wire fitted with a dome and ring finial.

The Sheffield plate fork was designed in several variations, all with three slender round tapering prongs with sharp points. The majority made after about

1790 were shaped and made as miniature harpoons without barbs but slightly curved. The centre prong was attached to the hollow socket with a small strengthening knop at the joint. The thick end of the prong was drilled with a hole through which passed the U-shaped unit to form the two outer prongs. It was soldered firmly in position.

By about 1800 toasting forks were made with telescopic handles in three or four sections of plated tube and rod. The grip was of polished hard wood or japanned wood enriched with gilded or bronzed ornament. When closed such a toasting fork measured no more than a foot in length, the prongs being shorter than usual. A silver example in the Victoria and Albert Museum is struck with the London hallmark for 1805. The collector will occasionally find a Thomason telescopic toasting fork. These date from 1809 and are described fully in the *Memoirs* of Sir Edward Thomason, the celebrated Birmingham silversmith and plater:

> 'I invented the sliding toasting fork, some with one, two or three slides, within a handsome japanned handle common now [1834] in all the shops. I also invented one that by the action of drawing the slide, raised a [face] shield from off the prongs, and upon shutting up again of the slides this action moved the shield flat over the prongs. I also invented a third kind, which was that the three prongs collapsed together, which, on the shutting up of the slides of the fork, drew the same into the mouth of a snake, the head of a silver snake being attached to one end of the outer slide or handle.
>
> 'These were made in silver, gold and plated and large quantities were sold by me, but as I did not protect the invention by patent, thousands were made and sold by other manufacturers.'

# Sheffield plate chronology

| | |
|---|---|
| *1742* | Thomas Bolsover discovered fused plating at Tudor House, Sheffield. |
| *1743* | Thomas Bolsover and Joseph Wilson established plating workshops at Baker Hill, Sheffield. |
| *1755* | Sheets of single-sided plate placed back to back. |
| *1758* | Single-lapped copper edge introduced by Joseph Hancock. |
| *1760* | Accession of George III. |
| *1762* | Matthew Boulton established a plating factory at Soho, Birmingham. |
| *1762* | Invention of swage block for shaping rims. |
| *c. 1765* | Piercing first appeared on Sheffield plate. |
| late *1760s* | Introduction of plate silvered on both sides. |
| *1768* | Introduction of double-lapped copper edge. |
| *1769* | First drop hammer invented by Richard Ford. |
| *1770* | Invention of solid plated wire. |
| *1773* | Assay offices established at Sheffield and Birmingham and platers prohibited from using makers' marks. |
| *1775* | Introduction of silver-lapped edge. |
| *1779* | English method of close-plating patented by Richard Ellis. |
| *1780* | Introduction of silver cast mounts. |
| *c. 1780* | Bright-cutting introduced on encircling bands of silver. |
| *1784* | Platers permitted to strike a maker's mark. |
| *1785* | Introduction of drawn silver and plated wires for joints. |
| *1790* | Soldered-in heavily silvered shield introduced for a coat of arms. |
| *1790* | Introduction of silver stamped mounts filled with lead-tin alloy. |
| mid-*1790s* | Cast tool steel harder than formerly. |
| *1796* | Telescopic candlestick patented by A. J. Eckhardt and Richard Morton. |
| *1806* | Close platers permitted to strike a maker's mark. |

*c. 1810*    The silver plate could be thinner than formerly.
*c. 1815*    Introduction of wide silver stamped mounts.
*1820*    Accession of George IV.
*1820*    Crown first struck on Sheffield plate.
*c. 1820*    Spinning introduced.
*1822*    Mechanical flat chasing patented by William Mitchell of Glasgow.
*1824*    Improved silver stamped mounts patented by Samuel Roberts, Sheffield.
*1830*    Accession of William IV.
*1836*    British plate patented by Anthony Merry.
*1837*    Accession of Queen Victoria.
*1840*    Electro-plating patented by George and Henry Elkington.
mid-*1840s*    Electro-type mounts introduced by the Elkingtons.

# Bibliography

Bradbury, Frederick, *History of Old Sheffield Plate*, 1st ed. 1902, repr. 1966
Caldicott, J. W., *The Values of Old Sheffield Plate*, 1906
Dickson, H. W., *Matthew Boulton*, 1906
Hayden, Arthur, *Chats on Old Sheffield Plate*, 1920
Sheffield Assay Office, *The Old Sheffield Plate Register*
Sheffield City Museum, Illustrated booklet, 1966
Singleton, H. Raymond, *Old Sheffield Plate*
Veitch, H. N. *Sheffield Plate, its History, Manufacture and Art*, 1908
Wyllie, Bertie, *Sheffield Plate*, n.d.
Young, W.A., *The Silver and Sheffield Plate Collector*, 1928

# Notes to the plates

1   Old Sheffield plate. (*top left*) Coffee pot with plain bulbous body and pineapple finial to the ogee lid. Capacity 1¾ pints. By Tudor & Leader, Sheffield. A similar example is in the Metropolitan Museum, New York. 1780s. (*top right*) Inkstand with cut-glass pots for ink and shot set in solid guard rings with plated wafer pot topped by taper socket and extinguisher. *c.* 1790. (*below*) Soup tureen with bombé body, ivory handles and paw feet. Cover encircled with fruiting vine mount. 13¼ inches overall. *c.* 1820. MAPPIN & WEBB.

2   Knives and forks with handles of stamped Sheffield plate weighted with loom, blades and prongs of steel: (*centre*) pistol butt design; (*top and bottom*) ends cut obliquely. In the VICTORIA & ALBERT MUSEUM.

3   Close plating. Knife blades and fork prongs illustrating the processes of close plating in silver on steel. The blades are shown, left to right: as received from the forging department; smoothed, polished and cleaned; covered with silver foil; after burnishing. By A. Hatfield & Son, silver cutlers, Pepper Alley, Fargate, Sheffield. In the SHEFFIELD CITY MUSEUM.

4   Close plating. (*left*) Knife with tortoiseshell scales inlaid with *piqué* silver, the folding steel blade close plated with silver. Patented by Samuel Colmore, 25 Digbeth, Birmingham. 1780s. (*centre and right*) Dessert knife and fork with blue jasper handles enriched with white jasper ware and silver ferrule. Struck with the registered mark of A. Hatfield, Fargate, Sheffield. Early nineteenth century. In the SHEFFIELD CITY MUSEUM.

5   Eccentric steel snuffers, showing the action patented by Christopher Pinchbeck in 1776, which cuts off, confines and extinguishes the snuff at one motion. Hand-worked at the forge with cast enrichments, the whole close plated. By Joseph Wilmore, Birmingham, 1807. In the VICTORIA & ALBERT MUSEUM.

6   Close plating. Folding knife, fork and spoon set. The scales of the handles are in a light-coloured mottled horn. The knife blade folds into its haft; the stems of fork and spoon slide into their hafts; the spoon handle is also fitted with a corkscrew. Each piece is struck with the mark of W. Scot, Birmingham, registered 1807. In the SHEFFIELD CITY MUSEUM.

7   Close plating. Four-pronged table forks with stamped handles in close-plated steel. (*left and right*) In king's pattern made by M. J. Gilbert, Legge Street, Birmingham, *c.* 1815. (*centre*) Threaded pattern struck with the mark of T. Harwood, Birmingham, registered in 1812. In the SHEFFIELD CITY MUSEUM.

8   Close plating. Two-pronged skewer in close-plated steel, used before the introduction of the carving fork for holding the joint firmly upon the serving dish. The prongs were hand-wrought from a single length of square-section steel. Struck with the mark of W. Scot, Birmingham. Registered 1807. In the SHEFFIELD CITY MUSEUM.

9   (*left*) Fork for serving and cutting fish, with ivory handle and silver ferrule. *c.* 1820. (*centre*) Fish slice by J. Linwood, Newhall Street, Birmingham, mark of a tree registered in 1807. (*right*) Fish slice by Henry Hall, Shadwell Street, Birmingham, 1829–35. In the SHEFFIELD CITY MUSEUM.

10   (*left*) Asparagus server with large bow-spring tongs and wide rectangular blades pierced with scroll pattern, *c.* 1820. (*centre*) Lobster crack resembling large nutcrackers. (*right*) Cheese scoop with ivory handle and silver ferrule struck with the hallmark of R. Silk, Birmingham, 1810. The scoop is heavily silvered and engraved with a crest. In the SHEFFIELD CITY MUSEUM.

11   (*above*) Sauce boat with high uprising spout curved downward at the tip. The handle has a spreading leaf attachment at each end. Capacity 1½ pints. 32*s.* pair. (*below*) Sauce tureen with a short stemmed foot and loose ring handles. 80*s.* pair. From a trade pattern book in the VICTORIA & ALBERT MUSEUM.

12   Teapots of 1½ pints capacity. Boxwood handles with leaf attachments and domed lids with flower finials. The plain body with leaf encircled base cost 42*s.*; the identical pattern with reeded body, 46*s.* From a trade pattern book in the VICTORIA & ALBERT MUSEUM.

13   Draught-proof chamber candlestick on rectangular tray with ball feet. The candle-socket is encircled with a pierced air vent which supports an engraved flint-glass candle-shade. The cone-shaped extinguisher has a long stem to extend down the shade to the flame. From a trade pattern book in the VICTORIA & ALBERT MUSEUM.

14   Chamber candlestick on rectangular tray with gadroon mounts in silver. The snuffers fit into a recess in the stem and the extinguisher hooks upon the thumbpiece. These sold at 40*s.* a pair. From a trade catalogue in the VICTORIA & ALBERT MUSEUM.

15   Cruet with diamond-cut flint-glass bottles on a revolving platform: the three cut-glass bowls also turn on the stem. Sprinklers to the peppers and the mustard pot rim are in silver. This was priced at eight guineas. From a 1797 trade catalogue of Roberts, Cadman & Co. in the VICTORIA & ALBERT MUSEUM.

16   Salt-cellars in elaborately pierced late eighteenth-century designs. Those with scroll and reeded feet cost 13*s.* a pair; the footed examples 18*s.* a pair. These prices did not include glass liners. From a trade pattern book in the VICTORIA & ALBERT MUSEUM.

17   A selection of salt-cellars fashionable from the late 1790s. The example with a hemispherical bowl, gilt inside and with silver edges, sold at 24*s.* a pair. The remainder were priced with tinned interiors and with plated interiors silver-edged. The scalloped rim was 14*s.* and 18*s.* a pair, the batswing design 20*s.* and 24*s.* a pair and the circular pierced examples 10*s.* and 14*s.* From a trade pattern book in the VICTORIA & ALBERT MUSEUM.

18   Illustrations of tea caddies from a trade catalogue of about 1795, with plated interiors and silver edges. The reeded example, oval, with lock and key, was priced at 48*s.* The oval and square caddies with pull-off covers are decorated with bright-cut engraving and cost 20*s.* each. In the VICTORIA & ALBERT MUSEUM.

19   A page from a trade catalogue of about 1795 illustrating a beaker costing 4*s.* 6*d.*; a simulated staved and hooped tankard with lid, 30*s.*; a mug in the form of a cask with a flat-sided D-handle, 18*s.*; a chamber candlestick with snuffers, 38*s.* the pair. In the VICTORIA & ALBERT MUSEUM.

20   Catalogue page of 1792 illustrating several small items. Here the period's pierced salt-cellars with characteristic dipped sides, scrolled and reeded feet and blue glass liners are priced at 13*s.* and 15*s.* a pair. Chamber candlesticks were also sold by the pair. Design shows circular tray with reeded edges and typical details of snuffer and extinguisher hooked upon a thumb-rest. Here the cost is two guineas a pair. Ornate fish server with silver edges and mounts is priced at £1. In the VICTORIA & ALBERT MUSEUM.

21   Catalogue illustrations of an oval fruit-basket in wirework priced at 42*s.* and two pierced mustard pots enriched with bright-cut engraving priced at 14*s.* and 16*s.* each. The ringed-and-washered corks cost 12*s.* a dozen. In the VICTORIA & ALBERT MUSEUM.

22   Urn-shaped wine cooler entered as an ice pail in old pattern books. Handles and applied ornament in stamped silver. When new it would be difficult to distinguish this from silver.

23   Teapot in British plate encircled with reeded ornament raised by stamping. Silver gadrooned mounts and cover finial. Square-section spout and handle. JOHN BELL OF ABERDEEN.

24   British plate jug in a design of the late Georgian period. This high-lipped spout dates it as much as the fact that its coating of silver has a basis of white-toned nickel alloy and will never betray rose in its silvery gleam. JOHN BELL OF ABERDEEN.

25   Candelabrum for three candles, one of a set of four, in British plate. The base is weighted with a filling of loom. Foliate arms, filled with a lead-tin alloy, are typical of the 1830s–1840s and mounts are of silver to take the rub of wear.

26    Pair of rococo candlesticks in British plate, reflecting the earliest candlestick design made in Sheffield plate of the late 1750s, itself adapted from a George I silver pattern. The scalloped outlines of socket and foot and the baluster moulding were well-suited to the sparkle of candlelight.

27    Teapot, sugar basin and cream jug, a matching set in British plate. The curved reeded ornament, shaped by the drop hammer, is found in association with a variety of handles and spouts. JOHN BELL OF ABERDEEN.

28    Tray in British plate, heavily silvered on nickel alloy, rimmed with applied flower and foliage ornament in deep relief stamped in silver. *c.* 1840. JOHN BELL OF ABERDEEN.

29    Teapot, cream jug and sugar basin, a matching set in British plate, difficult to find today, with a coffee pot of the same period, *c.* 1840. All are elaborately chased against a matted ground. Handles, rims and feet are exceptionally well designed.

30    A display of square-based candlesticks in designs of Adam influence, *c.* 1780. (*top left*) Roman-Doric columns and festooned pedestal faces. (*top right*) Set of four with tapering square columns, each face with applied ornament. (*below*) Richly ornamented Corinthian capitals and columns entwined with beading. S. J. SHRUBSOLE LTD.

31    Table candlestick with circular pillar and pyramidal foot, decorated in low relief. Made by Thomas Law, Sheffield, *c.* 1760. Height 12½ inches. In the SHEFFIELD CITY MUSEUM.

32    Table candlestick with die-stamped decoration in high relief. Made by Matthew Fenton & Co., Sheffield, from a design by John Flaxman. *c.* 1780. Height 11½ inches. In the SHEFFIELD CITY MUSEUM.

33    Square-stemmed table candlestick with urn-shaped socket and loose nozzle. *c.* 1780. This pattern was catalogued at 48*s.* in the early 1790s and 42*s.* extra with 'branch to suit'. Height 11½ inches. In the VICTORIA & ALBERT MUSEUM.

34    Table candlestick with a plain cylindrical stem entwined with garlands of leaves. The corners of the pedestal decorated with rams' heads festooned with swags. By Tudor & Leader, Sheffield, *c.* 1780. Height 11¼ inches. In the VICTORIA & ALBERT MUSEUM.

35    Table candlestick with square incurved stem and base, both decorated with die-stamped figures in low relief. *c.* 1780. Height 11¼ inches. In the VICTORIA & ALBERT MUSEUM.

36    Table candlesticks. (*left*) Stem in the form of a demi-figure. 1760s. (*right*) Constructed in the late 1750s from 60 individual units of plate silvered on one side only. Impressed mark on the edge of the square base which supports a spirally fluted foot. By Joseph Hancock, Sheffield. In the SHEFFIELD CITY MUSEUM.

37 Table candlestick with an arm that swings on a swivel to adjust the position of the light. Silver gadroon mounts. The base is weighted by loom and a disc of heavy wood covered with green baize. *c.* 1815. In the SHEFFIELD CITY MUSEUM.

38 (*left*) Dwarf candlestick showing seam down the pillar. (*right*) Table candlestick with oval foot, stem, socket and knops. Constructed from 15 units: foot 3, stem 2, socket 2, lower knop 3, upper knop 2, sconce 3. Weight 2 lb $3\frac{1}{2}$ oz. An inexpensive type first associated with the 1790s. In the COLLECTION OF MRS V. S. MITCHESON.

39 Pair of candlesticks with die work touched up by hand. Each base is struck from a die in six sections. The nozzles are struck from a die and the edges turned over. The base metal edges are so cleverly turned over that they are virtually invisible. Height $11\frac{3}{8}$ inches. 1760s. Coffee pot plated on one side of the copper only and tinned within. Seams may be seen on body, spout, handle sockets and finial. The decorations are flat chased with chinoiserie and fantastic flowers. Height 11 inches. 1760s. In the VICTORIA & ALBERT MUSEUM.

40–44 Telescopic candlesticks.

40 A pair of single-slide examples operating on the notch-and-catch principle, with fluted base and socket. Impressed PATENT. *c.* 1800. In the SHEFFIELD CITY MUSEUM.

41 Two-branch candelabrum with central urn that could be used for a third light. Double telescopic pillar. By Richard Morton & Co., Sheffield. *c.* 1800. In the SHEFFIELD CITY MUSEUM.

42 A pair of five-slide telescopic candlesticks with decorated urn sockets and gadrooned edges. Shown closed 12 inches high; open 21 inches. In the WAKEFIELD-SCEARCE GALLERIES.

43 Traveller's candlestick: a chamber candlestick, extinguisher and socket with a double telescopic pillar. These may be packed within the two bases which measure $5\frac{1}{4}$ inches in diameter and $3\frac{1}{2}$ inches high. Attributed to Roberts, Cadman & Co., Sheffield. *c.* 1805. In the SHEFFIELD CITY MUSEUM.

44 A double-slide pillar showing the slides extended. Impressed $^{\text{EKHARDTS}}_{\text{PATENT}}$ in one stamp. *c.* 1800. In the SHEFFIELD CITY MUSEUM.

45 Candelabrum, the circular pillar tapering downward, with typical vase-shaped socket supporting an urn-shaped finial and scrolled branches. Height $17\frac{1}{2}$ inches. 1790s. In the VICTORIA & ALBERT MUSEUM.

46 Candelabrum, one of a pair, each flat face of the tapering pillar decorated with two sunken panels with low relief patterns. Each corner is topped with a ram's head in cast silver. By Matthew Boulton. 1780s.

47 Pair of library candelabra with adjustable branches. Measuring $18\frac{1}{2}$ inches with the arms extended. Engraved with a coat of arms. Made by J. Green & Co., Sheffield, *c.* 1810. In the WAKEFIELD-SCEARCE GALLERIES.

48   One of a pair of two-light candelabra with rare Adam urn centrepiece, tapering square plinth with rams' masks, swags and foliage, vase-shaped sockets. Late eighteenth century.

49   Three-light candelabrum with scrolling reeded branches by Roberts, Cadman & Co. 24 inches high, 18 inches wide. *c.* 1820.

50   Sheffield plate dining table suite elaborately enriched with silver mounts. One of the pair of three-light candelabra is convertible to a single five-light candelabrum. The matching candlesticks are 13 inches high. Each piece is struck on the edge of the base with Matthew Boulton's mark of the double sun. *c.* 1812.

51   (*left to right*) Candlestick with shouldered stem tapering towards the base, reeding encircling foot, shoulder and nozzle. One of a pair of three-light candelabra with lower stem fluted, gadrooning around the sockets. The branches may be lifted off and the lower unit used as a table candlestick. Pair of exceptionally slender baluster candlesticks. Candelabrum with two branches and an urn-shaped centrepiece which may have its cover removed for use as an extra candle socket; the tapering stem with fluted mushroom shoulder. Floridly decorated candlestick with baluster stem, *c.* 1830.

52   Pair of chamber candlesticks with plain circular trays encircled by drawn reeded mounts of Sheffield plate. The cylindrical candle sockets are pierced for snuffers. The nozzles are of the same shape and design as the trays and are soldered in position. PRESTONS LTD.

53   Chamber candlestick with flat circular pan and looped handle. Rising from the centre and at right angles to the handle is a slotted support to hold snuffers, the finger loops of which would extend beyond the tray rim. Surmounting this are two outward scrolling branches each terminating in a candle socket with a conical extinguisher hooked into a tubular socket. The rims of the pan and candle sockets are decorated with lead filled gadroon mounts. Height about 16½ inches. *c.* 1810. In the SHEFFIELD CITY MUSEUM.

54   A set of four chamber candlesticks with vase-shaped candle-sockets. The rims of the pans and conical extinguishers are everted and decorated with wide silver mounts of floridly designed flowers and foliage. The thumbpieces fitted to the handles are also decorated with silver mounts. PRESTONS LTD.

55   Horizontal wax jack for desk use with scroll lifting handle and flat thumbpiece. The coil of wax taper is partially covered with a fluted shield to protect it from sealing wax droppings. *c.* 1800. In the SHEFFIELD CITY MUSEUM.

56   Horizontal wax jack with a rectangular frame of drawn wire, the taper held horizontally on a winding spindle. A plain trumpet-shaped stem hand-raised from a rectangular tray with gadrooned silver mount. The flame aperture is a short tube held in position with thick washers holding a smooth rectangular plate to catch wax drippings. 1780s.

57   Cylindrical bougie box encircled with reeded mounts and with flat slip-on cover. The projecting tube contains a tightly fitting nozzle to control the emerging taper. ASPREY & CO. LTD.

58   Vertical wax jack showing the scissor action by which the taper-end is clipped. The U-shaped spring is seen between the handles. Late eighteenth century.

59   Bougie boxes with pierced sides and reeded ribbon handles shaped from drawn plate. In this design the cone-shaped extinguisher is pegged into a loop and attached by a hand-made guard chain extending from the finial to an eye on the upper handle. With flat lid, 1790s; with domed and pierced lid, *c.* 1820. The central wax jack is in brass, 1780s.

60   Pair of candlestick sconces in the form of seven-petalled flowers; snuffers below are of close-plated steel with solid silver mounts. The gadrooned tray with plain platform was stamped from a die. *c.* 1830. The taper box has a vertical seam and separate bottom. The gadroon mounts are of silver with 'turn-over' edges. *c.* 1800. The four-lobed snuffer tray has snuffers and two extinguishers. This was intended to be placed between a pair of table candlesticks. *c.* 1800. In the VICTORIA & ALBERT MUSEUM.

61   Two snuffer trays with close-plated steel snuffers with silver mounts. The trays, shaped by the drop hammer, are in a design with an exceptionally deep well and the rim in a piece with the platform. (*centre*) Globe inkstand mounted on a round foot. The four curved supports terminate in silver flowers and are joined by pendant swags of drapery. The ink bottle and pounce pot mounts are also in silver. In the VICTORIA & ALBERT MUSEUM.

62   A pair of two-candle wall lights in Sheffield plate, with elaborate chased decoration. Height 15 inches, width 12 inches. Converted for use with electricity. In the WAKEFIELD-SCEARCE GALLERIES.

63   Lantern with five long, thin glass-filled sides and a wide door, the base fitted with a candle socket. Reeded loop handle at the back. The top is surmounted by a leaf covering an air vent. Height $6\frac{1}{4}$ inches. *c.* 1795. In the SHEFFIELD CITY MUSEUM.

64   Shaving mirror with an oil lamp and font. The glass may be adjusted as required. Height 16 inches. 1798. In the SHEFFIELD CITY MUSEUM.

65   One of a pair of plain wine coolers, with ring handles. Height 8 inches. *c.* 1800. S. J. SHRUBSOLE LTD.

66   Wine cooler encircled with five wide thread mounts and handles in silver. Height $8\frac{1}{2}$ inches. *c.* 1800. S. J. SHRUBSOLE LTD.

67   Wine cooler with gadrooned body and matching mounts. Applied silver escutcheon containing a coat of arms. Height 9 inches. 1820. S. J. SHRUBSOLE LTD.

68   One of a pair of wine coolers with mask and ring handles. Height 8½ inches. *c.* 1800. S. J. SHRUBSOLE LTD.

69   Wine cooler on round foot with decorated stem. The body ornamented with applied silver mountings and borders. Height 10 inches. 1825. S. J. SHRUBSOLE LTD.

70   Wine cooler, the urn-shaped body with shell and gadroon mount, the handles with acanthus leaf terminals. Height 9½ inches. 1820. S. J. SHRUBSOLE LTD.

71   Grecian urn wine cooler, one of a pair, by Kirkby, Waterhouse & Co., *c.* 1810. A similar pair is in the Mappin Art Gallery, Sheffield. S. J. SHRUBSOLE LTD.

72   Wine coolers heavily ornamented with fruiting vines; elaborate applied silver mounts and flat chasing suggest the second quarter of the nineteenth century.

73   A pair of double decanter stands connected with wire couplings containing rings for the stoppers. The design includes a handle at each end for moving around the table. 1800. ARTHUR ACKERMAN & SON INC.

74   Four coasters or decanter stands with turned mahogany bases. A trade catalogue of about 1800 illustrates 16 patterns including those with wirework and pierced and chased galleries as shown here. The top coaster with solid sides is of the Regency period. In the SHEFFIELD CITY MUSEUM.

75   Decanter wagon in the form of a naval 'jolly boat' on four wheels with a shaft for pushing it along the table. Sunken recesses for a pair of decanters and their stoppers. Length 12 inches from stem to stern. *c.* 1825. ASPREY & CO. LTD.

76   Wine wagon with widely reeded gallery and expansive fruiting vine mount, and loops for the decanter stoppers. T-finial to the swivel handle. Early nineteenth century. PRESTONS LTD.

77   One of a pair of wine wagons containing a pair of loose coasters with heavy mahogany slides. The decorative vertical shaft swivels beneath a smooth rigid coupling platform. The wheel spokes are of cast silver. *c.* 1830. JOHN BELL OF ABERDEEN.

78   Orange and lemon strainers with flat-based bowls about one inch deep. (*left*) Wire loop handle, late 1780s. (*right*) Close-plated double scroll handle, quatrefoil and circular piercing. 1770s. In the SHEFFIELD CITY MUSEUM.

79   Double-handled orange and lemon strainer for use with a punch bowl. This example is in sterling silver and was made in 1749 by Edward Aldridge, London, and was copied extensively in Sheffield and Birmingham from about 1781. PRESTONS LTD.

80 Orange and lemon strainer with shallow, four-inch diameter bowl and lyre-shaped handle. In sterling silver by Thomas Daniel, London, 1778. This pattern was copied in Sheffield plate from the mid-1780s. PRESTONS LTD.

81 Combined orange and wine strainer dismantled to show the orange strainer bowl, the funnel and the ring upon which hung the muslin wine straining bag. Early nineteenth century. In the COLLECTION OF MRS V. S. MITCHESON.

82 Early Victorian three-part wine funnel, the bail handle and cover with ivory accessories. Diameter of rim $4\frac{1}{2}$ inches. PRESTONS LTD.

83 Combined orange strainer and wine funnel with plate used as a cover. Height $5\frac{3}{4}$ inches, diameter of funnel $3\frac{1}{4}$ inches. Early nineteenth century. In the SHEFFIELD CITY MUSEUM.

84 Orange and lemon strainer in silver fitted to a Sheffield plate funnel, both with reeded rims and shell-shaped hooks. Height $3\frac{3}{4}$ inches. *c.* 1810. PRESTONS LTD.

85–88 These teapots illustrate the development of factory methods that cut costs and made Sheffield plate available to thousands who could never afford to own hand-fashioned ware made by the old silversmiths. Late eighteenth and early nineteenth centuries. All in the VICTORIA & ALBERT MUSEUM.

85 Octagonal teapot with vertical sides encircled with a saw-pierced gallery and mount, both of solid silver and applied. Pyramidal lid.

86 Octagonal teapot with narrow fluted panels at corners and on cover. Reeded mounts encircling top and bottom.

87 Octagonal teapot with fluted and flat-chased decoration. Seams are to be seen on the sides, handle sockets and spout. Handle and pineapple finial in ebony.

88 Oval teapot with gadroon mounts. Heavy embossing strengthens the thin plate where it is subject to most stress. Capacity $3\frac{1}{2}$ gills. Early nineteenth century.

89 Teapot in the 'revived rococo' style with ogee body, highly placed swan-neck spout, D-handle; pineapple finial and round stemmed foot. JOHN BELL OF ABERDEEN.

90 Teapot decorated with flat chasing, pyramidal hinged cover with pineapple finial; separate stand. The catalogue price in about 1795 was 58*s.* without stand.

91 The ornamental bands encircling top and foot of this teapot are of silver decorated with bright cutting. A full service in Sheffield plate to match this vessel consisted of tea urn, sugar basin, cream jug, tea caddy, oval teapot stand, pair of sugar tongs and caddy ladle. It was customary until about 1800 to include a separate stand under the teapot. Double plated, this teapot cost 58*s.* when new.

92    Three-piece set for a tea tray. Made by George Ashforth & Co. in the early nineteenth century. All vessel rims are strengthened with silver gadrooning. Capacity of teapot one quart. JOHN BELL OF ABERDEEN.

93    Four-piece tea and coffee service with matching tray. Teapot, sugar basin, cream jug and coffee pot are encircled with curved reeding and have silver mounts. *c.* 1810. S. J. SHRUBSOLE LTD.

94    Five-piece tea and coffee service including kettle with spirit lamp and stand. By Matthew Boulton. Nineteenth century. In the WAKEFIELD-SCEARCE GALLERIES.

95    Three-piece tea service, the teapot complete with stand. On right, cylindrical coffee biggin with stand and spirit lamp. D. J. WELLBY LTD.

96    Three-piece tea set. The collar or cape of the pot was an attractive late-Georgian innovation and the shaping of the handles shows the period's feeling for unusual design. The introduction of foot rings meant that the separate stand or ball feet were no longer necessary. Made by George Ashforth & Co. in the early 1800s.

97    Tea service with elaborate ornamental rim mounts and bodies encircled with wide grooves; harp-shaped handles and ball feet. 1820s.

98    Tea and coffee service, lower parts of the bodies encircled with deep gadrooning. The spherical body to the teapot was a revival of a style fashioned half a century earlier. Marked with the eight crossed arrows registered in 1811 by T. J. & W. Creswick, Paternoster Row, Sheffield.

99    A page from a Sheffield plate pattern book issued in 1797 by Roberts, Cadman & Co., Eyre Street, Sheffield. The globe of this tea and coffee machine contained six quarts of water and was heated by a box iron. This vessel was stationary, fixed to the lower base (D). But the lower vessel, divided into three compartments for teas and coffee, could be revolved so that water from the globe's base tap might fill the one required. The tray below could also be revolved independently so that cups placed upon it could be filled in turn from any of the three patent taps. With silver edges and engraved garter and shields this cost £31 10*s.* The pattern shown in the small drawing sold at £21.   In the VICTORIA & ALBERT MUSEUM.

100    Tea and coffee machine with spirit lamp beneath the large globular urn which swivels to fill the two smaller urns with hot water. These and the drip bowl may be removed and used separately. In the COLLECTION OF MR MARK J. SCEARCE.

101    Tea and coffee machine. The three plain globular urns have lion mask and drop ring lifting handles. Each is supported on a square plinth accommodated, together with a drip basin, upon a flat platform with a reeded rim. Height 21 inches. *c.* 1800.

102    Tea and coffee machine, each globe urn accompanied by a spirit lamp. Plate with an extra thickness of silver was used to permit the engraving of a decorative garter around the circumference of each. By Daniel Holy, Wilkinson & Co., Sheffield. Height 24 inches. Early nineteenth century. In the SHEFFIELD CITY MUSEUM.

103    Tea urn encircled with gadroons, each edged with chased outline and with cover decorated to match. Lion mask and ring handles. *c.* 1800. In the WAKEFIELD-SCEARCE GALLERIES.

104    Tea urn with spherical body and matching spirit lamp on shaped plinth. Mask and ring handles. Probably by D. Holy, Wilkinson & Co., Sheffield. 1790s. In the WAKEFIELD-SCEARCE GALLERIES.

105    Rectangular tea urn on strap legs with paw feet rising from a shaped plinth with lion mask attachments and ring handles. Late eighteenth century. In the WAKEFIELD-SCEARCE GALLERIES.

106    Tea urn by Matthew Boulton with heavy silver gadrooned edges and reeded body. The claw supports rise from a shaped plinth supporting a screw-on matching spirit lamp. In the WAKEFIELD-SCEARCE GALLERIES.

107    Tea urn heated by charcoal on square plinth with pierced rim and ball feet. The body lightly chased with a cartouche containing an engraved coat of arms. Pineapple finial and thumbpiece to the tap in green ivory. Capacity two quarts. 1760s. In the VICTORIA & ALBERT MUSEUM.

108    Tea urn shaped and chased to resemble a beehive. Silver mounts filled with tin-lead alloy. Four lion mask and claw supports rising from shaped plinth on ball feet. Tinned inside. Heated by red hot iron in jacket. *c.* 1815. In the SHEFFIELD CITY MUSEUM.

109    Tea urn containing iron and sleeve heater. Body encircled with reeding and a band of solid silver chased with a shell pattern. On spool stem rising from a square plinth with acanthus and paw feet. Early nineteenth century. PRESTONS LTD.

110    Tea urn heated with a box iron. The body encircled with a design in bright cutting. *c.* 1790. In the VICTORIA & ALBERT MUSEUM.

111    Tea urn with four curved legs shaped from flat plate, rising from an incurving square plinth. Decorated with bead mounts in cast silver. Capacity four quarts. 1780s. In the VICTORIA & ALBERT MUSEUM.

112    Tea urn with charcoal method of heating, on pierced plinth with claw and ball feet. The whole chased in relief. Green ivory handles and knob to the dolphin spout. Capacity four quarts. 1770s. In the VICTORIA & ALBERT MUSEUM.

113 (*left*) Pair of helmet cream jugs encircled with reeding on round feet. Catalogued *c.* 1780 at 17*s.* each. JOHN BELL OF ABERDEEN.

114 Hot water jug with bead mounts and dipped cover with flower and foliage finial. One quart capacity. By J. Younge & Co. 1780s. In the VICTORIA & ALBERT MUSEUM.

115 Hot water jug, catalogued in the 1780s as a pitcher. Octagonal body encircled with chased medallions and pendant swags on shaped plinth. Green ivory handle. In the VICTORIA & ALBERT MUSEUM.

116 (*left*) Adam-style jug, the engraved encircling silver band harmonising with plinth piercing. Hinged cover, square plinth on ball feet. By R. Morton & Co. 1770s. (*centre*) Coffee pot with chased body and double-domed cover. One quart capacity. By M. Fenton & Co. 1770s. (*right*) Hot-water jug with hinged cover and urn-shaped knob. Beaded mounts in solid silver. By J. Younge & Co. 1780s.

117 (*left*) Hot-water jug on three short acanthus legs with bead and acanthus borders encircling body and cover. *c.* 1770. (*right*) Hot-water jug plated on one side only: where double plating was necessary, as on the inside of the lid, two fused silver plates have been placed back to back. Decoration on the lip, lid and handle sockets is early die work, touched up by hand. The hinge is an example of the earliest 'book' style. The handle is wickered. Height 10 inches. Late 1750s. In the SHEFFIELD CITY MUSEUM.

118 Interchangeable coffee pot and teapot on stand with charcoal heater below: copper receptacle for the charcoal. To use as a teapot the percolator is removed and the lid placed on the lower vessel. 1790s. In the SHEFFIELD CITY MUSEUM.

119 Coffee biggin with reeded body and lid with stand and spirit lamp. Capacity $1\frac{1}{2}$ pints. By A. Goodman & Co., *c.* 1805. JOHN BELL OF ABERDEEN.

120 Plain coffee jug fitting into stand with reeded legs and paw feet supporting spirit lamp. *c.* 1800.

121 Tea canister with ogee body decorated with flower and scroll embossment. Domed lid with urn-shaped finial. 1760s. In the VICTORIA & ALBERT MUSEUM.

122 Sugar pail, the rim and swing handle decorated with beading. The acanthus leaves on body and foot are embossed and chased and the foot is loaded. Height $7\frac{1}{2}$ inches. *c.* 1780. In the VICTORIA & ALBERT MUSEUM.

123 Sugar basket made up of plain flat wire with pierced and flat chased border above. Contains blue glass liner. Made by R. Morton & Co., *c.* 1800. Height $5\frac{1}{2}$ inches. In the VICTORIA & ALBERT MUSEUM.

124    Boat-shaped sugar basket with fluted and pierced body, bail handle and oval foot. Height 7 inches. Late eighteenth century. In the VICTORIA & ALBERT MUSEUM.

125–129    Sheffield plate tea caddies, with locks, decorated with flat chasing. Lids are of solid silver and hinge on flush joints.

125    Oval with hinge and lock on narrow ends. Turned ebony knob. Height 4 inches. Capacity $\frac{1}{2}$ lb tea. In the VICTORIA & ALBERT MUSEUM.

126    Cube-shape constructed from flat plates soldered at the edges. Height $3\frac{3}{4}$ inches.

127    Pair with corrugated sides and scalloped edges to rims. Catalogued at 45*s*. each in 1795.

128.    Oval with silver knob stamped in two halves.

129    With low domed lid and ivory knob and engraved with crest. Length and height $5\frac{1}{4}$ inches. JOHN BELL OF ABERDEEN.

130    Coffee biggin with gadrooned lid and book hinge. Tinned inside. By A. Goodman & Co., 18 Hawley Croft, Sheffield. *c*. 1800. In the COLLECTION OF MRS. V. S. MITCHESON.

131    Coffee pot chased with flowers, foliage and scrolls. The body was raised from the plate and has a vertical butt joint. The seam on the finial is visible. Height 11 inches. 1760s. In the VICTORIA & ALBERT MUSEUM.

132    Coffee pot made from single-sided plate. Lid and foot worked from two pieces of fused plate placed copper to copper, the upper layer of silver turned over to conceal copper edges. Height 11 inches. *c*. 1760. In the SHEFFIELD CITY MUSEUM.

133    Collection of old Sheffield plate coffee pots: (*left to right*) by Tudor & Leader, $1\frac{1}{2}$-pint capacity, height 9 inches, 1760s; with bulbous body, two-pint capacity, height 10 inches, 1810; with exceptionally fine detail of handle and spout, height $10\frac{3}{4}$ inches, 1810; showing Adam influence with festoon ornament, height 12 inches, 1770; egg-shaped body and swan-neck spout on short spool stem, height $9\frac{1}{4}$ inches, 1775. S. J. SHRUBSOLE LTD.

134    Interchangeable epergne and three-light candelabrum with figure supports. De-signed by Sir Frances Chantrey, R.A. for Gainsford & Nicholson, Sheffield. 1812. In the SHEFFIELD CITY MUSEUM.

135    Epergne with reeded supports to the bowl ring rising from paw feet. Four branches curve out from the platform to support the smaller bowls. The vessels, diamond-cut with serrated edges, came from the Whittington Glass House. Made by Thomas & James Creswick, Porter Street, Sheffield. *c*. 1820. In the WAKEFIELD-SCEARCE GALLERIES.

136    Epergne with octagonal mirror plateau, its gallery pierced with vertical pales and edged with gadrooning. Eight scrolled and reeded branches support circular trays topped by a canoe-shaped fruit bowl, all decorated with pierced vertical pales and star motifs. The claw and ball feet were a fashionable feature. Height 20 inches. Late eighteenth century. In the VICTORIA & ALBERT MUSEUM.

137    Epergne with canoe-shaped top bowl and four small matching bowls rising from scrolled branches. Double-lapped copper edges. Height 18¾ inches. 1760s. In the VICTORIA & ALBERT MUSEUM.

138    Sweetmeat epergne with vertical stand rising from a wire base, two sets of branches terminating in rings holding glass bowls with scalloped rims and topped by a large fruit bowl. Height 24 inches. Early nineteenth century. JOHN BELL OF ABERDEEN.

139    Epergne rising from a tripod stand with six scroll branches bearing pendant baskets, each constructed from six pierced panels. The swing handles by which they hang from the branches have openwork arches. Ogee-shaped top basket. Late eighteenth century. JOHN BELL OF ABERDEEN.

140    Four-division supper dish by Matthew Boulton. *c.* 1815. In the WAKEFIELD-SCEARCE GALLERIES.

141    (*behind*) Wirework sugar basket with glass liner; pair of second-course dishes with warmers; argyle. (*front*) Two entrée dishes with warmers flanking a loving cup and a wire-work cake basket. All late Georgian. JOHN BELL OF ABERDEEN.

142    Set of four George IV entrée dishes, silver mounted with wide borders of flowers. Formerly in the collection of H.R.H. the Duke of Windsor. In the WAKEFIELD-SCEARCE GALLERIES.

143    Soup tureen with a hand-raised swelling body engraved with a crest. Silver mounts and gadroon borders with turn-over edges. Height 10 inches. *c.* 1820. In the VICTORIA & ALBERT MUSEUM.

144    (*top*) Vegetable dish with domed cover. Border, mounts, handles and scroll feet are of embossed silver. Trade price £6 11*s. c.* 1810. (*below*) Soup tureen and cover of six quarts capacity. Embossed silver mounts and handles and paw feet. Trade price £11 11*s. c.* 1810.

145    Soup tureen in the form of a turtle. The shell hinges upward from the neck to reveal the bowl and a double-lipped edge is visible. 22 inches long by 17 inches wide. Capacity ten pints. 1790s. In the SHEFFIELD CITY MUSEUM.

146    Rectangular entrée dish with gadrooned ornament. By Matthew Boulton. Wine cooler with plain body, flower and foliage rim mount. Oval second course dish and warmer with fluted cover and paw feet. Plain oval tea caddy, ¼-pound capacity. By Ashworth, Ellis & Co. All *c.* 1815.

147   (*top*) Oblong entrée dish and cover shaped by stamping. One of a set of four, with gadrooned borders and hollow ball feet. Early nineteenth century. (*below*) Two-handled oval soup tureen, bombé-shaped body on ring foot. Cover has flower petal finial. *c.* 1820.

148   Pair of oval steak and vegetable dishes with melon shaping to covers and dishes. Scroll mounts. By Kirkby, Waterhouse & Co. 1820s. In centre, one of a pair of oval soup tureens with stamped silver mounts, catalogued as 'oval canoes'.

149   Pair of oval entrée dishes with plain D-shaped handles and hand-raised reeded covers with ivory knobs. The dishes are edged with reeded silver mounts. Length 15 inches. *c.* 1790. JOHN BELL OF ABERDEEN.

150   One of a pair of entrée dishes and warmers, the cover decorated with silver mounts. The warmer has been constructed from separate ends, sides and inserted base. The handles and feet are of stamped silver. *c.* 1820. JOSEPHINE GRAHAME-BALLIN.

151   Covered dish of a type that had endless uses on table and sideboard. Folded shaping contributes strength and the applied rim, of silver weighted with a lead-tin filling, protects edges. *c.* 1820.

152   One of a set of four circular entrée dishes with two-handled vessel for hot water, on four ball feet. The cover is edged with gadrooning and similar ornament encircles the dome which is engraved with an expansive coat of arms. Diameter 10½ inches. *c.* 1795.

153   Plain entrée dish hand-raised entirely from the plate. The handle, of silver struck in two halves and filled, is screwed to an inner boss. On the rim of the lid the edge of the silver has been brought up to cover the copper edge without turning it over. By Roberts, Cadman & Co. *c.* 1800.

154   Entrée dish, one of a pair, with scroll ends. The body and cover were hand-raised including the gadrooning. The cover handle has a bayonet attachment. Length 14 inches. *c.* 1800.

155   Cheese toaster in Sheffield plate. This has a sliding cover to the hot water aperture in the handle socket. Pans 2½ inches square. Made by Tucker, Fenton & Co., Norfolk Street, Sheffield. *c.* 1805. In the SHEFFIELD CITY MUSEUM.

156   Cheese toaster with screw-in handle as plug for the hot-water compartment. Lifting handles to the toasting pans which betray evidence of much wear. Matthew Boulton, Birmingham. *c.* 1800. In the SHEFFIELD CITY MUSEUM.

157   Dish cover with wide melon shaping encircled with gadroon and foliage mount applied in sections. Handle in a foliate design. On meat dish rimmed with reeded mount. *c.* 1820. In the SHEFFIELD CITY MUSEUM.

158    Oblong bread tray encircled with wide flower and foliage mount. About 15 inches long. 1820s. In the SHEFFIELD CITY MUSEUM.

159    Dish ring pierced with two circuits of vertical pales and four narrow bands of scrolls, the centre chased with pendant swags. Struck with the mark of a cock, registered in 1785 by R. Morton & Co., Brinsworth Orchard, Sheffield. In the SHEFFIELD CITY MUSEUM.

160    A less expensive version of the style of dish ring shown on the left. This is encircled with bright-cutting. *c.* 1800. JOHN BELL OF ABERDEEN.

161 and 162    Sheffield plate adjustable dish crosses, constructed almost entirely from die work units and supporting spirit lamps. The arms swivel around the necks of the lamps. With moveable petal brackets and feet. 1790s. JOHN BELL OF ABERDEEN.

163    Folding dish stand with four knopped adjusters operating on swivels. Made by Watson, Fenton & Bradbury, Mulberry Street, Sheffield. Struck with the mark of a ship. *c.* 1810. In the SHEFFIELD CITY MUSEUM.

164    Revolving dish stand constructed of round wire and flat ribbon. Reversible to hold a round or oval dish and fitted with a double-sided heat disperser for the separate spirit lamp. 1790s. In the SHEFFIELD CITY MUSEUM.

165    Dish cross constructed almost entirely from die-struck units and assembled in sections. The adjustable arms are hollow and the ends unscrew for removal of the sliding legs for cleaning. Made by Ashforth, Ellis & Co., and marked A E Co in script letters each in a separate punch. 1770s. In the SHEFFIELD CITY MUSEUM.

166    Dish cross with fixed arms and sliding legs to fit a round dish of any size. Fitted with a heat disperser beneath which is placed a spirit lamp. *c.* 1800. In the SHEFFIELD CITY MUSEUM.

167    Sauce boat with oval foot raised from the plate – the seam is to be seen on the right. With silver edges and chased with flower, foliage, and scroll decoration. One-pint capacity.

168    Pair of plain sauce boats. Rims and feet with silver beaded mounts. Capacity $\frac{3}{4}$ pint. Late eighteenth century. JOHN BELL OF ABERDEEN.

169    Sauce boat with three hoof feet in early George II style. Height 5$\frac{1}{2}$ inches. One-pint capacity. *c.* 1820. Tea urn, early George III. Double-ended sauce boat in George I style with oval foot. Height 4$\frac{1}{2}$ inches. *c.* 1830. In the VICTORIA & ALBERT MUSEUM.

170    Set of four one-pint sauce tureens with oblong bodies and rectangular plinths. Covers topped with festoon ornament. By Tucker, Fenton & Co. Early nineteenth century. JOHN BELL OF ABERDEEN.

171   Oval sauce tureen with plain body on rectangular plinth. Body rim and foot strengthened with reeded mounts. Height 6 inches. Late eighteenth century. In the VICTORIA & ALBERT MUSEUM.

172   Sauce tureen with canoe-shaped body, domed cover and stand, all fluted. Late eighteenth century. In the VICTORIA & ALBERT MUSEUM.

173   Oval sauce tureen with bead mounts and applied festoons and medallions. One pint capacity. By J. Hoyland & Co. This pattern is also found with a matching stand. 1770s. In the VICTORIA & ALBERT MUSEUM.

174   One of a pair of sauce tureens with shaped body and cover. Filled silver mounts. By T. Bradbury & Sons. Catalogued at 15 guineas each. 1830s.

175   (*left*) Argyle with central box iron in cylindrical sleeve; with straight tapering spout, circular foot and lift-off cover. *c.* 1790. (*right*) Argyle with hexagonal body and double jacket for hot water. Teapot style spout with handle of flat plate at right angles to it. Mark, the hand of J. Watson & Son. 1830s. In the SHEFFIELD CITY MUSEUM.

176   Argyle with drum-shaped body encircled with matching silver mounts. With swan-neck spout and containing a hot water jacket with filling socket on upper handle. Height $4\frac{3}{4}$ inches. 1770s. In the VICTORIA & ALBERT MUSEUM.

177   Argyle with barrel-shaped body containing a double jacket. Hot-water inserted through beak-shaped spout (*left*) with hinged cover. Slender swan-neck pouring spout at right angles to handle. 1780s. In the COLLECTION OF MRS V. S. MITCHESON.

178   Argyle, the rounded portion of the body containing the gravy and the lower section filled with hot water through the projecting socket (*right, behind handle*) covered by a hinged lid. Height 7 inches. Late eighteenth century. In the VICTORIA & ALBERT MUSEUM.

179   Soy frame on oval platform with four ball feet. The guard rings fit cut-glass bottles with circular feet. Hung with crescent-shaped labels for Cayon, Elder, and Lemon, hall-marked 1800. In the SHEFFIELD CITY MUSEUM.

180   Soy frame containing three stoppered glass bottles and a fluted mustard pot with blue glass liner. By N. Smith & Co., Sheffield, 1790. In the SHEFFIELD CITY MUSEUM.

181   Spirit frame with platform of Sheffield plate with openwork frame containing two bottles and two tumblers in flint-glass. By J. Younge & Co. 1785. In the SHEFFIELD CITY MUSEUM.

182   Epergne and cruet frame on a revolving stand encircled with a pierced rim. This is fitted with a wirework frame containing cut-glass soy and cruet bottles, all silver mounted. With central canoe-shaped dish and four branches supporting pickle dishes. *c.* 1800. BIRCH & GAYDON LTD.

183    Epergne and cruet frame with octagonal platform revolving on a circular base: plain guard rings containing eight footed bottles of flint-glass, silver-mounted, including three intended for soy. The wire frame supports a central bowl and four branches with hanging pickle baskets. 1790s. In the SHEFFIELD CITY MUSEUM.

184    Combined epergne and cruet frame with eight flint-glass condiment bottles fitted with mounts of Sheffield plate, four canoe-shaped dishes which would have glass linings for pickles, and a fruit bowl. The tray with pierced and chased gallery revolves on a pedestal base. In the SHEFFIELD CITY MUSEUM.

185    Plain canoe-shaped salt-cellar, one of a set of six, with diamond-shaped plinth foot and spool stem. A style fashionable from *c.* 1780 to 1800. JOHN BELL OF ABERDEEN.

186    Salt-cellar of a shape unusual in Sheffield plate, with beaded rim. The stamped units composing the legs have been noted on small table-ware by John & Thomas Settle, Sheffield. JOHN BELL OF ABERDEEN.

187    Salt-cellar with blue glass liner. The pierced vertical pales display irregularities showing that each was cut separately. Flat chased ornament masking corners. *c.* 1780.

188    Oval salt-cellar on four reeded feet stamped from dies and hand curved. Gallery decorated with hand-sawn perforations and flat chasing. Original price was 13*s.* a pair. In the VICTORIA & ALBERT MUSEUM.

189    Pair of Scottish salt-cellars, the flint-glass wells with serrated rims supported in frames of plated wire. Early nineteenth century. JOHN BELL OF ABERDEEN.

190    Salt-cellars, two of a set of four, oval on claw and ball feet struck from dies. The galleries are saw-cut and flat chased, the beaded mounts being in silver. Blue glass liners. JOHN BELL OF ABERDEEN.

191    The Trafalgar inkstand with cut-glass pots for pounce and ink and a Sheffield plate wafer box. The flat-topped base, on ball feet, is weighted with bloom to give stability. The anchor and chain are of silver. Mark of Daniel Holy, Parker & Co. A design made from 1806. In the SHEFFIELD CITY MUSEUM.

192    Very early ogee-shape saucepan plated inside with unusually thick silver, the exterior copper. The socket to the wooden handle, plated and riveted to the body, is impressed JOS^H HANCOCK SHEFFIELD. Height with handle 8 inches. Late 1750s. In the VICTORIA & ALBERT MUSEUM.

193    Egg-cup stand constructed entirely from drawn wire, fitted with four egg-cups pierced with a circuit of vertical pales. *c.* 1790. In the SHEFFIELD CITY MUSEUM.

194   Egg-cup stand with guard rings for eight egg-cups, loops for eight spoons and a frame for a salt-cellar in flint-glass. The stand encircled with silver gadroon borders. *c.* 1800. In the SHEFFIELD CITY MUSEUM.

195   Egg-cup stand with four egg-cups and salt-cellar, all gilded inside and four egg spoons gilded all over. All rims encircled with gadrooning. Struck with a trumpet, the registered mark of A. Goodman & Co., Sheffield. *c.* 1805. In the SHEFFIELD CITY MUSEUM.

196   Egg stand combined with toast rack. When the eggs are removed from the frame the supporting guard rings may be swivelled to a vertical position to keep separate the slices of toast. Struck with a hand, the registered mark of N. Smith & Co., Sheffield. *c.* 1810. In the SHEFFIELD CITY MUSEUM.

197   Combined egg-cup and toast rack with four egg-cups in flint-glass. The wire frame also carries a pepper caster with a silver top. 1812. In the SHEFFIELD CITY MUSEUM.

198   Toast rack with a frame of reeded ribbon and wire dividing bars, on scroll feet. Early nineteenth century. In the VICTORIA & ALBERT MUSEUM.

199   Toast rack with wire loop divisions attached to a stand with an ornamental gallery on claw and ball feet. 1785. In the SHEFFIELD CITY MUSEUM.

200   Toast rack with pierced and chased platform on scroll feet. Six divisions formed with looped wire. *c.* 1800. In SHEFFIELD CITY MUSEUM.

201   Toast rack with hooped divisions of wire on an oval platform of flat ribbon with central stretcher; hollow claw and ball feet. 1790s.

202   Fish slices. (*left to right*) Silver edge and green ivory handle, *c.* 1800. Pierced and chased, with silver ferrule and ivory handle, *c.* 1790. Blade pierced and chased and engraved with fish; green ivory handle and Sheffield plate ferrule, 1790s. Fish-shaped blade pierced and chased, 1780s. Hexagonal blade pierced with borders of pierced pales enclosing engraved crest and fish, 1790s. In the SHEFFIELD CITY MUSEUM.

203   Oval fish plate or mazarine, each motif of the pierced design hand-pressed individually. Length 19 inches. 1780s. In the SHEFFIELD CITY MUSEUM.

204   Sheffield plate of the late eighteenth century including asparagus tongs; knife and fork voider flanked by punch ladles; and, below, a cheese toaster (*closed*) with a pair of steel knives with plated hafts. In the VICTORIA & ALBERT MUSEUM.

205 and 206   Plain rectangular tea-trays with ends extended to form hand-holds simulating scrolls and edged with beaded silver mount. Each engraved with coat of arms. (*right*) The hand-holds are decorated with expansive acanthus leaves stamped from silver. Late eighteenth century. JOHN BELL OF ABERDEEN.

207   Rectangular plain tray with coarsely gadrooned border in silver. The D-handles are stamped in silver and filled with lead-tin alloy. Early nineteenth century. JOHN BELL OF ABERDEEN.

208   Tea tray, its gallery pierced with vertical pales and edged with gadrooning. The hand-holds are decorated with silver mounts in the form of acanthus leaves. By Matthew Boulton, Soho, struck with a single garter star. Late eighteenth century. JOHN BELL OF ABERDEEN.

209   Tray entirely raised in one piece from double-plated copper, the sides being shaped by means of swages. The mounts and handles are of silver. The centre bears flat-chased decoration in the form of a rectangle containing an escutcheon enclosing an engraved coat of arms. Size 30 inches by 20 inches. *c.* 1830. JOHN BELL OF ABERDEEN.

210   Tray elaborately flat-chased and engraved with a coat of arms. Improved silver-stamped mounts and four claw feet. Struck with the bell mark of Roberts, Cadman & Co., Sheffield. Made between 1824 and 1828. JOHN BELL OF ABERDEEN.

211   Elaborately decorated tray with swaged sides and improved silver-stamped mounts. Mechanically chased central plate with stippled ground. Coat of arms engraved on a rubbed-in shield. Made between 1824 and 1830.

212   Salver on three claw feet. Piecrust edge decorated with filled silver mounts of shell and flower pattern. Crest engraved in the centre. Diameter 18 inches. Early nineteenth century. CHARLES WOOLLETT & SON.

213   An unusual Sheffield plate tea table on six scroll feet. The rim is bordered with silver mounts in the form of swags of wheat-ears pendant from a finely gadrooned edge. Diameter 30 inches. Early nineteenth century. JOHN BELL OF ABERDEEN.

214   Waiter with piecrust edge encircled with a silver mount of shell and flower pattern, the centre flat-chased with sprays of flowers and foliage and rococo scrollwork. The crest engraved on a rubbed-in shield. Diameter 9 inches. In the SHEFFIELD CITY MUSEUM.

215   Inkstand made from two sheets of plate silvered on one side only, stamped in a die and soldered back to back: cylindrical ink and pounce pots in cut-glass fitted into pierced guard rings. Late 1760s. In the SHEFFIELD CITY MUSEUM.

216   Inkstand with a pair of square cut-glass bottles for ink and lead shot, the central wafer box supporting a taper-stick with a cone-shaped extinguisher and guard chain. 1820s. In the SHEFFIELD CITY MUSEUM.

217   Plain inkstand with wire guard rings containing square ink bottles in flint-glass and an octagonal wafer box on a raised platform with central pen tray encircled with reeded mounts. *c.* 1785. In the SHEFFIELD CITY MUSEUM.

218   Inkstand, its platform encircled by a pierced gallery topped by a beaded mount, fitted with drum-shaped inkpot and shot container and vase-shaped taper holder with loose sconce. By J. Parsons & Co. 1785. In the SHEFFIELD CITY MUSEUM.

219   Combined inkstand and candlestick in the fashionable Adam style. With fluted plinth and chased pillar and vase. The cover is reversed to take the candle. Height 6½ inches. 1770s. In the VICTORIA & ALBERT MUSEUM.

220   Globe inkstand shown open: pressure on the top finial causes the upper half of the sphere to fall and reveal the contents which include ink and pounce pots, pen-knife and penholder. By Roberts, Cadman & Co. Height 9 inches. *c.* 1805. In the SHEFFIELD CITY MUSEUM.

221   Inkstand on mahogany base. Glass bottles for ink and pounce flanking wafer box topped by taper socket and extinguisher. Channel in front for pens and drawer for accessories. *c.* 1800. In the VICTORIA & ALBERT MUSEUM.

222   An amusing inkstand following the introduction of the railway locomotive. The dome finial opens to give access to the ink. 1830s. HARVEY & GORE.

223   Group of four snuff-boxes constructed of copper plated on one side only. The sides are seamed, invisibly outside. The covers are decorated with hand-chased ornament and the bases with die-stamped patterns: both cover and base lined with tortoiseshell to prevent the snuff from clogging in indentations. The cover of the example on the right is set with panels of aventurine. Diameter 2½ inches. 1750s. In the SHEFFIELD CITY MUSEUM.

224   Rectangular snuff-box of sturdy Sheffield plate. The cover with a five-lug hinge is set with a copper halfpenny of the third issue of George III struck by Matthew Boulton in 1799. This coin has been close-plated with silver which is seen to have proved far more susceptible to wear than the Sheffield plate box. *c.* 1800. In the COLLECTION OF MRS V. S. MITCHESON.

225   Snuff-box with pull-off cover fitted with a tortoiseshell panel, the rococo scrollwork worked in silver in the *posé d'argent* technique. Possibly by Thomas Bolsover in the late 1750s. A similar box is in the Sheffield City Museum. In the COLLECTION OF MRS V. S. MITCHESON.

226   Loving cup and cover. The hammer-shaped body with vertical seam and box or hollow handles similarly raised and seamed. Cover and foot each raised from a disc of plate. The pineapple finial is die work. Height 11 inches. 1760s. In the VICTORIA & ALBERT MUSEUM.

227   Tankard with hinged domed cover, shaped in three sections and invisibly joined. Body shaped and joined with a single vertical seam; box handle and hinge units also hand-shaped. The thumb-piece is die work. *c.* 1780. In the VICTORIA & ALBERT MUSEUM.

228    Pair of light-weight lidless tankards. The s-shaped handle has a thumb-piece attached to a strengthening piece concealing the join of the body seam. Late eighteenth century. JOHN BELL OF ABERDEEN.

229    Pair of presentation goblets with beaded mounts. The cups and trumpet sections of the stems were shaped by spinning in the lathe. The exteriors are heavily gilded to accept all-over engraved inscriptions within wreaths. George IV period. JOHN BELL OF ABERDEEN.

230    Loving cup engraved with a coat of arms within a flat chased cartouche. The imitation fluting is similarly tooled. Encircled with an applied strengthening band. Marked by Thomas Law, Sheffield, with the initials T L in upper case script struck three times with the name Law. Between 1758 and 1770. S. J. SHRUBSOLE LTD.

231    Oval cake basket, the sides saw-cut with perforated designs of ovals and diamonds enriched with embossed pendant swags and gadroon borders invisibly soldered on. The foot ring is encircled with bands of perforations in geometric designs edged with gadrooned silver wire. The bail handle displays perforations bordered by gadrooning. In the SHEFFIELD CITY MUSEUM.

232 and 233    Two views of cake basket showing side and interior. The hand-raised body and ring foot are decorated with saw piercing. The bail handle, of a type common in silver but rarely met with in Sheffield plate, is constructed from a combination of wrought and die-struck units. The interior perforations are enriched with embossed flowers from which hang embossed swags. Width 14 inches. 1760s. In the VICTORIA AND ALBERT MUSEUM.

234    Very similar basket to plate 231 but with more elaborate handle. The silver on the flat base is thick enough to be engraved with a coat of arms. Both are by Matthew Fenton & Co., Sheffield. ASPREY & CO. LTD.

235    Hot-water warming pans with screw-on handles of hard wood. (*left*) Encircled with reed-and-tie mount, engraved with coat of arms. 1790s. (*right*) Pan and cover hand-raised from plate silvered on one side only. 1770s. In the VICTORIA & ALBERT MUSEUM.

236    Pipe lighting bowls to burn smokeless court charcoal. 1780s. (*left*) Portable with deeply scalloped rim attached to plain bowl and claw and ball feet. (*right*) Bowl attached to footed salver for table use. In the SHEFFIELD CITY MUSEUM.

237    Portable pipe lighter with boxwood handle, the bowl rim pierced with two circuits of diamond motifs and encircled with reeded mount; fitting into reeded vase for table use. This burned peat, considered agreeable to smokers. In the VICTORIA & ALBERT MUSEUM.

238    (*top left and right*) Pair of pipe lighters: the bowls to hold the dishes of hot charcoal are bolted to the waiter plates which have pierced borders. Height $4\frac{1}{2}$ inches. G. Ashforth & Co. 1790s. (*centre*) Pipe lighter with handle. All would be fitted with loose copper linings.

(*bottom*) Snuffer trays with pierced galleries. By N. Smith & Co. 1790s. (*centre*) Vase-shaped mustard pot, chased and pierced, with blue glass liner. 1780s. In the VICTORIA & ALBERT MUSEUM.

239    Cucumber slicer with a silver mount encircling the stand. One end of the tube is fitted with a steel blade which could be made to revolve quickly by the hand crank. The plated tube protected the salad from the unpleasant flavour of acidic juice from the peeled cucumber on base metal. 1820. In the SHEFFIELD CITY MUSEUM.

240    Honey pot and plate in the form of a basket-work bee skip. The upper portion lifts off as a cover. *c.* 1800. In the SHEFFIELD CITY MUSEUM.

241    On the left a monteith used as a wine-glass cooler. Diameter 10½ inches. 1780. In front, a double decanter coaster with baize beneath and a loose ring for a cord or ribbon to pull it along the table. *c.* 1810. On the right, an egg-boiler suite complete with spirit lamp and egg timer. In the VICTORIA & ALBERT MUSEUM.

242    Lidded pipe-lighter with the base attached to a tray, both encircled with pierced and chased decoration. Made by G. Ashforth & Co. in 1785. In the SHEFFIELD CITY MUSEUM.

243    Urn raised on four legs shaped from reeded ribbon, its tray encircled with silver gadrooning. For burning pastilles to perfume a room. *c.* 1790. In the SHEFFIELD CITY MUSEUM.

244    Egg coddler with gadroon mounts, engraved with coat of arms and crest. Eggs were cooked or coddled by keeping them closely covered in hot water. *c.* 1800. In the SHEFFIELD CITY MUSEUM.

245    Egg-boiler. Cover and cup perforated all over with circuits of hand-worked holes. Joined at the circumference by a bayonet fastener. Struck with a bell, the mark of Roberts, Cadman & Co. Late eighteenth century. In the SHEFFIELD CITY MUSEUM.

246    Pipe-lighter for burning smokeless court charcoal. Pierced with a band of vertical pales and a circuit of pierced and chased medallions below. The copper liner is missing. *c.* 1785. In the SHEFFIELD CITY MUSEUM.

247    Table snuff-boxes. (*left*) Canoe-shaped for two qualities of snuff. Hinged covers with silver edges. *c.* 1800. (*right*) With a coco-nut shell vessel and lid mounted on trumpet-shaped base. By T. Law & Co. *c.* 1800. In the SHEFFIELD CITY MUSEUM.

248    Tea-table kettle on stand with spirit lamp. 1820s and 1830s. JOHN BELL OF ABERDEEN.

249    Two-bottle soy frame, the high galleries pierced with vertical pales, late eighteenth century. Four-bottle spirit frame with shell ornament on supports, *c.* 1820.

250   Centrepiece for dining table. The standard was hand-raised in sections and joined: the attachments and mountings were die-struck. *c.* 1840.

251   Page from a pattern book of the early 1790s, with the prices marked in ink. At the top is a canoe-shaped snuffer tray, priced at 16*s.* In quart size the teapot is priced at £2 10*s.* Mustard pot pierced and lined with blue glass is 14*s.*; egg-cup 4*s.* and pepper caster 6*s.* The simple bottle ticket at the top is priced at 12*s.* a dozen. In the VICTORIA & ALBERT MUSEUM.

252   Soup tureen with domed cover, heavy feet and handles, silver mounts, rubbed in silver shield engraved with crest. Six quarts capacity. By I. & I. Waterhouse & Co. *c.* 1820. JOHN BELL OF ABERDEEN.

253   Canoe-shaped cruet stand with cut-glass oil and vinegar bottles and a pierced muffineer with blue glass liner on pedestal. Priced 42*s.* A page from an early nineteenth-century pattern book in the VICTORIA & ALBERT MUSEUM.

254   Miniature tea equipage for dolls' house in Sheffield plate. Complete with footed salver, tea urn, teapot, cream jug, tea canister, sugar basin with tongs, and spoons. Early nineteenth century.

255   Cake basket with sides of hair-pin wirework, the remainder in plate enriched with elaborate silver mounts. 1820s. In the SHEFFIELD CITY MUSEUM.

256   Sheffield plate cake basket with sides of flat ribbon wire and an openwork bail handle. The base engraved with an expansive coat of arms. 1760s.

257   Cake basket composed entirely of wire-work intertwined in a honeycomb pattern between the gadrooned border and plain flat base. *c.* 1810. In the SHEFFIELD CITY MUSEUM.

258   Oval cake basket with foot ring and upraised ends. The rim is decorated with a band of pierced and chased ornament strengthened with a reeded border. 1790s. In the VICTORIA & ALBERT MUSEUM.

259   Wirework cake basket with hair-pin sides. A separate mount was made for the wire body. This was attached to the top mount with soft solder after the wires had been attached with hard solder. The wire ends were attached with soft solder below the bottom to a base mount.

260   Cake basket of plain interlaced wire with an openwork swing handle made from reeded ribbon wire. Struck with the initials of Samuel Kirby & Co. *c.* 1800. In the SHEFFIELD CITY MUSEUM.

261   Wirework cake basket with hair-pin sides and foot ring which stands on a loose crumb-plate encircled with a reeded gallery. The basket base is of wire. PRESTONS LTD.

262   Eight-sided sugar basket of hair-pin wirework strengthened by a rim of Sheffield plate displaying a band of perforated and chased ornament. Blue glass liner. *c.* 1790. In the VICTORIA & ALBERT MUSEUM.

263   Sweetmeat stand with three removable escallop shell dishes. Early nineteenth century. HARVEY & GORE.

264   (*top left*) Taper holder with handle and unusual wire frame to contain the ball of wax taper. (*top right*) Two-bottle oval inkstand with pierced galleries supporting the cut-glass ink and pounce pots separated by lifting handle. Late eighteenth century. (*below*) Pair of early tapersticks, 1750s, flanking the massive base of a candelabrum, its socket designed to support two or three branches. In the VICTORIA & ALBERT MUSEUM.

265   Group of late Georgian Sheffield plate showing (*behind*) a pair of muffineers and a sauce boat. In front, a pair of pierced decanter coasters with urn medallions and a pair of salt-cellars on claw and ball feet, with blue glass liners and bands of piercing and bright-cut engraving.

266   Trug tray with simple gadroon mount. Early nineteenth century. JOHN BELL OF ABERDEEN.

267   Three-light branch sold separately for a matching candlestick which might be fitted with candle sockets of other designs in the pattern book. The finial is removable. The factory price was 32*s.* The two-cigar cases with slip-on ends cost 3*s.* 8*d.* each. Late eighteenth century. From a pattern book in the VICTORIA & ALBERT MUSEUM.

268   Group of table ware in Sheffield plate illustrating the flamboyant ornament fashionable from the end of the Georgian period.

269   Banquet for the Prince Regent with the Emperor of Russia and the King of Prussia. At Guildhall, 1814. Much of the table ware is in Sheffield plate. Painted by George Clint, A.R.A.

# Index

The numerals in **bold** type refer to the figure numbers of illustrations